RECONCEIVING POSTCOLONIALISM

VISIONS AND REVISIONS

Edited by

Sunita Sinha

ATLANTIC

PUBLISHERS & DISTRIBUTORS (P) LTD

Published by

ATLANTIC

PUBLISHERS & DISTRIBUTORS (P) LTD

7/22, Ansari Road, Darya Ganj,
New Delhi-110002
Phones : +91-11-23273880, 23275880, 23280451
Fax: +91-11-23285873
Web: www.atlanticbooks.com
E-mail: info@atlanticbooks.com

Branch Office
5, Nallathambi Street, Wallajah Road,
Chennai-600002
Phones: +91-44-64611085, 32413319
E-mail: chennai@atlanticbooks.com

ISBN 978-81-269-1200-1

Printed in India at Nice Printing Press, A-33/3A, Site-IV, Industrial Area, Sahibabad, Ghaziabad, U.P.

Acknowledgements

Nothing compares to my grandfather, Dr. R.K. Sinha—the most truly humble teacher—whose very name casts a spell over all the lovers of English literature. Whether it was Eliot or Lawrence, whether it was Donne or Keats, whether it was Shakespeare or Shaw, it was with an equal felicity, ease and command that he dealt them all. I was privileged, no doubt, to have grown up amidst quotes from Milton, Eliot and Arnold, lines from Wordsworth and Shelley, that kept me familiar with the golden names of English literature since my earliest years. Whenever my imagination began to stagger, or when I was at a complete loss, all he would say was—"compare and connect".

This book is in homage to a profound admiration for my grandfather.

Sunita Sinha

Preface

Postcolonialism today, ushers in as an emergent discipline which constitutes a composite but powerful intellectual and critical movement and renews the perception and understanding of modern history, cultural studies, literary criticism and political economy.

The term "postcolonial" or "post-colonial" as a concept entered critical discourse in its current meanings in the late 1970s and 1980s but both the practice and the theory of postcolonial resistance go back much further. The postcolonial *avant la lettre*, Frantz Fanon in his text, *The Wretched of the Earth* (1961), presaged some of the positions now called "postcolonial". Fanon called for a cultural and national liberation and defined the central role played by language in shaping the consciousness of the colonized people. Michel Foucault, the French philosopher, in his *Madness and Civilization* exhibited an obsession with discourse as power. Inspired by Foucault's writing, Edward Said with his landmark text, *Orientalism* (1978), set the stage for the theoretical and critical corpus that would subsequently take shape under the "rubric of post colonial studies". Said's discourse locked East and West into an oppositional relationship by producing "the Orient" as the sensual, emotional, inscrutable and fundamental Other to the "Occident" defined by comparison as cerebral, rational, transparent and secular.

The growing currency of postcolonial thought was consolidated by the appearance of *The Empire Writes Back:*

Theory and Practice in Post Colonial Literatures (1989). The authors of this founding text, Ashcroft, Griffiths and Tiffin were concerned with the works of literature which were linked by their "having emerged in their present form out of experience of colonization and asserted themselves by foregrounding the tension with the imperial power, and by emphasizing their differences from the assumptions of the imperial centre". They denounced the methodology which involved "the fixing of texts in historical time and the perpetual search for the determinants of a single, unified and agreed meaning...proceed(ing) from a single ideological climate and "enthroned" in a "privileging norm" which ipso facto denied the value of anything from the margins". Further, Homi K. Bhabha in *Nation and Narration* (1990), Gayatri Chakravorty Spivak in *The Post Colonial Critic: Interviews, Strategies, Dialogues* (1990), and Arnold Harrichand Itwaru and Natasha Ksonzek in *Closed Entrances, Canadian Culture and Imperialism* (1995) have explored the ways in which literature served as an important site of struggle for self-determination, and for political, social and cultural power. For the moment, postcolonial theory seems everywhere.

Postcolonialism responds to more than merely chronological construction of post independence and to more than a discursive experience of imperialism. It is rather "an engagement with and contestation of colonialisms discourses, power structures and social hierarchies". According to Sandraa Ponzanesi, "post colonial" is a state of awareness and not a legal/ chronological term referring to the strict historical moment when different colonial societies became independent. Since long, therefore, postcolonialism has been appropriated by contemporary critical discourse in a wide range of domains. It has come to represent an attempt at transcending the historical definition of its primary object of study towards an extension of the historic and political notion of "colonizing" to other forms of human exploitation, normalization, repression and dependency.

Postcolonial studies addressing issues of race, ethnicity and empire have provided some of the most innovative and controversial contribution to recent scholarship. However, though this ever-growing expansion has proved a source of confusion and embarrassment for some, for others it has provided a useful tool of purposeful inquiry and for many others still, a source of overpowering influence in the academy in almost all parts of the world.

The book *Reconceiving Postcolonialism: Visions and Revisions* introduces us to the challenging and exciting range of postcolonial literatures in English, and focuses on the key issues of migration, racism, national identity, cultural hybridity, gender politics, etc. It collects twenty essays in this emergent field displaying both historical depth and theoretical finesse as they attempt innovative and vibrant readings. The divergent, complementary and competing viewpoints aim at providing a good exploration to the postcolonial studies. It is a comprehensive collection spanning the literatures of Australia, Africa, Canada, India and America, "which offers an extensive focus on the emergence of...innovative non-European English language literature originating from former British colonies".

In an exhaustive study, "Feminine Psyche and the Narrative Strategies", Neeru Tandon analyses the various narrative strategies that the woman novelists have adopted to probe into the inner recesses of the feminist psyche. Discussing at length the techniques employed in the fiction of Indian woman novelists like Anita Desai, Shashi Deshpande and Shobhaa De, Dr. Tandon also surveys the devices used by the Afro-American woman novelists, Toni Morrison and Alice Walker, for projecting the idea of woman's repression and her subsequent quest for self-actualization.

In their innovative paper, "Depiction of Childhood Friendship in Male and Female Novelists: A Comparative Study of R.K. Narayan's *Swami and Friends* and Shena Mackay's *The Orchard on Fire*", Tripti Karekatti and Rani Nalawade make a comparative statement on the depiction of childhood friendship in the two novels. Both the novels have almost the same story, about close friendship and eventual separation. However, while *The Orchard on Fire* has touches of seriousness and pathos, *Swami and Friends* reveals light-hearted humour and boisterous fun. Thus, Narayan paints a happy picture of childhood in his novel and Mackay reveals the darker one.

Hariclea Zengos chooses to write on a controversial novel in his paper, "Multicultural Melbourne: Mapping Identity in Christos Tsiolkas' *Loaded*". The paper discusses issues of sexual politics and "intercultural racism" while exploring twenty-four hours in the life of a young alienated and nihilistic bisexual working-class man from an immigrant minority culture. In the contemporary world that values wealth and well-defined categories, the angry and confused protagonist, Ari, tries to deal with his outsider status as an unemployed drug user determined to destroy himself on his journey through Melbourne's Greek, gay and pub cultures.

Sarbojit Biswas' paper, "Kim Scott's *Benang* and Doris Pilkington's *Towards the Rabbit-Proof Fence*: Conscious Racism and Identity De-orientation", offers a comparative study of Kim Scott's *Benang* and Doris Pilkington's *Towards the Rabbit-Proof Fence*. He traces in both the novels, a revolt against the powers of hegemonic white Australia, attempting to nullify Aboriginal identity through state power. Both the novels project the triumph against colonial hegemony by triumphing against all odds. As chronicles of half cast lives on the edge, the paper tellingly conveys the message of moving from "ignorance to knowledge, from resentment and indignation past injustices to a more sympathetic view...."

In "Cosmopolitanism vs Americanism: A Critique of American Cosmopolitanism in the Works of Margaret Atwood and Salman Rushdie", Garima Gupta offers an analysis of American cosmopolitanism in the works of Margaret Atwood and Salman Rushdie. The paper traces the origin of the term "cosmopolitanism", and further posits it against American capitalism. The comparative analysis of Atwood and Rushdie effectively brings out their common plea for an "unprejudiced" cosmopolitanism.

Esterino Adami in "The Terrorist in the Text: The Deictic Construction of Otherness", deals with the question of diasporic identity in the twenty-first century world as observed in Mohsin

Hamid's *The Reluctant Fundamentalist*. Written in the form of a long monologue, the paper recaptures the tensions and conflicts generated by the global fear of terrorism.

Prof. Subir Dhar's "Character and Fantasy in Mahesh Dattani's *Bravely Fought the Queen*" is a scholarly analysis of Dattani's plays focusing on the element of fantasy which indicated "an irruption within the changeless everyday reality".

Prof. Gauri Shankar Jha in his critical paper, "The Fashion of Post-colonialism and Karnad's *Hayavadana*", discusses the ethics of postcolonialism in the world of literature, particularly Indian English writing. The paper highlights the fashion of postcolonialism as a dormant inevitable current in Indian English writing refuting the Orientalist definition of Indians as "underdeveloped". Prof. Jha considers Girish Karnad as the only Indian English dramatist whose play *Hayavadana* is a "post colonial offshoot of a matured post colonial mind".

K. Mishra in "Borders don't Really Apply: A Note on Diasporic Dimensions in Amitav Ghosh's *The Circle of Reason* and *The Shadow Lines*", offers an insightful study of the dilemmas of diaspora and the problems of identity, alienation, displacement and rootlessness that inform significantly the novels of Amitav Ghosh.

Geetha B. in her innovative paper, "Theme of Cosmic Loneliness as an Extension of Individual Loneliness as Delineated in the Science Fiction Writings of Arthur C. Clarke", introduces the genre of science fiction as a literature of change focusing on "ideas". The paper begins with a brief outline on the thematic concerns in Arthur C. Clarke's fiction and goes on to explore the theme of cosmic loneliness which features extensively in his works. The paper relates the theme of cosmic loneliness to the existential questions and the angst in "the man within" which generates the sense of fragmentation and alienation in the modern man.

Mbuh Mbuh Tennu's comparative analysis of "De-Africanising Womanhood and the Dilemma of Africanity: Mariama Bâ's *So Long a Letter* and Buchi Emecheta's *Second Class Citizen*", offers an in-depth study of the dilemma of Africanity, which is apparent in the difficult position of a woman caught between a valuable heritage that she will not forfeit and an opposing need to express herself as a progressive woman straddling between tradition and modernity. The paper focuses on the dilemma of a woman who wants to reconcile the traditional exclusionism she endorses with the modernity she admires.

Vandana Datta in her well-researched paper, "Decolonization and the Politics of Language", states that the English language, which was the instrument of subservience, has now become a weapon of liberation, wherein, the much colonized people are using the same English language now to fight cultural imperialism or neo-imperialism thrust upon them by the West. As Datta effectively puts it, "The Empire started writing back and it wrote back with a vengeance effectively appropriating the language to suit their needs, to launch a struggle against cultural imperialism."

After the tyrannical reign of Ahmadou Ahidgo in Cameroon, the central African country, the "New Deal" regime succeeded it and ended the reign of ten which had stifled the Anglophone Cameroonians for four decades. In his well-researched paper, "Anglophone Cameroon Poetry: Poetics and the Politics of the New Deal", Nkemngong categorized the Anglophone Cameroonians into two groups. The first group celebrated the rupture of oppressive system and welcomed the era of political legitimacy and the later poets saw the change as betrayal of honest citizens.

Malti Agrawal's paper, "Women as Victims: Manju Kapur's *Difficult Daughters* and *A Married Woman*", studies the woman's need for self-fulfillment, autonomy, self-realization, independence, individuality and self-actualization as depicted in the novels of Manju Kapur. The paper effectively brings out Kapur's preoccupation with displacement and repression experienced by tradition-bound Indian woman. Here, the women described do not suffer from physical violence but fall victims to emotional-mental-sexual violence.

Saddik M. Gohar in his critical paper, "Navigating Myth and Tradition in Feminist Emirati Poetics: An Intertextual

Approach", examines Saleha Obeid Ghabesh as an eminent voice in feminist Emirati poetics. In this brilliant critique of the decadent traditions which aim at silencing the Arab women in an era of self-assertion, Saddik M. Gohar's analytical paper explores the reconstruction of myth and tradition to articulate the significant topics in UAE community. Dealing extensively with the Arab dreams, frustrations and feminist issues, the paper significantly places Emirati poetry in the contemporary global literary canon.

Prof. Emmanuel N. Ngwang's paper, "Re-Configuration of Colonialism or the Negation of the Self in Postcolonial Cameroon in Bole Butake's Plays", focuses on Bole Butake's plays, written against the backdrop of inhumane oppressors of the seemingly silent and marginalized masses of the fictionalized communities of the North-West Province of the Republic of Cameroon, Africa. The paper explores critically the legacy of European colonialism which aimed at the exploitation and degeneration of the formerly independent African people and ushered in a world where the concepts of freedom, equality and the pursuit of happiness have been negated.

Anju Bala Agrawal in her scholarly paper, "Nature and Man in Seamus Heaney", presents Heaney as a master poet who connects Nature, emotion and even plot in a brilliant and particularly Irish poetry. The paper explores the growing distance between the world of language and the physical world he sees around him. Dr. Agrawal analyses the various aspects of Nature as depicted in Heaney's poetry. Heaney, in his poems, brings out man's relationship with Nature, and "sees history, language and myth as bound up with Nature with territory and landscapes".

S. John Peter Joseph in his paper, "Need for Racial Harmony and Universal Brotherhood: A Critical Response to *The Nowhere Man*", focuses on the different aspects of the East-West encounter and analyses the problems arising out of Indian diaspora's inadequacy to adjust themselves to the alien culture. Kamala Markandaya's novel points towards a cultural and political synthesis between the East and the West which can be achieved through mutual respect, appreciation and understanding.

Basavaraj Naikar's innovative paper, "The Diasporic Poetry of G.S. Sharat Chandra", traces the gradual evolution in Sharat Chandra's poetic career beginning with native experience, passing through immigrant experience and ending up with American experience. Oscillating between the experiences of native Hindu culture and American culture and finally being completely absorbed by the latter, Dr. Sharat Chandra's diasporic poetry describes his expatriate experience—which makes thoughts from his native experience come back to him.

Koyel Chakrabarty in her comprehensive paper, "'Equating the other half of her equation': An Appraisal of Androgynous Subsistence in *Wuthering Heights*, *Debi Chaudharani* and *Sula*", traces the concept of androgyny lurking in individual patterns in these three novels about different races, decades and nature. Chakrabarty asserts that Emily Brontë, Bankim Chandra Chattopadhyay and Toni Morrison have all invested their characters with distinctive androgynous qualities that create the image of *Ardhnarishvara* as a blend of power and sensitivity and set for themselves new paradigms and patterns.

The book *Reconceiving Postcolonialism: Visions and Revisions* aims at deepening the awareness of current postcolonial debates and perspectives. It explores an array of established critical positions and evaluates new critical positions. The articles included in the book display both historical depth and theoretical finesse as they attempt close and lively readings.

I wish to express my gratitude to the contributors in this editorial venture, who enthusiastically contributed to this project and enriched the anthology with their perceptive papers.

I am particularly thankful to Atlantic Publishers and Distributors (P) Ltd. for the confidence evinced in me and for seeing the book through the press.

Sunita Sinha

Contents

Feminine Psyche and The Narrative Strategies

1

Neeru Tandon

> We have to find the means at all costs. No longer separate the speech act from the spoken, make the female subject surface in a language where we can meet ourselves. Represent the feminine sub-conscious. Grasp language and penetrate what it discloses jouissance.[1]
>
> —Dupre

Aristotle says that plot is the most basic feature of narrative, that good stories must have a beginning, middle, and end, and that they give pleasure because of the rhythm of their ordering. But what creates the impression that a particular series of events has this shape? Theorists have proposed various accounts. Essentially, though, a plot requires a transformation; there must be an initial situation, a change involving a sort of reversal, and a resolution that marks the change as significant. Some theories emphasize types of parallelism that produce satisfactory plots, such as the move from one relationship between characters to its opposite, or from a fear or prediction to its rectification. In each case we find the association of a development on the level of events with a transformation on the level of theme. The theory of narrative postulates the existence of a level of structure what we generally call 'plot', independent of any particular language or representational medium. The basic distinction of the theory of narrative, then, is between plot and presentation, story and discourse. There are many variables, and they are crucial to narratives' effects. Mostly narrative theory explores different ways of conceiving these variables. What I have particularly in the mind is to find the endeavour of women writers to speak in a 'female tongue'. At the level of enunciation there is an overt concern with the role of the narrator and the narratee. A plurality of narrative voices is introduced; in many cases the narrators are writers.

Theorists distinguish 'first person narration', where a narrator says 'I', from what is somewhat confusingly called 'third person narration', where there is no 'I' the narrator is not identified as a character in the story and all the characters are refined to it's the third person, by name or as 'he' or 'she'. First person narrators may be the main 'protagonists' of the story, they tell, they may be participants, minor characters in the story; or they may be observer of the story, whose function is not to act but to describe things to us.

Narrative voices may have their own distinctive language, in which they recount everything in the story, or they may adopt and report the language of others. A narrative that sees things through the consciousness of a child may either use adult language to report the child's perceptions or slip into a child's language. The Russian theorist Mikhail Bakhtin describes the novel as fundamentally polyphonic (multi-voiced) or dialogic rather than monological (single-voiced). The essence of the novel is its staging of different voices or discourses and, thus of the clash of social perspectives and points of view. Theorists speak of self-conscious narration when narrators discuss the fact that they are telling a story, hesitate about how to tell it, or even flaunt the fact that they can determine how the story will turn out. Self-conscious narration highlights the problem of narrative authority.

The academic study of literature fulfils a combination of three functions in relation to the student and the larger community:

1. The rhetorical function of providing linguistic skills which can be used for aesthetic pleasure, and for effective communication in a variety of professional contexts; oratorical, political, forensic, creative and so on.
2. The humanist function of individual and social betterment, in which a literary education acts as a civilizing and acculturating process which inculcates literary judgement, taste and critical discernment.

3. The cognitive function of providing knowledge, specifically linguistic and literary, but also broadly social, cultural, ideological and even moral, which is mediated, historically and enhances perception of specific aspects of the human condition.

A novelist presents the truth of life through her or his fiction as he/she perceives it. For this, she has to choose a particular mode so that she can strike a chord of understanding with her readers and make the reading of her work a complete and satisfying experience for them. The method adopted by the novelist to present life in the process of living may be described as the narrative technique. Though the novel gets its sustenance from the story it intends to tell, its success depends on how it is narrated and also what else it conveys. The value of the novel is judged as much by what it conveys as by how it is conveyed. A novel becomes a work of fiction, a part of popular literature in the true sense when there is compatibility between the narration and the narrative technique. For example, the question occurs in the mind of a common reader why some writers use first person narrative and some use third person narrative.

It may be easier for the writer to use the third person omniscient narrative method, for it allows her to dive into the minds of her characters, explain their acts and also to present her views on men and matters. In this context the important thing to be decided is the centre of vision. This method helps gain objectivity and panoramic view but at the cost of emotional intensity and involvement on the part of the readers. If the narrator is one of the characters in the novel and the narration is carried on in the first person, the novelist can gain the advantage of lending its authenticity, immediacy as well as shifting his responsibility to the narrator. It also provides the necessary distance between the writer and the narrator.

Most of the writers have chosen first person narration in their first novels. In Anita Desai's *Cry, The Peacock* and Alice Walker's *The Color Purple* women who occupy the central positions in the novels both Maya and Celie are narrator heroines and in them lays the central consciousness of the novels. Though in *Cry, The Peacock*, Part I and Part II are third person narratives, most of the novel is revealed through the interior monologue in the mind of Maya. In the case of Celie, who tells her own stories, the narration is purely subjective but gains poignancy and also makes the readers emotionally involved. The first person narration helps the reader identify himself/herself with the narrator and look at the happenings from her point of view which renders the experience an unforgettable touch. A feminist writer does not merely play with concepts, she deconstructs in order to reconstruct. Her writing is scriptable, open-ended, text rather than work, fragmented. Enunciation is foregrounded. Multiple narrative voices are heard; there is an awareness of a possible multiplicity of narratees. There is a break with traditional genre boundaries and narrative patterns. But all this is directed to a particular end. The female subject seeks release from gender pattering; she seeks to retrieve her position as subject of her own story.

Turning inward, Anita Desai's fiction grapples with the intangible realities of life, plunges into the innermost depths of the human psyche to fathom its mysteries, the inner turmoil, and the chaos inside the mind. The technique is very appropriately used by Anita Desai in capturing authentically a psychological realism, an intensified impressionism, a 'quickened, multiplied consciousness'. As a result of this eminent use of flashbacks and stream of consciousness technique, the form of Desai's fiction becomes coincident with consciousness. Primarily interested in exploring the psychic depths of her female characters, Desai may be said to be doing something unique among the contemporary Indian English novelists. She portrays her characters as individuals 'facing single handed, the ferocious assaults of existence'. Desai lays no special emphasis on the plot construction, on the well-made novel with the traditional notion of having a beginning, middle, and an end. Story, action and drama mean little to her except insofar as they emanate directly from the characters she writes about. In Desai's concept of the form, pattern, rhythm, perspective or the singleness of vision are of utmost value. She prefers the word 'pattern' to plot or plan.

Anita Desai's art of fiction may be compared with the artist's endeavour to create a sophisticated montage in an aesthetic form. Montage may be defined as the art or the process of making a composite picture by bringing together into a single composition, or art form, different pictures and arranging them in an aesthetic sequence. This generalized definition of a montage admirably fits in with and governs the pattern of Anita Desai's fiction along with process of its creativity, its development and its aesthetic projection. Anita Desai's fifth novel, *Fire on the Mountain* pervasively demonstrates the novelist's basic technique of fiction as montage. This novel is a mosaic of many patterns, a texture of many images drawn from botanical and zoological sources.

Traditional techniques such as point of view and narrative plot have been utilized, not to produce a lively world of action but to find formal analogues for a private world. Desai's novels explore the subconscious recesses of the human mind with a view of determining their influence upon conduct and character. Their plots are often merely an excuse for psychological research, and Desai sometimes allows a stream of thoughts and images to flow with little or no regard to the conscious ordering of a narrative. Novels of Desai's type have always existed as alternatives to the novel of adventure or narrative in imagery and portraiture. The manner of the lyrical novelist like Anita Desai has led to a more effective rendering of the mind and has opened up ranges of metaphoric suggestiveness that could not have been achieved by purely narrative means. The lyrical novel, by contrast, seeks to combine man and world in a strangely inward, yet aesthetically objective form.

In *Cry, The Peacock*, the hallucination of lizards and birds copulating also show her unfulfilled sexual desire. The dust storm symbolises her inner fury and her violent resolve to extricate herself from her critical situation. Here Desai has made effective use of the devices to the interior monologue and the stream of consciousness technique in order to portray the lonely life of Maya.

Thus, as far as the narrative technique of the novel is concerned, many things prove it as a lyrical novel. The protagonist

Maya has the narrative voice of the novelist. The novel portrays a poetic vision to reconcile Maya with the inner and the outer self by committing the final act. The plot of the novel moves with modulations of memory. The novel is mostly in thoughts; and action is very little. Maya is the symbolic protagonist. She absorbs the animate and inanimate objects into herself.

The first person narration adopted in this novel is most suited to reveal Maya's changing states of mind from neurotic to hysterical and then to one of insanity. Desai's concern is to portray Maya's struggle to grapple with the threat of the albino astrologer's prophecy, viz. death for one of the couple in the fourth year of their marriage. To explain the act of homicide on the part of Maya, her creator has to reveal her through the various stages of her consciousness. As Meena Belliappa says, "The nature of the central character is crucial to a fictional technique which places the centre of the novel within a single consciousness."[2] Desai here uses a highly charged and poetic language saturated with symbols and images to protect Maya's consciousness. R.S. Sharma observes:

> The various psychic status of Maya, chaotic and disordered as they are, have been unified into a pattern through a series of motifs and symbols which while externalizing Maya's inner crises lend the narrative the qualities of a tragic poem.[3]

Maya's predicament is revealed through her angel of vision by employing the technique of flashback. Anita Desai uses colour symbolism dexterously to present Maya's confused state of mind. The dance motif is also used repeatedly. The peacock dances like Shiva who stands both for life and death, destruction and creation. Even if the cry of the peacock is a myth, it effectively conveys Maya's predicament. Maya is often drawn to the moon a symbol of both love and lunacy. Desai has used beautifully the linguistic device as a narrative technique. As K.R. Srinivasa puts it: "She has tried to gorge a style supple and suggestive enough to convey the fever and fretfulness of the steam of consciousness of her principal characters."[4] Really what makes the reading of the novel an intense and disturbing experience is the narrative technique employed to convey Maya's predicament. Light and darkness in their various shades are employed symbolically throughout in Anita Desai's novel, *Where Shall We Go This Summer*? Light is mostly associated with the sky and is symbol of the romantic ideals that Sita, the protagonist, hankers after, while darkness which is attributed variously to some concrete earthly phenomena serves as a metaphor for her past which she is yet to reconcile with.

Anita Desai has concerned herself with the inner conflict of her characters, mainly women characters. She presents, sometimes the conflicts of her female characters as if she were sitting in the mind of these women. She expresses the ambitions, the fears, the dilemmas and the miseries of women as only a woman can feel and understand.

Fire on the Mountain is one such masterpiece wherein Desai concerns herself with the anguish of Nanda Kaul, a woman quite past her prime; the widow of a Vice-Chancellor. Nanda Kaul's suicide in the end may be justly recognized as one of the most beautiful scenes in English fiction. When the shocking news of Ila Das's rape and murder is broken to Nanda she bursts into frenzy. Her frenzied outburst may be interpreted in various ways and each interpretation helps to enhance the narrative beauty of *Fire on the Mountain*. The scene is highly suggestive and inconclusive.

Desai's *Clear Light of Day* is a study of youthful dreams. The novel tries to probe the subconscious where love and frustration create enormous shadows. Desai also shows through her narrative skill how the mind refuses to get trapped within the maze of shadows. The story moves from the murky atmosphere of decay and death into the clear light of day. Throughout the narrative, Desai uses several distinctive motifs, such as shadows against light and songs against silence to weave a rich tapestry in which her characters move. The novel begins with the song of koels ringing out from the dark trees like 'an arrangement of bells' and it ends with the rich nourishment of music at the Misras. They listen to Mulk's singing, his voice 'creeping out of the silent shadows like a skeletal bird making its swoop'. In portraying Bim's turbulent memories against a background of shadows and sounds; Desai has not just written a novel about family love, but also created a memorable work of art adorned with rich poetry.

Encouraged by the popularity of the new shift in treatment, Anita Desai experimented with another theme in her widely acclaimed novel *Journey to Ithaca* discussing socio-spiritual (cultural) experiences of the female characters as a possible threshold towards self-identification rather than pursuing the earlier subject matter of socio-psycho analysis. Similar progression in theme, that is identity solicitation by women through spiritual gnosis seems to be the central discussion of *Fasting, Feasting*, nevertheless, the fallacy to dispense with this recent novel as merely a religio-spiritual speculum into the life of modern Indian women must be eschewed. *Fasting, Feasting* is a well-formed, highly complex novel having several intriguing episodes. The title of the novel is explicitly symbolical. Fasting alludes to the life of self-discipline, renunciation and inner purification connoting essential rungs of the ladder culminating in spiritual gnosis. Through the character of Mira-Masi, Anita Desai focuses light on different types of women liberation. Uma's spiritual experience in the Ashram is described dramatically. Through her narrative Desai concludes categorically that whether it is the East or the West, in the absence of religious and spiritual anchorage neither family, nor society can sustain human beings.

This novel is important and distinct because of one more factor 'Food'. One of the major sources of life often generates a network of a writer's thoughts, carrying with it all the biological and primitive associations. This element makes images vibrant; it's the best tool of a writer in creating the desired effect. Desai works on surfaces, never intends to go beyond certain depth of human mind and that too, she searches here through stomach.

Thus, we have seen clearly that Desai has a subtle and inimitable style. Her fiction is symbolic, sensitive, and psychological. Anita Desai is a painter of sensitive poetic pictures. Her pictures are varied in hue and open to manifold interpretation. Moving deep into the works of Anita Desai one notices her food imagery. Going back to *Cry, The Peacock,* we remember the image of Maya sharing cool lemonade with her husband, of Maya sharing meals with her father; of the crowded dining hall of her-in-laws' home; each picture tells us of Maya's relationship with the other characters, whether cool, lukewarm, claustrophobic or dominating and torrid. *Fasting-Feasting* is full of food imagery; barbecues; ladoos and more and more food. Anita Desai uses these gustatory images to speak of her concerns with man and his psyche. Desai uses food imagery to show how men satisfy their psychological and emotional cravings with food. No doubt, Desai is subtle and sensitive and her style is one of suggestive symbolism.

Anita Desai is essentially a symbolist whose works are studded with exquisite symbols employed functionally and artistically. She has been able to accomplish this because she had pursued, and has been deeply influenced by, the symbolic European and American literatures. To Anita Desai, the extensive use of symbols is necessity and writing is an effort to discover and then to underline, and finally to convey the true significance of things.

Anita Desai, being the modern psychological novelist is concerned with the exploration and delineation of psyche, with the examination and presentation of the inner being of people, and not with the external life of systematic thinking, coherent speaking, and intelligible actions based on the principle of causality. She is a psychological novelist in thought, content and technique. She adopts the symbolist technique in her writing out of sheer necessity to portray the inner mystery, the unconscious and the subconscious of the characters. She says in an interview with Ramesh K. Srivastava, "I use (symbols) unconsciously. I mean I employ metaphors and images which acquire significance and suggest deeper meanings than they state, i.e. turn into symbols."[5] Inevitably, Anita Desai's novels are permeated with brilliant symbols. All of her novels from *Cry, The Peacock* onwards with the exception of the last two via. *In Custody* and *Baumgartner's Bombay*, which only sporadically concentrate on the inner life of the characters and mostly deal with the external, reality, are deeply embedded in symbolism. Quite a good number of symbols are extensively used by her to bring out the essence of life, particularly the feminine psyche and sensibility and this within the framework of the art of the novel.

Shashi Deshpande utilizes dreams as a literary device to portray the psychic reality of her characters. Shashi Deshpande is a careful and conscientious writer. Her writings nevertheless give the impression of spontaneity. She does not try to run after technical innovations or stylistic deviations, but her use of language is fresh and characteristically precise. Deshpande learnt the secrets of craftsmanship assiduously. As a mature writer, she has been conscious of the significance of this aspect of fiction writing right from the beginning. She told Lakshmi Holmstorm:

> I learnt about language. Craftsmanship is so important in writing, and you only learn it by doing it. And the short story was the perfect form to learn from, because one had to be brief. One had to be careful. And that training is still with me. I am very careful about not using any extra word.[6]

Deshpande's writings once again prove that art lies in concealing art. The highly functional language with telling economy that she uses, is an important asset of her as a fiction writer.

In her modesty, Deshpande thinks of herself as an ordinary woman 'who writes sitting at home'. But she is honestly concerned with expressing herself in English as clearly and effectively as possible. Deshpande concedes choices to a fiction writer in technical matters: "There are some, maybe several, choices in the technique; in the way you 'tell' the story". About her travail in developing the right technique for herself, Deshpande told Holmstrom:

> Technique is something which I have to worry a lot about. I have to work at it and think about it and it takes me a long time to hit upon it exactly. Its' like setting the tanpura... before a concert begins.[7]

Deshpande has been so much careful about the technique in her fiction. Her writings are singularly free from strain and form has never been allowed to smother the content of her works. Consequently, despite their serious tone, her novels make a fascinating reading. One may find in some of Deshpande's novels occasionally autobiographical strains, but her characters and incidents are not directly lifted from her own life. What the novelist does is to make creative use of her experiences and memories in her works.

Memory plays a significant role in her novels. The narrative keeps on moving back and forth in time. The non-linear arrangement in her novels gives them the integrative structure they have. The novelist also uses some devices of the stream of consciousness flashback; light of memory, interior monologue and so on to probe into the psyche of her characters. Deshpande does not write for foreign readers and there is no attempt in her novels at 'window-dressing'. Her novels have an interesting beginning, and both the beginning and the end are convincing. Most of her novels and short stories are open-ended, and the reader is free to supply the conclusion the way they deem fit, for her fictional concerns and narrative.

Technically speaking, the novel *The Binding Vine* can be called a pure novel. It has the action divided into four evenly balanced parts. As in the novels of Jane Austen, there is very scantly physical action shown. The action of the novel begins in part one, gathers gear and develops in part two and three and reaches the Aristotelian end in the last para. The narrative technique is the first person autobiographical one. Urmila, the narrator heroine, is the pivot of the plot, who connects all the threads, in the plot. It is Urmila's agony at the death of Anu which weaves all emotions and themes into unity. The novelist has skillfully protrayed her characters, especially her women. The central symbolism in the novel is contained in the title of the novel. Urmila is like an Oak and the infant Anu is like a creeper around her. She is a sensitive vine and needs Kishore as an Oak to entwine herself around. The fragrance of the night queen is the departed Anu.

Thus, it becomes clear that Deshpande's narrative mode of social realism and her avowed interest in limiting herself to small social landscapes, especially that of either joint family or a nuclear family, her preference for a narrator who uses the first person narration, the absence of issues which directly deal with questions regarding nation, imperialism, neocolonialism or the conflicts and differences between cultures could act as resisting blocks in claiming her to be either postcolonial or postmodern.

The feminism depicted by her novels seem to end where they began with only a changed protagonist who has followed the tortuous route of self-examination and self-realization. One striking feature of her novels is that the re-presentation of a woman belonging to a particular class of the Indian society is very realistic.

Shashi Deshpande's novels encapsulate her artistic vision of femininity. In her fiction she explores and exposes the long smothered wail of the incarcerated psyche of her female protagonists imprisoned within the four walls of domesticity and sandwiched between tradition and modernity, between illusion and reality and between the mask and the face. Shashi Deshpande has dealt graphically with problems that confront a middle-class educated woman in the patriarchal Hindu society. *Roots and Shadows*, explores the inner self of Indu, who symbolises the 'New Woman' who is educated and who lives in close association with society brushing aside all its narrow conventions. Through the character of Indu, Deshpande has portrayed the inner struggle of an artist to express herself, to discover her real self through her inner and instinctive potential for creative writing. Indu perceives herself as a shadow of the female self, a negative, and an object. Indu recognizes her displacement and marginalisation as a woman and a process of ego-dissolution begins. She finds herself merging into others, experiencing a loss of boundaries. The authoritative and dominating male has not only suppressed the female voice but also brought silence, dullness and repulsion to the houses women live in. Indu exists and yet does not exist. Indu plays the role of an ideal housewife but the role of a wife restricts, rather circumscribes her self-development; firstly, by taking away her freedom of thought and expression, and secondly, by denying her the scope of giving free play to her artistic potential Indu cannot unburden herself, and her feminine instinct is curbed and suppressed.

Indu's is the paradoxical situation in which Indian women are enmeshed. Indu's problematic of 'becoming' expresses Deshpande's feminist polemics against sexual and gender roles imposed upon women in a patriarchal culture. It reduces Indu to a mere thing or a mind less body, for her feminine instinct for articulation is suppressed. She realises that marriage had stunted and hampered her individuality because she had regarded it as a 'trap' and not a bond. As a feminist novel, *Roots and Shadows*, gives expression to feminine discourse all through; revealing the pure voice of woman herself. One may ask why Indu, a feminist herself, is so critical of Akka who is also a woman. The answer here is that feminism does not mean a feminine reaction against whatever is masculine in order to accept whatever comes from femininity or females. It has got its own right or wrong.

Shashi Deshpande exposes the male prejudice against female children. A characteristic feature of feminist writing is not only to articulate woman's voice but also to present a critique of the canons of patriarchy. It scrutinizes the position of woman in a male-dominated social context. Deshpande brings out the boiling and broiling problem of marriage as an evil social practice. Deshpande's mode of representative writing goes here along with a technique of weaving together stories from the past and the present as well as stories of different women. In *The Binding Vine*, the network of familial relationships is presented in a manner which seems to be 'natural' for the story of an Indian woman. It is mixed with other stories, gossip and narrations. Thus, Urmi's narration of her own story is interwoven with carefully selected stories of other women; some belonging to the family, some belonging to the larger society, who accidentally draws her into their own narrative structures. Through analogies, similes and metaphors, an author renders his or her expressions concise, concrete and condensed. Of all the literary devices employed by an author, metaphors speak volumes of his or her mental attitude and concentration of vision. Obviously, a metaphor is very helpful in image making, in concretizing emotions and in crystallizing moods.

Shashi Deshpande also used metaphors like 'the dark' and 'the sunlight', 'death' and 'life', 'silence' and 'the binding vine'. They tend to neatly summarize the fluctuating moods and the mysterious emotions of a sensitive woman. Metaphors clearly reveal the inner workings of the protagonist's minds and the emotional ripples in their hearts. 'The dark' and 'the light' are frequently used as the contrastive metaphors. While the former denotes fear and sorrow, dejection and estrangement, the latter signals joy and fearlessness, company and compassion. Another dominant metaphor operating in Shashi Deshpande's fiction is 'death', which remains in sheer contradiction to 'life'. In *If I Die Today* and *Come up and be Dead* the metaphor of death becomes powerfully evocative and assertive. Another metaphor 'silence' is also operative. In her novels Deshpande makes a powerful study of female psyche and its problems. She unmistakably highlights women's helpless and hapless situation, their existential dilemma, their want of understanding or compatibility with their husbands. In fact, Shashi Deshpande has woven a delicate and subtle texture of her fictional world with a good deal of thought and dexterity. Though the metaphors used in her novels are not many, they powerfully highlight the dichotomy of human life.

Shashi Deshpande uses a beautiful image to describe Jaya's married life in *That Long Silence*; "A pair of bullocks yoked together, a clever phrase, but can it substitute for the reality?" The images employed by Deshpande are appropriate to the theme of the novel. These are recurrent images—'a pair of bullocks yoked together and 'sheltering tree'—and these images explain the meaning of the novel in a subtle way.

One of the most enjoyable features of Deshpande's writing is the unselfconscious list of literary allusion, myth and folklore. Her fiction offers a startlingly vivid perception of the inner world of Indian womanhood, forced to remain silent for so very long. Since many of her novels have woman for the central consciousness, these devices are especially useful to the novelist as a means of illuminating the inner landscape of women's minds. She does not use myth and legend as embellishment or for local colour or ethnic applique work. These factors are deeply engrained in the Indian psyche—especially those which are found in the epics and the puranas. They are so much a part of our psyche and our collective unconscious that it is in terms of these myths and legends that we try to order our inner world. One of the best instances of the pervasive significance of these elements is to be found in DHNT, where the story of Dhruva serves as an analogue to Sarita's story. The Tulsi-Cult, an important part of women's lives in India, finds its proper place in her novels.

The themes of domination and cunningness are illustrated in *That Long Silence* through a folktale, i.e. story of the sparrow and the Crow—one of the earliest fable heard by Indian children. The novelist's use of mythic material requires the reader to do his homework in order to get the most out of Deshpande's fiction. She has created a familiar world anew in which authentic experiences of the interior landscape of Indian woman is powerfully projected through devices including myths, folktales and so on.

Shobhaa De as a creative writer is becoming immensely popular day by day. Most of the readers enjoy her extraordinary narrative technique as well as her subject matter. She was the first person to popularize the now much read and heard Indian Esperanto: 'Hinglish'. She is essentially a feminist writer. Like Nayantara Sahgal and Shashi Deshpande, she concentrates on women's problems and gives a new approach to them. She is a modern novelist who recognizes the displacement and marginalization of women and attempts to turn this pattern upside down through her writings. Adding to the interest value of her fiction is De's sharp eye for detail, her piercingly accurate characterization, her perceptive insight of the secret depths of the human psyche. Each novel is encompassing its own exquisite world of passion, romance, fantasy and inevitably hard reality.

The contents of her novels, her mastery over the art of story telling and her use of the language is very significant. In fact, her novels seem to be the modern version of picaresque novels of the eighteenth century. The picaro in this case is a woman, may be partly on account of her experience as a journalist that she is able to say things interestingly and with a courage of conviction in a language uniquely her own. Her novels owe their incomparable popularity to her intimate understanding of the psyche for women and their problems. Shobhaa De is very careful about words and their order. She says 'That she has always found words very seductive; if they're arranged in a startingly original way'. She verbally reenacts scenes and situations. Her innovative flair for using words can be easily guessed from a few pairing like 'fluff' and 'flippery', 'grime and grit, pegs and pakoras', pariahs and parasites etc. She used the kind of language and the explicit sex scenes that caused 'major shock waves' among readers when it was first published: this was the first time that an Indian woman wrote in this manner, and it was difficult to accept. But in her need to write and be read easily and quickly, she is frequently slipshod and often so informal as to be meaningless and superficial; her fondness for the epithet 'Lousy', for instance, that she can apply to everything. But, in spite of all the sleaze and the slime that she portrays, in spite of producing pulp fiction that only too often titillates rather than entertains, she, is paradoxically enough, a serious writer with her clear-eyed honest appraisal of human relationships and her overriding concern for female psyche.

De's novel *Socialite Evenings* offers a few pointers for us to view it as a feminist work. This novel relies upon stereotypes. I suggest that the reduction of women characters into stereotypes is an overall narrative strategy. On De's part Karuna, Anjali and Ritu are flat and stereotyped because they are made so in a male dominated social context. De is suggesting that such a discourse about women reduces them and assigns them to these types. It denies individuality to the women, and forces them to adopt attitudes, envisioned for them by the males.

De's choice of the cinematic technique is not just to popularize her novel and bring it into the tradition of the fiction of the media but an attempt to communicate a vision of life. De owes much to two techniques-montages and editing, both of which, incidentally, have a snapshot like effect.

In *Snapshots*, the influence of film editing is seen particularly in the use of cross-cuts, contrast-cuts, dissolves, flashbacks, and the occasional substitute image, while the shifting point of view achieves a multiple view point that gives the novel a feeling of synchronicity, so that in the end the experience of one becomes a metaphor for life and society as a whole. The novel consists of fourteen chapters, each divided into a number of sections separated from one another by cuts, so that each section is as if it were complete in itself and each chapter a montage of snapshots, the entire novel being linked together by the thematic montage.

Her novel *Sisters* deals with the fast emerging urban culture and its evils. It is a piece of literature with absorbing narrative, well knit plot, dramatic structure rich in images and psychological realism, in characterization and intense individual awareness of self and social predicament. Very significantly, the novelist used images of 'vultures' and 'sharks' for the corrupt business tycoons and 'lousi' and 'fish' for their women victims.

De's *Starry Nights* can be analyzed in the light of the contemporary feminist critical theories put forth by Sandra M. Gilbert and Susan Gubar. Shobhaa De is not content with only protest and petition formula hence her separation is visible from the 'mirror' category. The second category in which Gilbert and Gubar place the more vocal and violent feminist critics/ authors is that of vamp. Truly speaking, Shobhaa De flaunts a frightening flippancy in flagrantly flouting the conventional canons of morality and decency prevalent in the patriarchal social order. Shobhaa De's striving affinity with the 'vamp' group of feminist authors is clearly visible in her novel especially *Starry Nights. Socialite Evenings* was her first experimental attempt at the vamp ideology. Anjali is the first sketch of Aasha Rani of *Starry Nights*. Shobhaa De displays the first sign of being a vamp artist in *Socialite Evenings*, in which the troika of female characters symbolize the absolute freedom of woman kind from all types of patriarchal restraints.

The vamp approach to feminism is at full play in the novel after Aasha Rani's first surrender to Kishanbhai. Thereafter, Shobhaa De makes Aasha Rani embrace upon a dazzling round of sexual encounters with her rather persistent references to the erotic zones and the private parts, and characteristics of the female body. With her seductiveness, Aasha Rani breaks all sexual taboos. *Starry Nights*, furthers the theme of a liberated woman. It is but an extension of the frontiers of feminism. She, with an unfeminine vehemence, becomes a liberated woman who lives for her own pleasures and knows no value system. Shobhaa De as a vamp author explores the female psyche and candidly and boldly puts forth in her novel what a woman always feels but is ever afraid to express.

Shobhaa De conforms to the vamp ideology of feminism in the sense that she shows how self-destructive the attempts to achieves liberation have been for Aasha Rani and Sudha and will be for others as well. It is precisely because of the inherent lopsidedness and orthodoxy of the patriarchal system that perpetuates male hegemony. But even then the ending of the novel does not sound a note of despair; it is symbolic of a new beginning once again. This time it is Sasha, Aasha's daughter, who has to continue the show, the struggle and the survival of a woman against the predatory male dominated society.

Shobhaa De's vamp brand of feminism admits of no redemptive formula for the 'fallen women' and no millennium for the liberated women. Her women characters who endeavour to liberate themselves often meet with disaster. In another novel *Snapshots* De introduces Swati, who is apparently no victim, but a survivor. De's *Snapshots* seems to be written in haste: there are several lapses in style and occasional slips in time sequence, and episodes and characters are sometimes quite gratuitously introduced without being integrally linked to the story and having, therefore, quite frequently the effect of mere titillation. Its picture of society is apparently based on popular women's fiction and soap operas of the west rather than on the Indian reality. True the rape, incest, lesbianism, perversions described in the novel do exist in India, but the overemphatic exclusion of everything else, the occasionally contrived situation, and the crude language the characters speak, are unrealistic, and cheapen the impact of the novel. De is, moreover, surprisingly careless about details.

Not surprisingly, the novel reads like a film that depends largely on montage itself resembling a series of snapshots significantly juxtaposed against one another and editing for its effects. It is here that the interest of *Snapshots* lies in its technique of narration. In her earlier novels, De has generally followed the more traditional linear mode, occasionally branching out into the archetypal feminine cyclic narration; *Snapshots* marks a definite change in her technique, and consequently, a change in her vision of life.

Women writers often over exploit the technique of emphasis through accumulation of characters and incidents reinforcing the idea of women's repression, making the author seem over eager to make her point. Anita Desai and Shashi Deshpande both successfully project the evolving feminist consciousness of the Indian women of the today. Through the a depiction of their questioning self while Shobhaa De is more direct in her feminists sympathies than the other writers being studied.

II

In this thesis, I attempt to demonstrate intertextual connections between major novels by Afro-American women, e.g. Toni Morrison's *The Bluest Eye* and Alice Walker's *The Color Purple*. These connections enter largely around subsequent women's re-figurations of Hurston's delineations in her novel of a female protagonist's quest for self-integration and a supportive community.

I focus on these authors's use of language and apply socio-linguistic theory to my analysis. I argue that the history of black women in Black America, a history framed by racism and sexism, has contributed to the development of a language that reveals black women's consciousness. The language used by the black women characters in the novels discussed in the study, demonstrates this consciousness and communicates culturally specific meanings to those black women who share the same consciousness. Finally, it discusses how the black woman, who rarely recognizes herself in the faces of Euro-American women literary characters, has become an insider as she reviews literature written about her and in her own language. The signs and symbols she encounters are no longer arbitrary, they are loaded with culturally specific womanist meanings. The style of Morrison in *Song of Solomon* is effective because the reader has real sense of accomplishment as he travels through various levels of awareness. These levels increase in complexity as Morrison tackles issues in black history and life. The one drawback to the style she utilizes here is that many clues and important images can be missed by a careless or confused reader. But even then after each reading, the reader achieves a higher level of understanding and appreciation of Morrison's narrative craft.

Jazz, Morrison's new novel, serves to redefine the very possibilities of narrative point of view. Morrison has found a way to create an ensemble of improvised sound out of a composed music. *Jazz* is made up of rhythmic paragraphs, subsections and sections that together compose a musical score. She also uses her language-instrument to try out some daring modes and techniques of play and to create the informal, improvisatory patterning of *Jazz*. Elements of blues, march, rag, spirituals or hymns get fused into the matrix of *Jazz*. The music produced is a combination of melody, rhythm and harmony with a basic theme or composition which provides for a large scope of improvisation.

What is, however, compelling in *Jazz* is not the novel's plot, but how the story is told. In the telling of the story of *Jazz*, Morrison has adopted a unique narrative method in which the omniscient narrator addresses the reader, but at times allows other characters to relate their stories from their own point of view. *Jazz* has several narrators, or points of view, whose speaking consciousness bring forth harmony to the novel. Morrison gives us a multi-faceted view of Joe's neighbour, Rose Dear, Violet's mother, True Belle, her grandmother, Alice Manfred, Dorcas' aunt. Action, her boy friend and Felice, her girl friend—by the seemingly simple device of letting different voices tell the story or related episodes of the same story. The vision of Morrison's nameless narrator frames the love story, and this anonymous voice slowly draws readers into the rhythm of the city, especially Harlem, where *Jazz* casts bewitching spells on people's psyche. A disembodied narrator slips easily and guiltlessly from third person all knowingness to first person lyricism, without ever relaxing its grip upon our imagination. Just as the musical mode of *Jazz* uses familiar material to express various sentiments, uniting performer and audience, the fictional mode of *Jazz* establishes an instant contact between the characters and the reader.

The opening lines are 'bluesy' in the way they 'talk around' a direct emotional response to murder and description of a corpse. Such use of implication or suggestion, rather than direct acknowledgement of emotion are the fundamental trope of the blues musical technique. The novel's language is Jazzy as it has an improvisational tone with its multiplicity of 'solos' relating itself to the central incident. The opening line of each chapter is a direct continuation of the closing line of the previous one and acts as the 'jazz' metaphor connecting it to the psychological vortex of Joe-Violet relationship. Joe's search for his emotional needs is portrayed thus not through traditional constructs of aesthetic beauty but through his murder of Dorcas. She symbolizes the happiness which they could have shared and have murdered with their own hands. Violet's retreating to her silence with her monosyllabic uttering of 'ahs' and 'ums' and 'have mercys' and her clinging to her dolls and parrots objectify her acute alienation.

Among the narrative strategies employed by the writer to represent collectivity; is her use of group dialogues, which serve to convey the idea of a social body and at the same time communicates its values. This once again has a dialogical function to play in its mode of articulation and is very close to the choirs in the black churches. The adult voices overheard by the two sisters and also by the young Cholly in *The Bluest Eye* represent the children's main source of understanding their world. In the final scene of exorcism in Beloved, the community chorus reaches its fullest dramatic potential. In the chorus, Morrison assembles the collectivity and concentrates its efforts. Among the functions which constitute social action, are those of the natural processes of nourishing, healing, conjuring and that of representation: joking, storytelling and singing. As opposed to the trafficking of goods vital to the dominant white community, Morrison institutes the exchange of food as the norm in society centering on the concept of nurturance.

Joking and storytelling, too have therapeutic effects on the community. Laughter is both self-deprecating and self-healing. *Sula* uses humour to raise Jude from self-pity. The barber shop conversation in *Song of Solomon* also discovers the peculiar irony in black existence. By joking about one's fears and indignities, one can extract laughter from the masses so as to make them bearable. Like the joke, storytelling also acts as a means of coping with the existential pain and remembering it for other's benefit. As in jazz, the music tells a story; it can express the complex chemistry of life in the city. Dorcas lives and dies to its sound.

In the novel *Beloved*, there is instability or rather an inadequacy of language in the passages of interior monologue recorded from the points of view of Sethe, Denver and Beloved. Mingled with the voices from the past are the voices of Sethe, Denver and Beloved, first separated and then interwoven, polyphonic and heteroglossic at the same time. Beloved's monologues reveal the recollections and desires of one who is at once in and out of time, alive and dead comprising past and present to defy interpretation. The linguistic units in this section, whether they are sentences, phrases or single words are separated by spaces and not by marks of punctuation:

> I AM BELOVED and she is mine. I see her take flowers away from leaves...she puts them in a round basket...the leaves are not for her...she fills the basket...she opens the grass.[8]

Only the first person pronoun and the first letter in each paragraph are capitalised. Toni Morrison writes of 'the complicated psychic power one had to exercise to revert devastation'.

Morrison's narrative art in *The Bluest Eye* is something different. Morrison's dilemma as a writer is that she cannot retell three hundred years, she must make Pecola's story relevant to that history and yet be her own story. She must create both a sense of intimacy with her characters, yet enough distance to give the theme its expansive substance, if she is to communicate the tragic complexity of such a 'single' theme. Perhaps, even more than the usual novel, the way in which this theme is presented is crucial to the theme itself. Morrison's narrative technique in the construction of the book is essential truth more than the particular events within it.

The speed, the frequency with which the words are said, run together, set the tonal modalities for the structure of this story about Pecola Breedlove and her mother and father, and Claudia and Frieda Mac Teer and their mother and father; about Junior and his mother, Geraldina, etc.

Morrison begins the objective part of each chapter of this book with a run together fragment from the Dick and Jane primer, a fragment appropriate to the subject of that particular section. By removing the punctuation from these fragments, she heightens the lack of internal integrity essential to their simplistic order. For example, 'Autumn' the chapter about the house Pecola Breedlove lives in, begins with 'HERE IS THE HOUSE IT IS GREEN IT HAS A RED DOOR IT IS VERY PRETTY'. These undifferentiated words are juxtaposed to Morrison's integral description of Pecola's house.

Morrison effectively transfers to her readers, especially her black readers, her sense of the images and cosmology of black language. Whether song or story, the universe of this novel comes though the metaphors of its language, its synthesis or rendering of families and events, its myth making or spiritualism—all of this we find at the centre of the novel *Song of Solomon.*

Irony—is the chief device, used in the novel to explain the behaviour of the characters. Morrison's ironies, however are always gentle, meant to heal rather than to wound, to correct rather than to punish. Her humour, like her use of language in general and like her departures from stylistic tradition, is nonetheless subversive, often sexually implicit, certainly gendered. She takes her novelistic pleasure and provides the same for her readers, for her language is always a celebration of the laugh of the Medusa, even when her subjects are so serious, so tragic and intense, that they turn us to stone.

Even more sombre is the image of candy in *Song of Solomon*, Guitar grows ill even at the smell of sweets. The peppermint stick, his mother buys for him on the day of his father's funeral, is surely a surrogate penis, but one that only serves to emphasize his own impotence to protect his mother, or any woman; therefore, he discards the candy as he discards the women, "he could not eat it or throw it away, until finally, in the outhouse, he let it fall into the earth's stinking hole".[9]

Milk and the image of motherhood are most particularly associated with male impotence in *Beloved*. Male impotence and images of castration, whether created by female submission or female power are certainly problematic for a great many readers, writers and critics of Morrison's work.

The image of three prostitutes in *The Bluest Eye* also presents a deep psychological study. "These women hated men, all men, without shame, apology or discrimination." They found all men, whether black or white, Mexican or Jews, old, inadequate and weak. They took delight in cheating them.

These three whores are prototype for their more sinister sisters. Morrison is giving a warning to women readers and feminist critics that, if women participate in the castration of men, whether through love or malice, they will end up with no men at all, only children.

The image of female characters is represented through houses. The houses in her novels themselves exude exoticism, just as do the women who live in them. The 'house of many rooms' in which Sula lives with Eva and Hannah is as whimsically constructed, with gratuitous stairways and doorways, as the lives of its inhabitants, and it is a testament to female power and autonomy in its refutation of male logic and practicality. Similarly Pilate's house, which she shares with Reba and Hagar, is defined as female space, empty of furniture, on the edge of the black community and therefore, of both the black and the dominant cultures. However, the persistence of the female triad as image in Morrison's fiction has also to do with an inquiry into the dangerous secrets of women's lives, their ways of knowing, their language and the wisdom and truth it expresses.

Traditionally, critics have either ignored song as a legitimate vehicle for establishing slave humanity or have limited their appraisal of song. Ashraf Rusholy in his article "Daughters Signifyin(g) History" argues that *Beloved's* narrative structure takes on 'a dialogue form that is like music or black preaching', but never identified the role of song in what he calls a 'musical narrative'. Morrison establishes song as imperative to her characters' survival during nearly every chapter of *Beloved*. *Beloved's* victims use song to reclaim and affirm their personhood in an aggressively inhuman world. Paul D's horrific experience at prison camp in Georgia is an episode in which Morrison shows the power of song to combat even the worst and most dehumanizing despair. Paul D uses song to defend his humanity. Morrison's inclusion of the specific topics of the slave songs from Gerogia allows the readers to identify more closely with incredible complex ideas of identity and worth during and after the chattel experience. Sixo establishes his humanity in front of the white men with his song, and the fact that Morrison does not record the words of this song is testimony to the higher significance of its sound. Beyond this, Morrison's inclusion of the juba song at such a grave and desperate section of the novel reinforces the expansive range of emotion harboured within the 'Sorrow Song'.

Always in Morrison's texts, there is a possible kind of redemption through that which is erotic, it lies in her language, resonates in her imagery, provides meaning and texture to structure. In fact, Morrison writes the female body, that her texts imitate and recreate the feminine orgasm, that they constitute what Cixous calls 'the flesh of language' the 'feminine style'.

It's true that because of the newness of themes and style of writing and use of language, black women's writing has been claimed to be a separate branch of literature by many black feminist critics. Lorraine Bethel is one such critic who believes that there is a separable and identifiable tradition of black women writers, simultaneously existing within and independent of the American, Afro-American and American female literary tradition. To prove the separate identity and features of black women's writing. Mary Helen Washington has stated "They use specific language, specific symbols, specific images, with which they try to record their lives, and try to claim their own name and their own space".[10]

A consideration of language is primary in the development of theoretical paradigms as these relate to all literatures, but particularly to the African-American feminine/feminist text. Toni Morrison's language is the language of black and feminine discourse-semiotic, maternal, informed as much by silence as by dialogue, as much by absence as by presence. Morrison seems to conjure her language, to invent a form of discourse that is always at once both metaphysical and meta-fictional. Morrison claims in her novels, freedom to move beyond language. Morrison sings her novels, images of music pervade her work, but so also does a musical quality of language, a sound and rhythm that permeate and radiate in every novel.

All women's songs, Morrison indicates, are 'just outside music', often also they constitute a protest. Cixous writes, in *The Laugh of the Medusa*, "In women's speech, and in their writing, that element which never stops resonating, which, once we've been permeated by it, profoundly and imperceptibility touched by it, retains the power of moving us—that element is the song: first music from the first voice of love which is alive in every women".[11]

Like music, but even less intelligible, far more mystical, is Morrison's recurrent evocation of a sound that transcends language, a primal cry that echoes from prehistory and also breaks 'the back of words'.

In one sense, Morrison's novels serve as the reader's own dreams, where that which is repressed, contained, becomes consciously expressed. Irigaray writes about the dream quality of the feminine text as a reflection of the feminine sensibility. Perspective and narrative responsibility in *Sula* are similarly 'feminized' by being fragmented and multiple.

The next prominent novelist of African-American fiction is Alice Walker. As a craftsman Walker sorts out the throwaways and stitches them into a tapestry of society. Walker uses thrifty sentences, knotted questions, tight metaphors and terse sections. Her novels continually stitch a fabric of the everyday violence that is committed against her characters.

Walker used the often unheralded heritage of black women, the creative sparks as well as the history of restrictions, as the foundation of her artistic vision. As a feminist, she explores the relationship between this tradition and societal change as crucial to the search for freedom—not only for woman, but for man, the child, the society, the culture, the land.

The theme is revealed through Walker's skillful, often subtle narrative. She is at her best a storyteller. We can feel her delight in telling stories in mingling bits and pieces of hard reality and lyrical fantasy. Like a quilter, she is economical; her stories are thrifty, there are no bulges or long stretches of the same material, no waste. Her craft of words, in fact, becomes a potential model of regeneration.

In her first novel, *The Color Purple* Alice Walker used epistolary form which calls attention to the act of writing by using letters to construct a tale. Once aware of the conspicuous presence of writing, we cannot help but note that a transformation occurs in terms of both its function and form. In the first half of the work, Celie uses writing to effect self-actualization, and its standard form is modified; as elements of the oral are injected into it. In the second half of history of Africa and Afro-Americans, and its function as a cultural element whose appearance generally signals the disappearance of the oral is altered. Thus, within this novel, two black women employ a device traditionally used by a white male culture to insure its authority.

Walker is very aware of the power of writing and by extension, literacy, to preserve and value one culture while destroying and devaluing another. We also see that her concern focuses on the particular experience of black women under a system in which writing is used for cultural devaluation. The importance of narrative technique was clearly understood by Walker. It can be judged by the way Walker has written the novel, *The Color Purple*, where both Celie and Nettie learn to master the written word and to modify its form and function so that they, as black women, are no longer complete victims of the racial and sexual oppression dictated by a white, ethnocentric use of writing. By mastering and modifying writing, Celie and Nettie change it into an implement that is no longer solely the property of men and whites, but one used by black women to gain a greater awareness of themselves and to preserve their oral history. The more Celie writes, the more she is able to analyze her experience and subsequently herself. She uses writing to fix the events of her life, thereby lending them coherence and making their review and understanding possible. She renders her writing in an oral manner. The spelling, syntax, and grammatical construction all evoke the way Celie sounds. The use of the black English to be verbal conjugation and the omission of 'are' in the sentence, 'she be my age but they married' serves as an example. We have the following characteristics of oral expression; rhythmic balanced patterns, repetition-antithesis, assonances, use of proverbs known to a large body, conservative use of language due to the need for repetition of tried and true expressions. All of these traits, to varying degrees, are evident in Celie's letters.

Celie's entire style of expression consists of rhythmic balanced patterns. Most of her sentences follow the same basic structure of, subject first then predicate. In Celie's hands, an antagonistic device once used to conquer and repress her now becomes an instrument assisting in her deepest self-examination. As she creates her own writing form, she also becomes more artistically expressive. She no longer merely states situational facts, she invents metaphors for her feelings. Often, she speaks of her experiences in terms of nature. Like Walker, Celie takes the written word and makes it her own, she is able to use it to crystallize her thoughts and come to realizations concerning her world.

Traditionally, the standard form of a language is used primarily to impose unity on the community which employs it. The capacity of writing as a communicative link, is thus overshadowed by its capacity to lend stasis to human experience so that it can be assessed and its capacity for recording and creating permanent history. Thus, it is the forceful narrative technique used by Alice Walker in the novel *The Color Purple* through which she has told the story of African, Afro-American, and Afro-American female experience. She has created a unique monument to these sagas, as her characters take the written form which ignored Afro-American history and culture and use it to preserve both.

The symbolism of colour has been effectively used by Walker in the novel. Purple and red symbolize happiness and independence—the colours which Mr.... Does not permit Celie to wear and she is forced to choose from browns, maroons and navy blues. Later on, she decorates her room with purple. Colours also denotes personality traits as far as Celie is concerned 'a pair the color of sunset' suits squeak, camel suits Jack, soft white is appropriate for Nettie, soft dark blue with patches of red is ideal for Shug. Celie thinks of moods and emotions in terms of colours. Paule Marshall, another Afro-American novelist of high repute, is known for her narrative technique in her works, and in talks, she had given her point of view about the craft of novel writing. She emphasized her need to create distinct human beings who are affected by culture and society, and who also affect these two important elements. Her works are pieces of sculpture; the shape and rhythm of her characters can scarcely be detached from the space around them. Her first novel *Browngirl, Brownstones*, explores areas in the world of technique with the enthusiasm of a novitiate and the carefulness of a serious student. Plot, narrative, imagery, setting, character development, interrelatedness of design, can be done in any number of ways. It establishes Marshall as a relentless analyst of character within the context of a particular culture. Everything else; setting, plot, imagery, narrative is subordinated to this end. Because she sees characters in a context rather than isolated from society, she uses setting as a major indicator of character. Her lucid descriptions of the spatial environment permeate her prose, not as elegant fillers but as substantive to the theme. Her prose, usually profuse and lush, is sensual not for its own sake but as signals of her character's composition. Even the titles of her novels emphasize spatial relationship as a major indicator of character. The words, browngirl and brownstones set up a special relationship. The title *The Chosen Place, The Timeless People* is a concentrated outline of her second novel.

The interrelatedness of complex shapes and settings is so fused in Marshall that her books are verbal sculptures. Form and space and humanity and culture cannot be separated. The intricacy of detail is maintained, even extended, in Marshall's panoramic novel. The characters in *Browngirl, Brownstones*—Selina, Silla, Deignton, Suggie—are psychologically related to Merle, Leesy, Vere and Lyle. In the first novel, the protagonist seeks an understanding of her world to find herself, as woman; in the second novel, we examine the many characters' psyches according to their sense of themselves as woman or man, black or white, oppressor or oppressed, to understand the particular world of Brownehills. As Marshall herself matures, her emphasis moves from the way the world affects an individual psyche to how our many psyches create a world. Paule Marshall's works, as psycho-political images, elucidate the people who affected in turn by their creation. Because of this thrust, her works remind us that all of us compose our own experiences in our minds and that our individual shapes are kinetically poised in a unified sculpture called the universe; that we all are continuity and process, shape and space, and that our sculpted creations are ourselves; whether or not we want it to. Marshall's novels manifest history as a creative and moral process, for she graphically describes how we compose our own experiences in our minds as well as in the objective world, how we as individuals and whole cultures decide upon the moral nature of an act, a series of acts, a history.

Thus, we find that Hurston originates the aesthetics of community by using a 'folkloric ethos' to displace traditional male versions of African-American folktales, transferring the voice of the storyteller from men to women. Morrison, while providing feeling glimpses of alternative 'rooted' storytellers and legendary stories, primarily uses negative example to illustrate the destructive effects of the dominant culture's language constructs on African-American identity and art. Walker conjoins the concerns of Hurston and Morrison, positioning herself, as Morrison does, in a desolate present, while retrieving, as Hurston does, a viable past to create a future state of soundness, a viable, global community.

On the other hand, the narrative style of each of the Afro-American women writers reflects certain qualities of the community in the novels as well as in their own personal vision. The allegorical approach is especially strong in the novels of Toni Morrison, where nature and human beings converse and where the images of the stories dance to create their own structure, their own parables. Especially in her novels the process of naming, of capturing the spirit through the word is paramount. Although the novels of Marshal are more psychological than imagistic, she, too, investigates the folk history of her characters as they grope toward self-understanding. Walker's theme is the pursuit of personal and societal wholeness, as she analyzes a major dilemma of black southerners, the relationship between one responsibility for one life and the restrictions of sexism and racism. By revealing the fantasies, myths, and dreams of her characters, she attempts to penetrate what she calls 'the historical subconscious of their communities.

Whatever their differences, and there are many, the novels of Paule Marshall, Toni Morrison and Alice Walker, Anita Desai, Shashi Deshpande and Shobhaa De tell stories of women who came before them. Their novels are the literary counterparts of their communities oral traditions. Not that any of these novelists are merely reporting stories, they are obviously creating fiction. Their style, the merging of images and events, constitute a particular value system.

In Shashi Deshpande's case her novels move in space as well as in time, through internalized beliefs. Deshpande writes a variety of Indian-English that is rooted in the ambience of regional culture, those of the states of Maharashtra and Karnataka. For example, her characters have names and pet names that immediately 'place' them for Indian readers as being Maharashtrian or Akannadige—Saru, Indu, Jaya, Chandu, Kamat. She also uses Marathi or Kannada words to describe various characters and their relationships to each other; such as Chandu Mama and Ajji. The culturally specific words and sentences set easily and naturally in her boy of work, so that the work reflects a contemporary, middle-class, Indian-English. Deshpande avoids foregrounding the indianness of the writing through the self-conscious use of 'local colour', but writes in an English with which her readers would be familiar and comfortable.

The use of a language other than the mother tongue or the 'spoken' tongue of the society one lives in, is in itself a narrative strategy. It at once, shifts the divisions between readerships; it also simultaneously opens out spaces for communication between the two cultures of the two languages and writers cross over from one to the other in different ways. While women have had difficulty formulating a coherent identity because of their immersion in an alien symbolic system, they are gaining new understanding of feminine subjectivity through openness to the multiple realities of women's lives and their psyche. The feminist creating of a multi-faceted subjectivity through interrelated voices repeatedly enacts a process of feminine self-discovery.

NOTES

1. Dupre, Louise. "The Dobly Complicit Memory", Tessera, *Room of One's Own*, p. 9.
2. Belliapa, Meena. *Anita Desai: A Study of Her Fiction*, Calcutta: Writer's Workshop, p. 6.
3. Sharma, R.S. *Anita Desai*, New Delhi: Arnold Heineman, 1981, p. 24.
4. Srinivasa, Iyengar K.R. *Indian Writing in English*, New Delhi: Sterling, 1934, p. 464.
5. Anita Desai in an Interview with Ramesh K. Srivastava.
6. Holmstorm, Lakshmi. (ed.) *The Inner Courtyard: Stories by Indian Women 1990*, New Delhi: Rupa Paperbacks, 1993, p. 22.
7. *Ibid.*, p. 25.
8. Deshpande, Shashi. *That Long Silence*, New Delhi: Penguin Books, 1978.
9. Morrison, Toni. *Beloved*, New York: Signet, 1991, p. 289.
10. Morrison, Toni. *The Bluest Eye*, London: Chatto and Windus, 1979, p. 28.
11. *Ibid.*, pp. 47-48.

Depiction of Childhood Friendship in Male and Female Novelists: A Comparative Study of R.K. Narayan's *Swami and Friends* and Shena Mackay's *The Orchard on Fire*

2

Tripti Karekatti and *Rani Nalawade*

Some of our best fiction has been an outcome of writers' interest in the depiction of childhood, childhood psychology, pleasures and anxieties of childhood, etc. For example, Mark Twain's *The Adventures of Huckleberry Finn* and *The Adventures of Tom Sawyer,* David Mitchell's *Black Swan Green*, Wole Soyinka's *Aké: The Years of Childhood*, Roddy Doyle's *Paddy Clarke, Ha-Ha-Ha*, L.M. Montgomery's *Anne of Green Gables*, Alexander Fuller's *Don't Let's Go To The Dogs Tonight,* Harper Lee's *To Kill A Mockingbird*, etc. Twain's *The Adventures of Huckleberry Finn* and *The Adventures of Tom Sawyer* are noted for their innocent young protagonists and the exploration of entrenched attitudes, particularly racism. *Black Swan Green* by David Mitchell depicts numerous problems of its thirteen-year-old protagonist Jason, where as, *Aké: The Years of Childhood* by Wole Soyinka, is an account of one boy's attempt to grasp the often irrational and hypocritical world of the adults. Roddy Doyle's *Paddy Clarke, Ha-Ha-Ha* gives the reader the vivid impression of listening to the memories of a ten-year-old Irish boy from the 1960s. In *Don't Let's Go To The Dogs Tonight,* Fuller remembers her African childhood with candor and sensitivity. *To Kill A Mockingbird* by Harper Lee is a moving story of Scout and her brother Jam set in Maycomb, Alabama at the time of Depression. Sometimes children in this fiction are used just to give us a fresh insight into the difference between the perspectives of the grown-ups and that of the children, as is often done by R.K. Narayan.

Sometimes, the author uses child characters to expose some social evils, as in Charles Dickens' fiction or in Arundhati Roy's. Charles Dickens' Oliver brings to light the horrible world of orphans in a workhouse. Charlotte Bronte's Jane Eyre reveals the pains of a girl growing up in an orphanage. Arundhati Roy's novel *A God of Small Things* depicts childhood overshadowed by the rigid caste and class structure and by politics.

These works are not only noted for their insight and wonderful depiction of childhood world but also for the place they give to friendship. Most of the protagonists in these works are accompanied either by devoted friends or siblings and many of the happy as well as anxious moments involve acceptance/non-acceptance of the protagonist by his/her friends. Some novels follow the friends to adulthood to show sometimes the brake-up, sometimes the continuation of the friendship. Sometimes we find that friendship provides the much-needed strength even after loss of contact with the friend. Some novels depict the loneliness that engulfs once that friendship is lost. Authors have handled various shades of friendship, especially, adolescent and adult friendship, starting from normal to gay/lesbian relationships.

The present paper is an attempt to make a comparative statement on the depiction of childhood and especially childhood friendship in two novels—R.K. Narayan's *Swami and Friends*[1] and Shena Mackay's *The Orchard on Fire.*[2] R.K. Narayan has deep concern for children and also a wonderful ability to observe childhood in all its nuances. R.K. Narayan's works explore the various factors that affect the mental makeup of children. He gives due importance to friendship in childhood and to the crucial role it plays in the life of a child. The novel *Swami and Friends* revolves round the friendship of classmates Swami, Somu, Mani, Rajam, Sankar, etc., especially, the close bond that develops between Swami and Rajam and the eventual separation of the two at the end of the novel. The novel gives us a glimpse not only into the daily routine and wanderings, fears and anxieties of these children, but also into the world of fantasies and imagination of middle-class children of semi-urban India. The novel *The Orchard on Fire* (short-listed for the 1996 Booker prize) written by the British novelist Shena Mackay has the same story-line: close friendship and eventual separation of two girls living in a quiet suburb of England. In both the novels, the authors explore normal middle class childhood and have at the center childhood friendship—the only difference being that in one it is male friendship, in the other, female. It will be interesting to study whether the depiction differs in the two novels keeping in mind crucial time and culture differences as well as the difference in the authors' and their protagonists' gender.

I

R.K. Narayan occupies a significant place in Indian English literature. Not only common readers but renowned critics and acclaimed authors like Graham Greene have appreciated his depiction of rural and semi-urban life in India in his novels and short stories. R.K. Narayan is especially known for his deep concern for children. This concern is reflected in his literature. His views about schooling, physical load of school children, freedom of children, their education, place of play and fun in the child's life are well reflected not only in his speech delivered in the Rajya Sabha but also in his works like *The English Teacher*. Through his other works like the short story "Uncle", novel *Swami and Friends*, etc., the reader gets an opportunity to see the world through the perspective of a child. His novels and short stories are enlivened by a touch of humour and the ability to reveal the wonderful in something very common place. For example, the story "A Hero" makes wonderful use of children's fear of darkness whereas the story "The Hoard" reveals that children's happiness lies in very simple things like sweets and sometimes in taking the freedom to not to obey the elders. In a slightly serious story like "Leela's Friend", he shows the ability of children to cross the barriers of master-servant relationship. The novel *The Dark Room* depicts the misfortunes faced by children due to an uncaring brutal father and a helpless mother.

The novel *Swami and Friends* is about a school-going boy Swaminathan, his friends and events that happen within his age group. Reading the novel reminds one of one's childhood, its curiosities, its surprises—both good and bad—and its idiosyncrasies. The story revolves around the friendship of the classmates Somu, Mani, Rajam, Sankar and Samuel. In many ways, reader finds strong resemblance between himself/herself and Swami. Swami becomes the child the reader used to be once, but now has forgotten and has recollected again, thanks to the vivid portrayal of childhood by Narayan. Narayan is highly successful in bringing back the reader to the level of child.

The author, through seemingly minor incidents, vividly brings out the typical perspective of children of looking and interpreting the world around them. Whether it is the incident of Swami wanting a hoop desperately or believing that the coachman can really change his coins to gold through magic or Swami in extreme fear imagining wild animals and demons surrounding him at night when he runs away from home, or his unwillingness to go to school on Mondays, Narayan very successfully reminds us of our childhood days and way of thinking.

The protagonist of the novel—Swaminathan—is a happy and cheerful boy who is neither very good at studies nor a muscle-boy like his friend Mani. He comes from a well-to-do Brahmin family. His is a perfectly normal childhood: caring parents, loving grandmother, loyal friends. There are no major upheavals in this childhood life. Simple joys and simple pleasures fill his life. Major anxieties and fears are never bigger than getting expelled from the school and his closest friend leaving the town for ever.

Swami doesn't like to go to school very much. It is more for his friends than for studies that he goes to the school. Even if he is not a naughty boy, we find him getting into some or the other trouble again and again. It is mostly because of his concern for his friends that he falls into trouble. He is loved very much by his parents. He also loves them but as is the case with the boys of his age, his friends mean more to him than either his parents or his grandmother. His life revolves around his classmates—Somu, Sankar, Samuel, Mani and Rajam. Somu, a confident and calm boy is the monitor of the class. Sankar is the most brilliant boy in the class. Samuel or 'Pea' is as ordinary as Swami—weak in Arithmetic, apprehensive and nervous about the same things as Swami. Mani is the muscle-boy of the class—elder and physically bigger than any one else. He fails in each class many times and has been in the school for a long time now. Everyone is afraid of him. Rajam is the last one to arrive in this group. He is good at studies, confident, and fearless. Son of the police superintendent, he is the best dressed, best English speaking boy in the class. He is ready to fight with Mani. Swami gets attached to him so much that he gets teased in school as the 'tail' of Rajam.

The novel revolves around the ups and downs in the friendship of these children. Initially, Rajam is not accepted by the group of Swami's friends. Even if Swami wants desperately to be his friend, being loyal to Mani, he feigns he hates Rajam. These small political intricacies of childhood life are brilliantly handled by R.K. Narayan. So are the incidents that bring out the innocence of children in matters of money. When they decide to organise a cricket team, they write a letter ordering the required goods to a company—Messrs Binns. The idea that some advance payment has to be made, doesn't even cross their mind. When Messrs Binns reply demanding 25% of the money in advance, they are unable to understand the meaning of the letter. They keep on wondering about it and ultimately conclude that they have been sent a letter meant for someone else and return the letter. Their childish interpretations and doubts are all very convincingly portrayed.

When they receive a letter from Sankar (who has left the town), all friends become very emotional and immediately write three letters to Sankar only to realize that Sankar has not written his address on his letter.

Rajam emerges as the most sensible of the boys. He accepts Mani's challenge to fight but ends up making him his good friend. When Swami is teased and isolated by other friends for his attachment with Rajam, Rajam brings them all together and by giving his own toys and other things as gifts to all of them, he makes them forget their enmity and become friends again.

These friends, especially Mani and Swami are ready to do anything for each other. When Swami tells Rajam and Mani about how the coachman duped him, Mani plans to kidnap the coachman's son.

It is for the sake of Rajam and cricket practice that Swami gets into trouble in the new school too. The only major serious development in the novel is this incident. Afraid that his father will be very angry and he will be expelled from this school too, he decides to run away. But he can't leave without meeting his friend Rajam. He dares to call out Rajam from school to talk to him for a few moments, but is unable to tell him that he is going to run away. He keeps on roaming outside the town and when night falls, gets so much afraid of darkness that he collapses unconscious. He is saved by the forest officer. Even in that condition, he is worried about the match on Sunday. But keeping in mind his condition, the officer tells him it is Saturday and Swami fails to turn up for the match. Rajam is not ready to forgive Swami for not turning up on the day of cricket match even after coming to know of Swami's misadventures. He does not leave his childish whim to not to forgive him for letting him down even when leaving the town for ever.

When swami comes to know about Rajam's father's transfer, his grief knows no bounds:

> A great sense of desolation seized Swaminathan at once. The world seemed to have become blank all of sudden. The thought of Lawley Extension without Rajam appalled him with its emptiness. He swore that he would never go there again. (*Swami and Friends,* p. 174)

Rajam is so angry with Swami that he doesn't want even to see him again. But Mani is not able to contain himself. Only because he violates Rajam's ban that Swami comes to know that Rajam is leaving the town the next day. Even on the station, Swami doesn't get any opportunity to talk to Rajam. At the last moment, when the train is almost leaving, he cries out:

> Oh, Rajam, Rajam, you are going away, away. When will you come back. (*Swami and Friends*, p. 178)

Until the end, Rajam doesn't reply. Swami is actually convincing himself when he says to Mani:

> Mani, I am glad he has taken the book. Mani, he waved to me. He was about to say something when the train started.

Mani, he did wave to me and to me alone. Don't deny it. (*Swami and Friends,* p. 178)

Rajam's departure and his denial to talk even when leaving leaves Swami heart broken. It is Mani who we find trying to calm his friend with the hope that Rajam will write him letters.

'But he does not know my address.'

'He asked me and I have given it', said Mani.

'No. No. It is a lie. Come on, tell me, what is my address?'

'It is—it is—never mind what.... I have given it to Rajam'. (*Swami and Friends,* p. 179)

At the moment, the world appears empty to the young boy without his friend Rajam. Mani's attempts to console him do not have any effect on him. Nor do other friends, even parents, school mean anything to him. This close involvement of children with their friends is brilliantly portrayed by Narayan. So are childish whims in the form of Rajam's resolution not to forgive Swami.

II

Shena Mackay was born in Edinburgh but lived and conducted her writing within the Kent and Surrey suburbs of London. She has been admired by authors like Iris Murdoch and has won many prizes and awards: Fawcett Society Book Prize in 1987 for her book *Redhill Rococo*; Scottish Arts Council Book Award in 1994 for *Dunedin*; her novel *The Orchard on Fire* was short listed for the Booker Prize for Fiction in 1996; *Heligoland* was short listed in 2003 for Orange Prize for Fiction and Whitbread Novel Award.

There are numerous similarities between R.K. Narayan's *Swami and Friends* and Shena Mackay's *The Orchard on Fire.* The protagonist of Mackay's novel is an eight-year old girl April Harlency. The story revolves round her life and friendship with Ruby Richards. Just as in *Swami and Friends*, Swami, Rajam, Mani are close friends, so also April and Ruby are inseparable friends in Mackay's novel. They are ready to do anything for each other. When Ruby's father cuts off her plait of hair, April cuts off her own hair too to prove camaraderie. Just as in *Swami and Friends* Swami gets a new brother, so also April in *The Orchard on Fire* gets a new brother—Peter. In both the novels, the close friends part suddenly never to meet each other again.

However, Mackay's novel, unlike Narayan's, doesn't revolve only around the events that happen within the age group of April and Ruby. The Kent village of Stonebridge, its typical social and cultural life, its residents with their own beliefs, habits and idiosyncrasies figure in the novel. Most importantly, even if the imaginative focus of the novel is the joys, fears and fantasies of a young April, it is a grownup April remembering nostalgically her childhood. The author succeeds in reminding us of our childhood but as it is an adult recollecting her childhood, a number of adults' concerns enter the novel. This does not happen in *Swami and Friends*.

April Harlency's parents come to Stonebridge to run the tea house Copper Kettle. April immediately develops close friendship with Ruby Richards, whose parents run the pub Rising Sun. They go to the same school, play together, read together the same books over and over again, and even have a secret hide-out place in the abandoned railway carriage in the orchard. Ruby's parents do not treat Ruby properly. She is often beaten up, made to work hard in the pub and locked up in the cellar. She is forbidden to meet April and to go to her house. But even then, the two friends manage to meet and to spend hours together.

Publicly humiliated and completely 'frightened out of her wits' by her drunken father in the garden party given by the Silvers, Ruby runs away and hides in the railway carriage throughout the night. Only April has an idea where she can be. Everyone is worried about Ruby and search parties are sent. Elders ask April again and again about where Ruby might be but April does not want to 'betray' Ruby and their friendship. The childish fear that both of them will be punished if Ruby is found, stops her from disclosing any information. She thinks:

> If Ruby was found she would get into the most awful trouble with all those people looking for her. And so would I. We would both be sent to an approved school. I had to find her before they did so that we could run away together. Please

God don't let Ruby be murdered or trapped by fire before I get there. (*The Orchard on Fire*, p. 190)

For Ruby's sake, April is ready to run away from her house. The fact that she will be leaving her house and will be separated from her parents (whom she loves very much) doesn't matter to her at that moment:

The baker and the milkman came next and I ran upstairs to pack a few clothes and Bobbity in a carrier bag. I would have to steal food when I got the chance and some money... I hid the bag under my bed and looked round my bedroom through tears. (*The Orchard on Fire,* pp. 191-92)

However, the two never get the opportunity to run away, as Ruby accidentally sets the orchard on fire and is some how saved by the search party and carried away by her father:

Her face and arms and legs were black. Her gingham dress was scorched. One bare foot dangled where a laceless plimsoll had fallen off.

'It wasn't me! I didn't tell!' I was running alongside Rex.

'I knew you wouldn't' Ruby's smudged face said.... (*The Orchard on Fire,* p. 194)

To avoid facing the public after the incident and to avoid possible police action for violence against Ruby, Rex and Gloria flee the village the very next day secretly. So, Ruby and April are not able to meet before parting. They are able to keep contact through secretly written letters for some time but then they loose contact completely.

The novel opens with middle-aged divorced April who still thinks continuously of her friend Ruby. She visits Stonebridge without knowing exactly why. All people she knew there as a child are either dead or have left but April seems to see them still:

Walking back to the station, I pass or am passed by various imposters who imagine that they live there, but I know that the real people of Stonebridge are all about me, in Brownie uniforms or their mothers' shoes, wearing rhubarb leaves as sunhats and painting their lips with a Smartie, pursuing their concerns as they always do.... (*The Orchard on Fire,* p. 211)

Seeing the sign "ANTIQUES, BYGONES KITCHENALIA" on Copper Kettle she feels:

> People are rummaging through the boxes outside the shop, I know what they are upto, with their kitchenalia, purchasing pieces of our lives. They are trying to buy their way into the past they think we had, they want to be snug and safe down Rabbit Lane. A thousand bus tickets faded to the colours of old ration books won't get them there and they can force all the carrots in the world through a Mouli grater, but they'll never find their way into the burrow where Bobbity and Sandy live.... (*The Orchard on Fire,* p. 211)

This wish to reenter the past seems more true of the grown-up April herself who has never been able to adjust with a life without Ruby and Stonebridge and seems herself eager than the 'strangers' to 'buy [her] way into the past'.

At the churchyard in Stonebridge, she suddenly sees the grave of Ruby and discovers that Ruby came back to live in Stonebridge, married a Robert Coppard, had two children whom she called April and Peter, but, had never tried to find out April:

> She came back. She was within two hours' reach and I missed her by just two years. (*The Orchard on Fire,* p. 209)

Through her tears, April wonders:

> Why did Ruby never try to contact me when we were older? There aren't so many Harlencys in the London phone book that she shouldn't have located me.... Did she write to the Copper kettle and were her letters returned, or did she think that I just hadn't bothered to reply to her or that I had found a new best friend? Perhaps, as I did, she thought we had all the time in the world to find each other again.

When she is back in her London apartment that evening, she thinks:

> Ruby and I lost touch. In half a century we never celebrated her birthday together. Now I have to think about Ruby's extraordinary present to me, the names of her two children and how to honour it.... (*The Orchard on Fire,* p. 215)

The childhood in *The Orchard on Fire* is not completely rosy and cheerful and 'innocent' as is the case in *Swami and Friends*. It is correctly described as "a fine balance of pathos and comedy".

The children's numerous wanderings, dreams and fantasies, fears and anxieties, idiosyncratic behaviour of the Stonebridge citizens provide ample humour to the novel. However, the dark side of the life—even of childhood—seems to outweigh these light moments due to the seriousness of the incidents—the issue of physical and sexual abuse of the children. Ruby is physically tortured by her parents, whereas April is mildly molested by Mr. Greenidge, an elderly rich man from Stonebridge. Mackay conveys April's fear so starkly that the reader feels as trapped as April. Ruby, brutally beaten up by her parents once says to April:

> I wish we lived in the little house in the snow. Just the two of us, and Peter. No grown-ups. Nobody could get us through the glass. (*The Orchard on Fire*, p. 122)

It is the grown-ups, who dirty the beautiful rosy childhood days. At the end of the novel, the grown-up April remembering how Mr. Greenidge forced her to endure his embraces and kisses feels:

> And then I remembered how Mr. Greenidge corroded my childhood with fear and anxiety and deceit. (*The Orchard on Fire*, p. 210)

III

The childhood emerging from *Swami and Friends* is a rosy, beautiful, carefree condition that any one would want for oneself. On the other hand, none would want for oneself April's experiences with Mr. Greenidge or parents like Ruby's. *Swami and Friends* is entirely written in a light mode. There are very few serious incidents in the novel. It is a world of children from white-collar middle class families with perfectly normal childhood and loving parents. These children have no serious worries and problems. The children in this novel are troubled only by matters like tension of the approaching exams, or tension of losing the cricket match, or worrying about father's reaction over the 'missing' cap or over how to collect the money coachman has asked to help get a hoop, or about obtaining permission for cricket practice from the head master of the school, or about reaching on time for the match, etc. There are numerous moments when these children are troubled by childish fears, for example, Swami doesn't pay attention to his grandmother when she asks him to get for her some lemons and later on is gripped by the fear that she may be dead because of his neglect. When he sees coachman's son at the club, he is sure that the boy will certainly murder him and so is very careful to stand in between his father and father's friend until he returns home safely.

There are such moments of childish fear in *The Orchard of Fire* too like April worrying that she will have to marry Mr. Greenidge if Mrs. Greenidge dies. But these moments always have dark lining. There are numerous incidents when Ruby and April are worried by real, big problems. Secondly, even the light and happy moments of the novel make the two girls stumble on some profound truths of the adult world. For example, after birth of her brother Peter, April understands one truth:

> It was already clear to me that Peter had done something extraordinarily clever by just having been born a boy, and all he had to do was lie there in a pale-blue knitted helmet and even old Ma Vinnegar worshiped him. (*The Orchard on Fire,* p. 128)

Even if both the novels have almost the same story, there is much difference in the depiction of childhood and childhood friendship in the two novels. *Swami and Friends* reminds the reader of childhood and succeeds in taking the reader to the level of the child. On the other hand, as it is a grown-up April nostalgically recollecting her childhood days, the perspective is not entirely of a child. The not-so-normal experiences of the two girls in *The Orchard on Fire* give it touches of seriousness and pathos whereas *Swami and Friends* just has light-hearted humour and boisterous fun.

Even if Swami is heart-broken and in tears after Rajam leaves at the end of the novel *Swami and Friends*, we can be sure that he will recover soon and again engage in the same kind of life as he was leading before Rajam came. On the contrary, life for April has changed completely after Ruby's departure. Throughout her later life, we see that April pines for Ruby and waits for her. She feels that others—even her mother—do not understand her and do not believe her. She feels only Ruby would have perfectly understood her if she was present. The childhood friendship has left a permanent mark on her mind and the separation from Ruby too has affected her whole life.

On comparing the two novels, we find that R.K. Narayan opts to linger on the happy side of childhood and to treat the subject in a light-hearted mode whereas Shena Mackay takes up also the dark side of childhood and a serious subject like child abuse in her novel. Friendship between the two girls in *The Orchard on Fire* emerges as an enduring bond, a sustaining force giving the much needed support throughout the later lives to both the friends even after actual contact with each other is long last.

NOTES

1. Narayan, R.K. (1935). *Swami and Friends*. London: Hamish Hamilton. First Indian Edition: 1944. Mysore: Indian Thought Publications.
2. Mackay, Shena (1995). *The Orchard on Fire*. William Heinemann Ltd. (All the quotations from the Minerva Edition of 1996).

Multicultural Melbourne: Mapping Identity in Christos Tsiolkas' *Loaded*

3

Hariclea Zengos

In Christos Tsiolkas' novel *Loaded* (1997), Melbourne is a city divided by racial, class and ethnic differences. The novel explores a day in the life of its protagonist, Ari, a nineteen year old, Australian-born homosexual male of Greek descent. In the twenty-four hours that frame the story, Ari cruises the suburbs of Melbourne searching out clubs, drugs and anonymous sex. As he provides a running commentary on his life, Ari also concurrently produces a politically loaded map of the city which reflects not only his deep understanding of the hierarchies of class, race, and ethnicity, but also his ambivalence concerning sexuality and identity.

The text is divided into four sections—East, North, South, and West—offering a geographic as well as cultural map of Melbourne. A maelstrom of racial, class, sexual and ethnic tensions, Melbourne is a space of difference that is neither a crucible of ethno-racial relations (that is, a "melting pot" of unity in diversity) nor a multicultural mosaic of harmonious cultural plurality. Divided into ethnic communities or subcultures that create invisible yet tangible borders, Melbourne is a portrait of modern urban fragmentation, displacement, conflict and alienation. As he cruises Melbourne's suburbs, Ari debunks various myths of solidarity and community as well as the official discourses of Australian multiculturalism. The reader comes to see that Ari's nihilistic pursuit of casual sex, drugs, and music, is a manifestation of Melbourne's desolation and emptiness. The city, like the protagonist who wanders within it, resists definition and identity.

In the novel, Melbourne exhibits distinctive geographies of social differences, divisions and power relations; the city's space, in other words, is hierarchical as is evidenced by Ari's wanderings in the East, an area of Melbourne that he detests because, as he says, it is "the whitest part of my city, where you'll see the authentic white Australians" (Tsiolkas 41). Characterized by wealth and white privilege, the East is for Ari, a Disneyland of capitalism where "Television rules" (Tsiolkas 42). It is also where "the wogs with money" live in their "brick-veneer fortresses", but on the margins, "bordering the true Anglo affluence, never part of it" (Tsiolkas 41). While ethnic minorities have achieved material success and have realized the so-called Australian way of life—suburban, middle-class homes and cars—they are still excluded from Anglo-Celtic Australian society. In the East there is a spatial duality—of being inside and outside fortresses of privilege—that demarcates the self and the other, and represents the restrictions of mobility and access in Australian society. Tsiolkas' representation of the city suggests that assimilation is a failed ideology as it has not led to social integration but marginalization.

From the East Ari moves North, to that part of Melbourne that "isn't Melbourne, it isn't Australia", but rather "a little village in the mountains of the Mediterranean transported to the bottom of the southern hemisphere...[a] sore on the map of the city...where the wog is supposed to end up" (Tsiolkas 81-82). The North of the city is a diaspora space, representing the displaced position of the migrant, whom Ari considers "a conman, a trickster or a deluded fool" (Tsiolkas 83) for perpetuating "the old country" in a new land, and for emphasizing collectivity and ethnic identification. Ideologically inhabiting this diaspora city-space are Ari's Greek-born father, who is so nostalgic for the homeland that he claims that he cannot breathe in Australia, and his Australian-born, Greek mother, whose hybrid identity finds her unhappily living a border life on the margins of different nations, "in-between" contrary homelands. Ari sees his parents' old world values and traditions as having "no place or meaning in this city at the bottom of the world" (Tsiolkas 83). Thus, Ari hates the North in part because it is a failed replica of the migrant's homeland, and in part because his family expects him to end up there, living the conventional life of the good Greek boy within the ethnic community, a destiny he resists by cruising the North for anonymous sex with men.

From the North, Ari turns to the South, where Melbourne casts its unwanted and socially unacceptable. Among the South's "[a]rtists and junkies and faggots and whores, the sons and daughters no longer talked about, no longer admitted into the arms of family" (Tsiolkas 132), is where Ari could potentially belong should he decide to come out of his closet and be truthful with his family about his sexuality. The South is the opposing space to the North not only geographically but ideologically: sexual openness and family rejection are the polar opposites of the North's conventionality and family acceptance. That these sections are juxtaposed structurally in the middle of the novel suggests the potential for a border crossing, should Ari choose to confront his parents.

The novel's concluding section is the West, a ghetto area that Ari describes as "a dumping ground; a sewer of refugees, the migrants, the poor, the insane, the unskilled and the uneducated" (Tsiolkas 143-44). Geographic space demarcates the city's class differences. The Yarra River that separates East from West is the "chasm" that divides pastoral suburbia from urban industry. In the East "there are green parks rolling down to the river, beautiful Victorian bridges sparkl[ling] against the blue sky". In the "West...there is the smoke-scarred embankment leading towards the wharfs. The beauty and the beast" (Tsiolkas 144). For Ari, the working-class West is evidence that Australia's promise of solidarity and a "fair go" are all an "urban myth" that "goes something like this; we may be poor, may be treated like scum, but we stick together, we are a community" (Tsiolkas 142). Solidarity, as Ari's shrewd political analysis highlights, is impossible in a society driven by capitalism and its spirit of "getting ahead". As far as Ari can see, the only objective of immigrants is to "get money, enough possessions to rise above the community [they] are in" (Tsiolkas 143). This section of the novel particularly supports Joan Kirkby's claim that *Loaded* is "a powerful and sustained critique of modern industrial capitalism" and its alienating effects.

Melbourne as a central presence in the novel emerges, then, through a description of its multi-ethnic inhabitants and the spatially segregated areas in which they live. Melbourne is multicultural in so far as its citizens are of different races and ethnic backgrounds, but its multiculturalism is not one of social cohesion; rather, it is a plurality of cultures operating separately yet co-existing (not necessarily harmoniously) in what could be called a plural monoculturalism that is one cause of Melbournian alienation and marginalization, the other being the loss of solidarity both within and between ethnic groups themselves. Not surprisingly, as a consequence of his alienation, Ari rejects all forms of community and identity. "Ethnicity is a scam, a bullshit, a piece of crock" (Tsiolkas 43), he insists. Through Ari, Tsiolkas undermines the idea of Australian multiculturalism as a kind of melting pot since the novel dramatizes that economic and social inequality are very much a reality for Melbourne's ethnic communities.

The novel's episodic structure also calls into question the conception of the city as a totality, pointing to its lack of coherence and legibility. The text's four sections—East, North, South and West—are in turn divided into a series of scenes that create a kind of montage on race, class, ethnicity and/or sexuality, key features of Melbourne's postmodern urbanism. With the plot focusing on six random sex encounters that take place in or around two parties, three bars, a night club and a public lavatory, the city is represented in fragmented, netherworld spaces. Moreover, as Jean-Francois Vernay points out, "Ari is often found alone in secluded places and mostly indoors," a detail which further emphasizes the protagonist's alienation and self-containment. In addition, the plot is static—nothing of special note occurs but quite the opposite; the events retold clearly do not constitute an unusual day for Ari but a boring, routine one. The novel, then, is a kind of anti-rite-of-passage or coming-of-age story—Ari neither experiences a revelation or epiphany nor decides to act to change his life. It is significant that his nomadic crossings of Melbourne end where they began—with Ari lying in bed contemplating the ceiling—emphasizing his static character and suggesting that his nihilistic view of life is self-defeating.

Ari's cultural mapping of Melbourne in part reflects his ambivalence regarding his ethnic identity, which is tied up with Melbourne's Greek community. Ari describes this community as "backstabbing, money-hungry, snobbish, [and] self-righteous", with "no time for losers or deviants" (Tsiolkas 43). His volatile relationship with his unsupportive family represents on a microcosmic level his refusal to participate in the ethnic community. Ari may live with his family for economic reasons, but he is "estranged from them and the traditions of Greek culture to which they maintain what he perceives to be a crippling allegiance" (Hunn 114). When he declares, "I'm not Australian, I'm not Greek, I'm not anything," he rejects national and ethnic identity as agents of unity and belonging, refusing to restrict identity to fixed or essentialized notions. While society is intent on codifying and oppressively inscribing identities, Ari is intent on resisting or describing them, constantly refusing the labels and names that people attempt to attach to him. As Ari informs the reader, "It's not that I can't decide; I don't like definitions" (Tsiolkas 114). His engagement in transgressive acts becomes Ari's way of denying or effacing categories and labels that produce collective meanings.

As the title of the novel suggests, Ari is "loaded" with volatile emotions: anger, fear, guilt, and anxiety, to name a few. The title also refers to Ari's conviction that words and expressions are loaded with meaning, and that he must resist their power to define and confine him, largely by avoiding being labeled or categorized at all. When his friend Angie boldly asks him, "So what are you, […] gay, straight, or bi?", he declares himself a "slut" (Tsiolkas 94). It is in keeping with Ari's character that he is ambivalent about sexual preference because to commit to one preference would be to exclude another. Moreover, Ari recognizes that should he accept any conventional label such as gay, homosexual, straight, or bi—he would then be confronted by a swarm of tacit assumptions about who he is as well as be expected to perform the behaviors and attitudes that society ascribes to such signifiers. As Diana Fuss argues in *Inside/Out:*

Lesbian Theories, Gay Theories, "To be out [of the closet] is really to be in—inside the realm of the visible, the speakable, the culturally intelligible" (4). In other words, rather than offering liberation, coming out constructs the closet it supposedly destroys and the self it supposedly reveals. Ari knows that to come out as a homosexual, he has to make himself "an object of derision and contempt" (Tsiolkas 132) like his drag queen friend Toula, also known as Johnny. Toula refuses to disguise her sexuality and this is an obvious form of resistance; her dresses and skirts are, in a sense, her battle fatigues. Ari tries to convince himself that keeping his sexuality private is a form of resistance as well, but Toula begs to differ. In her view, Ari is in drag too, except he is in camouflage. Ari is unable to settle into a rigidly defined, conventional category, yet in Toula's view this does not constitute resistance. While Ari admires Toula/Johnny for standing up to his father and publically revealing his sexuality, Ari chooses to maintain his privacy and silence. His fear of parental rejection and social censure motivates him to remain self-contained and, as a consequence, unfulfilled.

Significantly, Ari prefers to use politically incorrect if not racist terms to refer to himself such as "wog", "faggot", "queer", and even the Greek slang word for homosexual, *pousti*, because they are "words [that] have guts" (Tsiolkas 115). Ari's self-referential terms maintain his difference from the normative and allow him to embrace his abjection. Paradoxically, his self-labeling is not an act of identification but resistance: "Those insults have formed me, they have nourished me. In latrines and underneath piers I have enjoyed pleasures that are made sweeter by the contempt I know they bestow on me in the eyes of the respectable world I abhor" (Tsiolkas 132). Ari sees language as a social tool that imposes normative and normalizing power over the individual. By using these slurs, he appropriates language to gain power and control rather than have it imposed on him.

In "Assimilation and Integration: Colonial(ist) Questions for Australian Lesbian/Gay/Queer Writing," Bronwen Levy argues that Ari "cannot find adequate words to explain or describe his own sense of self or identity" (21). I disagree with her view because I think the point of the novel is that Ari is trying to avoid social inscription. If I must use a term to define Ari, it would be "queer". David Halperin has defined queer as "whatever is at odds with the normal, the legitimate, the dominant. *There is nothing particular to which it necessarily refers.* It is an identity without an essence" (65). Queer then distinguishes Ari's position of resistance to the normative, not his identity. As Mandy Treagus points out, *Loaded* rejects "the subjectivities on offer—migrant, Australian, gay, straight—in favor of an undefined but predominately queer and Melbourne-identified persona...." Indeed, Tsiolkas advocates a queer way of being, seeing identity not as determined and fixed, with borders and boundaries, but fluid and contingent. In other words, identity is not a matter of being, but a continuous process of becoming.

Urban space and subjectivity are intricately related in the text, as Ari's view of Melbourne is influenced by his anxieties. The cartography of Melbourne also serves as a map of Ari's desires and ambivalence concerning sexual identity, which is informed by ethnicity. Ari expresses his contempt for the North by having casual sex with Greek men who symbolize his destiny (Hunn 115). "I roam the North so I can come face to face with the future that is being prepared for me," he says. As Deborah Hunn argues, rough, casual sex becomes for Ari a form of resistance to convention and social expectations that is enacted through the body (115). Sex is also Ari's response to the uneasy emptiness he feels, but the sexual act always remains emotionally and physically sterile. However, it is in the South that Ari is confronted with an opportunity to move toward a more serious and fulfilling relationship with a man he genuinely cares for, George, his brother's roommate. Ari thinks he might be in love with George, and fantasizes about telling his parents that he is moving out of the family home to move in with his lover—but to become part of a couple would result in a collective identity and no doubt emotional exposure, vulnerability, and social censure. Ari's closet, though complicated, is a space of his own choosing and keeps him safe from social pressures and expectations, from "the thousand and one things that people say you have to be or should want to be" (Tsiolkas 149). Ari prefers displacement to communal identification: "My silence and secrets allow me to move freely around the landscape of my city" (Tsiolkas 132-33). Thus, Ari's resistance to labels allows him to traverse boundaries and categories as easily as he crosses the borders and boundaries of Melbourne. Belonging nowhere and to no one, he can go anywhere. Paradoxically, then, the city can be "his" only through displacement.

While Ari is intent on resisting categories and labels, he is ironically caught up in heteronormative discourse as well as received notions of identity which depend on fixed, binary definitions (gay/straight, Greek/Australian, wog/white). He has internalized the stereotypical correlation of effeminacy with homosexuality as well as society's homophobia. He remarks at one point in the novel, "I don't like Johnny calling me a girl" (Tsiolkas 84), and while he considers drag queens cool because they "are not hung up on being a man" (Tsiolkas 92), he is not sexually attracted to them because "they act like schoolgirls". "I get off on real men, on masculinity" (Tsiolkas), he explains. Ari wants to live by the belief that "Thou can have a man and be a man" (Tsiolkas 101), but it is not a view held by Australian or Greek culture, where manhood is equated with virile heterosexuality, what Ari calls "macho shit". Yet Ari consciously performs the behaviors associated with male heterosexuality: "I do a good job of talking-like, walking-like, being a man. I've got the build, the swagger, the look.... Faggots love sleeping with me, they think they've scored a real man" (Tsiolkas 92). Ari illustrates Judith Butler's main premise in *Gender Trouble* that gender, rather than being an essential category of being, is a constructed identity based on the repetition of culturally gendered acts; gender, being an impersonation, is always drag. In keeping with his performance of masculinity, Ari, like a "real man", will not express his emotions. His inability to tell George that he loves him has much to do with his belief that to love a man and enter a committed relationship would feminize him: "I love you. I want to say those words, but they are an obscenity I can't bring myself to mouth. I've never said those words. I'm never going to say those words" (Tsiolkas 131). Sadly, it is this failure to love and be loved that does not allow Ari to transcend the alienation and desolation of the city.

Ari's sense of self, like the city through which he wanders, is characterized not by strength in diversity, but rather by a geography of incessant division. Melbourne as a city is a social product, with its multi-ethnic inhabitants creating community borders that divide and separate. Yet, while borders divide, they can also connect. As Homi Bhabha argues in *The Location of Culture* (1994), borders are important thresholds, full of contradiction and ambivalence, both separating and joining different spaces:

> What is theoretically innovative, and politically crucial, is the need to think beyond narratives of originary and initial subjectivities and to focus on those moments or processes that are produced in the articulation of cultural differences. These "in-between" spaces provide the terrain for elaborating strategies of selfhood—singular or communal—that initiate new signs of identity.... (2)

For Bhabha, borders are intermediate locations where one contemplates crossing or moving beyond a barrier. Ari, however, is unable to see borders as having this potential, a view which the novel, I believe, criticizes. Ari is engaged in endless transgression and performativity that atomise experience and deny the categories that produce shared and collective meanings. In short, he becomes disconnected from all collective associations. Because of his inability to think beyond the prevailing discourses of power, which fix and marginalize identity and to construct solidarity with others in both different and similar positions to his own, Ari remains alienated. Ultimately, resisting identity does not prove to be liberating for Ari; rather, it is a tyranny of its own because collectivity is replaced by dislocation, marginalization, and exclusion as Melbourne's cartography emphasizes.

WORKS CITED

Bhabha, Homi. *The Location of Culture*. London: Routledge, 1994.

Butler, Judith. *Gender Trouble: Feminism and the Subversion of Identity*. NY: Routledge, 1990.

Fuss, Diana. *Inside/Out: Lesbian Theories, Gay Theories*. NY: Routledge, 1991.

Halperin, David. *Saint Foucault: Towards a Gay Hagiography*. NY: Oxford University Press, 1995.

Hunn, Deborah. "It's not that I can't decide; I don't like definitions': Queer in Australia in Christos Tsiolkas's *Loaded* and Ana Kokkinos's *Head On*." *Territories of Desire in Queer Culture: Refiguring Contemporary Boundaries*. Eds. David Alderson and Linda Anderson. Manchester, UK: Manchester University Press, 2001, 112-29.

Kirkby, Joan. "The Pursuit of Oblivion: In Flight from Suburbia." *Australian Literary Studies*, 18.4 (Oct. 1998): 1(1). *Expanded Academic ASAP*. Gale. The American College of Greece, 11 Feb. 2008. http://find.galegroup.com

Levy, Bronwen. "Assimilation and Integration: Colonial(ist) Questions for Australian Lesbian/Gay/Queer Writing." *Queer in the 21st Century: Perspectives on Assimilation and Integration*. Eds. John Argus and Stephen Cox. Brisbane: Gay and Lesbian Welfare Association, 1999, 15-23. Available at www.glwa.org.au/docs/GLWA_Q21C-1999.pdf

Treagus, Mandy. "Australian Literature and the Teaching of 'Nation'." *Southerly* (Spring-Summer 1999): 16. *Expanded Academic ASAP*. Thomson Gale. The American College of Greece. 19 Mar. 2007. http://find.galegroup.com

Tsiolkas, Christos. *Loaded*. London: Vintage, 1997.

Vernay, Jean Francois. "Only Disconnect—Canonizing Homonormative Values: Representation and the Paradox of Gayness in Christos Tsiolkas's *Loaded*". *Antipodes*, 20.1 (June 2006): 41(5). *Expanded Academic ASAP*. Thomson Gale. The American College of Greece. 8 Dec. 2006. http://find.galegroup.com

Kim Scott's *Benang* and Doris Pilkington's *Towards the Rabbit-Proof Fence*: Conscious Racism and Identity De-orientation

4

Sarbojit Biswas

Give us Christ not crucifixion
Though baptised and blessed and Bibled
We are still tabooed and libelled
You devout Salvation-sellers
Make us neighbours not fringe-dwellers
Must we native old Australians
In our land rank as aliens?[1]

Oodgeroo of the Tribe Noonuccal

New Literatures in English emerging from the colonized continent of Australia are replete with postcolonial musings on problems of lost homeland and identity and in such a context, the role of 'historical fiction' as a mode of self-discovery is developing into a writer's tool for creation of "a focal point of cultural consciousness and social change".[2] Such an act is undeniably a symbolic 'writing back' to the hegemonic centre and is latent with a myriad of complexities in an increasingly multicultural world. The colonized continent of Australia practises multiculturalism or is multicultural in the sense that it has demographic conditions for ethnic and cultural diversity, though in reality it is just the opposite leading to a number of writers like Kim Scott and Doris Pilkington writing about the multicultural past. Kim Scott's *Benang* is a novel, which traces his family history, in the face of colonial oppression and racial prejudice, through efforts of breeding the first white man in his family of half-castes, while Doris Pilkington's *Follow the Rabbit-Proof Fence* is a heart-rendering tale of the writer's mother and her family as they try to escape forced colonial assimilation by running away. Both are novels of revolt against the powers of hegemonic white Australia, which is intent on breeding out and nullifying Aboriginal identity and life through state power; and ironically, both novels are success stories of surviving the odds and emerging triumphs against colonial hegemony which doles out only injustice and no compassion.

In this regard, a little history would not be out of place. There is no doubt that Australia originally belonged to the Aborigines or coloured people who had been living in the island continent for hundreds and thousands of years. The white man invaded the continent on January 18, 1788, when a fleet of 12 British ships landed at Botany Bay on the eastern coast of Australia and overran the continent for empire extension. To legally dispossess the native population, the British officials created the legal fiction of 'terra nullius' or Australia as an empty land in order to perpetuate colonial control. Along with forced land acquisition and spreading of a million sheep by pastoralists in Tasmania, the British also started stealing Aboriginal children from their families as a mechanism of dispossession.

Between 1910 and 1970, the Australian government detached forcefully 'half-caste' children from their families and sent them to settlement camps where they were to be 'nurtured' in British manners and manufactured to be servants of white Australians. Thus, such children, who were born of white and aboriginal parents, were removed, apparently for their own good and progress in a munificent policy or law referred to as Western Australia's Aborigines Act of 1905. Also, between 1869 and 1911, almost all states of Australia had set up a Board for the protection of Aborigines which was armed with a number of 'protectionist' laws and had at its helm a Chief Protector who protected by removing a young child from its mother or by deciding whom a person could marry and whom not, or whether one could work at a certain place or not.

The chief villain in both Scott's and Pilkington's novels is the Chief Protector A.O. Neville who is also the most famous of all chief protectors to have graced the post. Pilkington's novel traces the efforts of the young girls to run away from the policies of Neville which had put them under forced detention in the River Moore settlement and even goes on record quoting Neville in a newspaper article which appeared in 11 August 1931. Neville is quoted by the newspaper as saying that he is concerned about three native girls, ranging from 8 to 15 years of age, who ran away a week ago, apparently scared of their new quarters and in the hope of getting back home. In Scott's *Benang*, Neville's attempts at cultural assimilation is the primary focus and is linked to Scott's grandfather Ernest Solomon Scat who worked under Neville and was in the belief that he could breed out colour from his family. Thus, the novel traces the attempts of his grandfather at producing the 'first white man in the family'[3] through him and his fervent attempts at being just the opposite. As a consequence, the central villain of both the novels is A.O. Neville, a proponent of Eugenics, who believed that it was the duty of the white people to save the coloured people who would otherwise bring about their own downfall. Neville's validation for the elimination of "mixed blood" children rested on the Euro centric conviction that the native people of the colonized countries were "dying races" and that aboriginality should be "bred out" through forced assimilation into the racially superior white community.[4]

Kim Scott's *Benang* is a narrative straight from the heart as evident from the subtitle—"From the Heart" and Scott wants to make one understand the viewpoint of the whites: "Oh, they are not really human. Not like us. We are superior (and here is our proof)."[5] Thus the message that runs through the length and width of *Benang* is that day in and day out, always, the Whites are oppressors and consciously at that. They are unrelenting in their heaping of abuses and slurs on the Aborigines and are single minded in the persecution of the Aborigines. The white way is the creating and formulating of new rules and regulations to keep the Aborigines out of the mainstream and any attempt to be a part of their society, was viciously stubbed at the butt with laws, sometimes totally unreasonable.

So what do the Whites want? They want servants. And to that effect, they set up the Department for the Aborigines. And while a Department dedicated to a certain weaker section of society would naturally try to uplift and make better the lives of those who fall under its auspices, the Aborigines Department of the Australian government does the entire opposite. It has its own views on how to uplift—by separating young children (read infants) from their mothers and rearing them in missions (read prison camps), where the accent is on British mores and manners. It's rules makes it keep a hawk like eye on the movement of the Aborigines and where they settle, so much so that if they come too close to White settlement, they are driven out like flocks of sheep, being everywhere avoided like the plague.

And if the Aborigines Department was not enough, the appointment of a Mr. A.O. Neville to the post of Chief Protector of Aborigines further compounded and made life miserable for the Aborigines. Neville's policies as mentioned earlier are unique and seem hell bent upon severing any Aboriginal existence from the very roots. Scott also narrates how his grandfather caught on the Traveling Inspector of Aborigines, a Mr. James Segal. His opinions on Aborigines and the role of Settlements can be used a foreword to what Whites think about the natives:

> The Settlements give the natives a chance. They're a Child Race. It's our duty to train them for Useful Work, and keep them from harm, from causing harm. They can be an embarrassment. An ideal camp, he continued, is near enough to town to allow the natives to call for rations when they are indigent, to come under the surveillance by police and other local protectors, and to provide a ready labour force when necessary. However, it must always be far enough from White inhabitations to avoid complaints and to discourage unwelcome visits by White men.[6]

His words sum it all. The Settlement was the perfect place for Aborigines according to him. Its utilities would be manifold, like keeping them at arm's length but still within reach when needed as bonded labour, keeping them out like garbage but within limits so that the local guardians like protectors and police are able to keep track. But most hurting is the reason why they are there. The White mentality, from the very beginning, is that they are superior and being so, it is their God bestowed duty to help the Aborigines by giving them props. What is appalling is that they consider the natives to be a Child's Race, synonymous to a blank slate. And just like a newborn baby is reared and cultivated by its guardians, so want the Whites. They want to train them to be useful. But what type of usefulness would it be? Obviously useful enough to serve as servants of the White populace, while it is embarrassing to think that the Aborigines might shame them, for historically and ethnically, the Aborigines stretch far further than their colonial guardians—an opinion echoed throughout the books.

Thus, it was government policy that there be separate camps for the Aborigines, to be set up far away from White settlement and the children be transported to the missions. The treatment meted out is terrible, for as Scott's narration suggests, they were just herded off like sheep and cattle:

> In the morning, you saw a series of unconnected carriages which had been released of their human cargo. Not just your family's. You were rounded up by a few fellas in half uniforms; a jacket, a whip, a spear upped with glass, and waddies.
>
> 'This way,' they indicated. 'This way.' You were driven to the settlement like animals, really, but of course it was not for slaughtering. For training? Yes, perhaps. Certainly it was for breeding, according to the strict principles of animal husbandry.[7]

The sarcasm, when Scott tongue in cheek says, not for slaughtering, is very much evident along with their aim—to have total control over the process of birth and death.

While Scott mentions the Moore River Settlement a number of times for narrating the conditions that exist there, Pilkington's *Follow the Rabbit-Proof Fence* begins from the infamous place itself. Pilkington narrates the plight of her mother Molly, Molly's sister Daisy and their niece Gracie after they are forcibly taken by the police officers from their mothers in the community of Jigalong and transported some 1600 kilometers to the Moore River Native Settlement. At the settlement, the conditions are harsh and inhuman with padlocks, rock-like beds and barred windows. The living quarters are deplorable and the punishment cell is a tin chamber where a misbehaving native is kept chained in the sun without food or water. The Settlement set about its task of turning the girls into whites by forbidding them from speaking their mother tongue or Aboriginal language. There are also forcefully made to get rid off their Aboriginal heritage and taught to be culturally white. On not going by the discriminatory rules, the girls are forced into days of solitary confinement and it is then that the girls, living like prisoners, frightened and homesick, decide to change their lives. They plan to run away and go back to their mothers and what follows is unprecedented in human history. They plan to trek the entire 1600 kilometers on foot following the Rabbit-Proof Fence, a fence erected by the government to keep out rabbits. The Fence of 1834 kilometers was erected in 1907 from the Great Southern Ocean to the coast on the top side primarily for preventing rabbits from invading Western Australia from the eastern states. The next part of the narrative is the story of great grit and determination, of survival despite the greatest of odds and the victory of human spirit over all things in the world.

Thus, the two novels present the aboriginal stance to the 'white problem' and their reactions are both similar and different. In *Benang*, the revolt can be felt at two levels: first, in the mental solutions of problems of the uncles of the narrator and second, in the narrator's own attempts at resisting being the white man of the family. In *Follow the Rabbit-Proof Fence*, the point of revolt is direct and aims, almost similarly, at being converted into whites as well as running away from it all. Thus, more often than not the oppressed Aborigines resist but unfortunately, very few of these cases shape out into an open show of resistance. After every oppression, every act of brutality, the oppressed dream of what could be compared to what is. They are always mentally aspiring for better lives, but in most cases do not have the guts to come out into the open with their aspirations. Their needs and demands are very simple—they just seek better handling from the Whites, which would bring about a sea change in their life.

Benang should be praised for bringing to the forefront, in front of the world's eyes, these aspirations of the natives which more often than not, remain deep inside and unrealized. Scott charts the attempts of the Aborigines to get out of the Aboriginal Act. The most active in this regard was the narrator Harley's Uncle Jack. His efforts to come out of it all have been described symbolically:

> It was not a deep shaft, but still coming up, he saw the entrance as a fissure in the darkness. He saw a wound bleeding light, and imagined inserting his fingers in the opening. The back of his fingers would be together, and then, opening his arms slowly, in an arc, as if they were wings about to launch him, he would thrust them down. He would pull the world inside out. It would be another world.[8]

Scott presents his epistolary efforts towards getting himself a Certificate of Exemption. The letters follow on after another to A.O. Neville, The Chief Protector of Aborigines but to no effect. And after a long drawn process of correspondence through letters, the Chief Protector offers a few unacceptable reasons to Jack for not granting him Exemption. Thus, Jack Chatalong's dismissal left a deep and indelible scar on his psyche and increased his antagonism towards the Whites which would be apparent in his behaviour throughout his life. And he was not alone in his desire to be liberated, to escape the clutches of the Whites—his brother Will was with him. Will, a half-caste, too wanted the White rules concerning their lives to go. He felt that to improve his present state, he himself would be best, and that the interference only led to mistrust and further degradation of his condition. He yearns for total freedom, wants state control over his family affairs to stop but his moves boomerang on him, for he has no chance to mix with either the Whites or the Aborigines, thus making him a very lonely creature. And so what does this constant oppression and subjugation do to the psyche of the natives? It leaves them scarred for life. It leaves them repudiating and rebutting all things White. The scarred psyche makes them believe that they would be free from this oppression only when dead. And after death would they take their revenge seeking divine intervention:

> ...One of the native boys who, sick and tormented lay in bed, swore that after he died he would ask God to come down and burn them all up.[9]

And looking at the torture, most probably even God would accede to such a request. In this, Scott may have made a subtle suggestion for the use of 'dues ex machina' of Greek theatre for such a deplorable state of affairs would surely make God come down and turn right all the wrongs.

Benang is based on the accounts of the narrator Harley's attempts at tracing and revealing the past and making correct the present. During his efforts, he had to face a lot of public scrutiny, but he used his special ability to hover above others like a bird, to good effect. He accepts that the process had not been very easy for "the birth of even an unsuccessfully first-white-man-born-in-the-family-line has required a lot of death, a lot of space, a lot of emptiness."[10] And in time, all the sacrifices, all the sufferings bore fruit. He realized who he was—"Uncle Jack said to me, 'To start with, what you are is a Nyoongar'."[11] That is what he understood when he started out but the world would also have to understand and hence his efforts. In fact, the point which he wants to drive home into all onlookers is that looks and skin colour does not matter. What matters is what the heart says. And the heart says that he was not a White man but a Nyoongar. He accepts that he caused some embarrassment and may have made people uncomfortable but he does not care. What he cares for is the way people look at him and understand him. That has to change and towards that he says "I have written this story wanting to embrace all of you, and it is the best I can do in this language we share. Of course, there is an older tongue which also tells it."[12] He wants others to understand that it not for himself only that he is doing this, it is for the general good of all, and the all must understand that and appreciate his efforts and change themselves to their new identity. He wants all to understand that whatever he is saying is coming straight from the heart. The strength to continue, be themselves comes "from the heart of all of us".[13] Any reversal is bound to cause a lot of heartburn and even burns of the fire kind and he feels it all in himself: "There is smoke and ash in my skin, and in my heart too."[14] But whatever has to be sacrificed has to be, and in the end he triumphantly extorts both his identity and their presence: "We are still here, Benang."[15]

Molly Kelly was just 14 in 1931, when she led and engineered one of the greatest escapes, lasting nine weeks, of all human history. Her story presented by her daughter Doris, is, according to her daughter, the story of probably every one of the lost and stolen generations of that time. The children were of mixed race and their father Thomas Craig was English who worked, ironically, on the very fence they would later follow like a beacon light. Growing up among natives, Molly would often wish that "she didn't have light skin",[16] most probably because "the common belief of the time was that half castes were smarter than full blood blacks".[17] Later on, when they were being taken away to be trained as maid servants, they were under the belief that "they were going to the settlement to go to school. Rain clouds were gathering and by the time they reached the bend where large grey boulders loomed along either side of the road, the sky was black with rain clouds"[18]—ominous clouds which wonderfully summed up their dark unknown fate. On reaching the settlement camp, they slowly but surely became aware of the reality and as Pilkington writes: "it was more like a concentration camp, than a residential school for aboriginal children".[19] Chapter 8 of the novel, aptly and simply titled 'Escape' reveals their plans: "we'll find Rabbit Proof Fence, and follow it all the way home. We're gonna walk all the way,"[20] and in the face of all odds, they complete their journey evading the police, the local whites on the way and wild animals and even the 'marbu'. In the end, "these two girls had overcome their fears and proved that they could survive. It took a strong will and a purpose—they had both"[21] and their big sister "proved herself to be a worthy leader. Her self control and courage, had never faltered throughout the trek."[22] Thus, this story of revolt and survival is littered with instances of de-orientation and complete re-orientation of the three young girls. Having decided to follow the fence, they re-orient themselves for the fence was an important landmark for their clan, the Mardudjara people. They also overcame their fear of the 'marbu; the sharp toothed flesh eating spirit mentioned in the Dreaming of Aboriginal religion, for it proved less frightening than the fear of the River Moore settlement. Ironically, the escaped Molly would have to return to same place some ten years later with her daughters and would again escape, this time with her daughter Annabelle in her arms but leaving her other daughter Doris, the writer, in the settlement. Still later, Annabelle would be snatched away from her and trained in white manners so as not recognize her mother in later years, though the writer, Doris would come back to her mother.

Thus, the two novels by two colonized aborigines walk along almost the same lines and move towards some sort of redemption, some sort of reprieve from the white subjugation. Both their tales are real narrations of disturbed past histories of their families and are recounted through concrete evidences. While Scott used actual archival material, Protector's reports and first person accounts of his uncles, Pilkington used her mother and aunt's personal descriptions as well as newspaper and archival materials. Interestingly, the narration of any story of past oppression becomes a sensational account but Scott and Pilkington try to do away from such a practice in their novels. As Scott mentions, the reason for his penning his family history is not for sensationalizing but for letting the world know. For Pilkington, the story of her mother would have remained buried somewhere had she not given it literary oxygen to become an iconic novel for all the stolen generations. Also, by making the world know, it is less of an attempt to shame the whites than to present the reality. For history underlines the fact that history belongs to the rulers and the powerful and is always narrated from their point of view. Accordingly, the novels also seem trying to change the 'made-up' history of the masters and reframe the history of the servants, the colonized. For history retold is history revealed, for the creation of a new history from the colonized's point of view. But most importantly, they are also attempts at moving the readers and making them think of history and representation and being involved at the level of effect, the readers are expected to generate emotions of anger, shame and compassion and a denouncement of the past.

Central among all interests of the two writers seem their intention at revealing and reshaping their own identity in an ambiguously fashioned multicultural world. Multiculturalism offers a lot of apparent space, especially for the oppressed but as is evident, multiculturalism appears to a farce. 'Multi' cultures never exist side by side as Siamese twins but always create hegemonic formations with parasitic intentions. Multiculturalism offers space to the people in the lower part of the pyramid but such a space is open to violation by the masters who abuse to rule and gain control, so much so that, a time comes when the diminishing space becomes suffocating and disgusting to live. And then it is the fight for space as well as rights which tend to destabilize the apparently multicultural setup, a fight which again is unfortunately loaded in favour of the masters. Consequently, both the novels give the impression that they are attempts at recovering Aboriginal spaces lost in time so that new spaces are fashioned out.

The two novels are chronicles of half-caste lives on the edge, straddling two worlds. Their situation is bizarre and pathetic for they cannot fit into either culture, being neither totally coloured nor white. This dilemma of not fitting anywhere makes them some sort of a taboo, for, as in Scott's case, his fair skin draws looks of suspicion from his Nyoongar clan when he tries to be one of them. Their situation is worth pity; they are rejected by their Aboriginal mates as whites and herded by the whites as outcastes who need training to fit into white culture. From such a sense of loss, from being unable to find their true coordinates in society do the writers try bridging the man made boundaries and relocating their identity for the loss of identity drives anyone to madness. Hence, identity formation is one of the main objectives and in that they seem to be successful for in the end— they are once again part of their own people, the very people they were not supposed to become and bring about a down fall of all white intentions. Simultaneously, the message which runs through the fabric of both the novels is that the exploration of one's individual history presents the chance and highlights the significance of moving from ignorance to knowledge; from resentment and indignation at past injustices to a more sympathetic view of the oppressors of the past; from a sense of being psychologically dented and morally dispossessed to a therapeutic recognition with the people and the land.

NOTES

1. Oodgeroo, *My People* 3rd ed. Milton: Jacaranda Press, 1990, pp. 36-37.
2. Minh-Ha Trinh, *Woman Native Other*. London: Routledge, 1989, p. 6.
3. Kim Scott, *Benang*. New Delhi: Penguin Books India, 2003, p. 131.
4. Mitchell Dean and Barry Hindess, *Governing Australia* Cambridge University Press, 1998, pp. 177-86.
5. Scott, p. 177.
6. *Ibid.*, p. 47.
7. *Ibid.*, p. 93.
8. *Ibid.*, p. 84.
9. *Ibid.*, p. 329.
10. *Ibid.*, p. 496.
11. *Ibid.*
12. *Ibid.*, p. 497.
13. *Ibid.*
14. *Ibid.*
15. *Ibid.*
16. Doris Pilkington, *Follow the Rabbit-Proof Fence*. University of Queensland Press, 1996, p. 38.
17. *Ibid.*, p. 40.
18. *Ibid.*, p. 50.
19. *Ibid.*, p. 72.
20. *Ibid.*, p. 78.
21. *Ibid.*, pp. 119-20.
22. *Ibid.*, p. 96.

Cosmopolitanism vs Americanism—A Critique of American Cosmopolitanism in the Works of Margaret Atwood and Salman Rushdie

5

Garima Gupta

Cosmopolitanism: The Idea and the Practice

Cosmopolitanism can be defined as the idea that all human beings are governed by the same moral standards. This by implication rules out the notion of a world government as a prerequisite for cosmopolitanism. A more inclusive moral, economic, political, cultural relationships between nations or individual or different nations can also perpetuate a cosmopolitanism state.

Cosmopolitanism can be traced back to Diogenes who claimed to be a world citizen, a kosmopolities. Stoics who later took Diogenes' idea and developed it into a full blown concept asserted that each human being, "dwells…in two communities—the local community of our birth, and the community of human argument and aspiration" (24). A similar line of argument can be seen in Hierocles' circular model of identity which stresses that we should regard ourselves as concentric circles, the first one around the self, next immediate family, extended family, local group, citizens, countrymen, humanity. The task of world citizens becomes then to "draw the circles somehow towards the centre, making all human beings more like our fellow city dwellers and so forth" (1: 349). This idea of cosmopolitanism entails blurring of boundaries on a moral terrain and not on a geographical one.

Contemporary philosophical cosmopolitans too are moral universalists. They believe that same moral standards govern all humans irrespective of their nationality, culture or race. Thus, the geographical boundaries are morally irrelevant. A widely cited example of a contemporary cosmopolitan is Kwame Anthony Appiah.

Kwame Anthony Appiah's Cosmopolitanism: Ethics in a World of Strangers propounds cosmopolitanism which is based on the principles of the existence of different people governed by the same standards of values and humanity. As can be gathered from the title Appiah is of the view that in a world full of strangers, cosmopolitanism is a universal trait of humankind. Citing works by ethnographers, the writer stresses that people in far-flung places are the same in that "they have gods, food, language, dance, music, cravings, medicines, family lives, rituals, jokes and children's tales. They smiled, slept, had sex and children, wept and in the end died" (137). Thus, they are all governed by the same morality.

Critics and theorists have differentiated amongst the various types of cosmopolitanism on different grounds. Thus, while some categorise it as cultural cosmopolitanism, political cosmopolitanism, sociological cosmopolitanism, etc. others speaks of categories like neoliberal cosmopolitanism, postcolonical cosmopolitanism, postmodern cosmopolitanism, etc. Dwelling into the detail of these categories lies outside the scope of this article. However, what I have attempted is to outline the moral ground of the cosmopolitans which they use in propagating it as desirable alternative to provincialism and nationalism and a panacea to all ills of the contemporary world order.

This then is the ideas of cosmopolitanism or rather the ideal concept of the term which if implemented would no doubt usher in a utopian world order. But then, does the practice can form to the idea? Diogenes would have never dreamt that the noble concept of 'Kosmopolites' would acquire a snobby connotation in the sense of the well to do inhabitant of a large city where different cultures meet. A very relevant question one must ask is what does cosmopolitanism mean in a world where one-half of the world's population lives, "in urban rather that in rural areas". The synonyms of cosmopolitanism spelt out in the oxford thesaurus are 'international', 'multicultural', 'sophisticated', 'universal' and 'urbane' and one might add 'global' to this list.

This list clearly implies an urban setting without any rural connotations. Thus, one needs to distinguish between affluent urban cosmopolitans and blue collar and rural cosmopolitans. One also needs to keep in mind the affluent urban cosmopolitans of the first world and those of the third world. These are the categories which blur and are ignored by the moral cosmopolitans.

We trace the origin of the term to the Greek and find its parallel in the Indian ideology of 'Vasudev Kutumbkam', but when someone mentions a cosmopolitan person, the image that flashes across our mind is of a person with a good spoken English, a western attire and correct western manners. If a person speaks good English but is dhoti-clad will he be considered a cosmopolitan or if he dons a denim jeans but cannot speak English, does he fit the profile or if he is wearing a western attire, speaking good English but eats with his hands (not using spoon, forks, etc.) will he be accepted as a cosmopolitan citizen! If you have given an honest answer to these, then you agree with me that today the term in vogue is entirely western in its conceptualization and not limited to the moral terrain alone.

Cosmopolitanism and Americanism

Malik Solanka, protagonist of the novel Fury is characterized by Salman Rushdie as a truly cosmopolitan person (as is the present day connotation of the term). Malik Solanka is an Indian (as the name reflects) who has a British citizenship and who eventually moves to American which serves as the main setting of the novel. He is a truly cosmopolitan individual as he is at home anywhere, where his credit card is accepted. He is an affluent product of a capitalist society and his affluence guarantees his cosmopolitanism. Thus, a far cry from the original idea, today the practice of cosmopolitism is an effort to homogenize the world to the gain of capitalists or capitalism, an attitude which I am designating by the term Americanism.

However, in using the word 'Americanism', I am to quote Dr. Sucheta Pathania in her explication of Atwood's use of the term, "not attacking Americans as individuals...but attacking the attitude first developed by American Corporations, that the world is to be exploited freely for the benefit of the consumer society..." (46). To put it in the words of Jaidev, "Americanism is an ideology and it infiltrates the minds and life-styles of the people of the less powerful, less affluent submissive countries..." (66). Thus, I am using the term Americanism as an ideology. Even India can be said to be practicing Americanism when it tries to infiltrate the tribal communities with the (so-called) dominant ideology of the country. So Americanism refers to the American capitalism as well as the ideology it perpetuated.

Beneath the scintillating cloak of cosmopolitanism, one can discern the gradually spreading roots of American cultural imperialism. Benedict Anderson minimizes the impact of American cultural imperialism on youth who, "as they get older...conform more and more to older domestic cultural expectations" (24). But then what he fails to notice that "domestic cultural expectations" are getting diluted everyday with the McDonald culture. Cosmopolitanism, if implemented in its pristine sense is indeed the need of the hour but one needs to be wary of its distortion by the capitalist forces for their own profit and this is what I propose Atwood and Rushdie try to attempt in their novels.

Critique of Americanism by Atwood and Rushdie

I would like to reinstate that to these writers a critique of Americanism is a critique of its practice of homogenizing the world under the rubric of cosmopolitanism.

Surfacing by Atwood begins like a detective story. The narrator/protagonist, who is unnamed, comes back from Toronto after nine year's absence to Northern Quebec where she had lived as a child. She has been told that her father who lived alone on a lake island has vanished without a trace, and through she has not been in touch with him for many years, she feels bound to go on an attempt to find what has happened to him. Enroute with her friend Joe and another couple David and Anna, she finds that Canada is being victimized by Americanism. As soon as she takes the road to Quebec she discerns signs of change. Under the guise of progress, or sometimes globalization, or cosmopolitanism, Americanism has made deep inroads into the Canadian culture.

Quebec, the narrator, suspects, has always enjoyed a kind of cultural authenticity that has been long fortified by English, "American" Canada. It has always basked in romance, colour and legend in contract to the English Canada's staid cultural heritage. Though the protagonist is alienated from this land, her refusal to accept as genuine the trite folk tales she has been commissioned to illustrate reveals the sort of cultural authenticity she wants Quebec to have.

However, the protagonist discovers that no shields—those of language or religion or tradition—can save Quebec from the impact of Americanism. The distinctiveness of Quebec renders Americanism more starkly visible than it is in English Canada. Wherever she looks, the narrator finds signs hat her childhood version of Quebec is being violated by Americans and Canadians who have assimilated the "American" values of material progress and self-centered ecological destruction. The road to the village has been straightened and shortened; the gas station is decorated with stuffed moose, one waving an American flag; the village economy depends on catering to American holiday fisherman, businessmen in plaid shirts still creased from the cellophane packages.

At first the narrator assumes, like David, that in the wilderness the Americans will be easy to identify. They are the ones who scare away the fish with their souped-up speedboats, who violate the game laws by catching far more than they can eat, and who want all their camping equipment to be automatic and collapsible. But in northern Quebec, Americanism reveals itself to be not a nationality, but a state of mind. This is best illustrated by the following conversation in the novel between the supposed Americans and the protagonist and her friends.

> "We aren't fishing" I said, my lips clipping the words. My arms wanted to swing the paddle sideways, blade into his head: his eyes would blossom outwards, his skill shatter like an egg.
>
> The corners of his mouth wilted. "Oh" he said. "Say, what part of the states are you all from? Its hard to tell, from your accent. Fred and me guessed Ohio".
>
> "We're not from the states", I said, annoyed that he'd mistaken me for one of them.

"No kidding?" His face lit up, he'd seen a real native. "You from here?"

"Yes" I said, "We all are."

"So are we" said the back one unexpectedly. (138)

I have quoted this conversation at length because the writer has made a very interesting point here. All the characters in this conversation are actually Canadians but mistake each other for Americans because of their speech and looks. In this incident when the narrator's party and the Ontario fishermen mistake each other for Americans, the narrator suddenly realizes that in North America it is impossible to be a non-American.

In the entire novel, Atwood brings out how Americanism is slowly but surely invading Canada—ripping apart social fabric (the protagonist hadn't spoken to her father for nine years), destroying nature and natural resources (which is visible as soon as the protagonist takes the road to Quebec) and transforming the land and its people. Through her protagonist, Atwood both detests as well as resists this American intrusion be it in the person of Malmstrom interested in buying the protagonist's childhood home, or exposing David as a hypocrite who apes the American ways while verbally criticizing them or the Americans fishing in their power boats; infact, every small little way in which Americanism is infesting the Canadian national identity. As the protagonist disgustingly says, "It doesn't matter what country they're from, my head said, they're still Americans, they're what's in store for us, what we are turning into" (139).

Atwood, however, is not alone in her critique of the global American culture. Salman Rushdie echoes this critique as well. America begins to figure prominently in Rushdie's novels from his *The Ground Beneath Her Feet*. As a person stung by love at first sight, Rushdie univocally eulogizes the country and his culture as a true embodiment of cosmopolitanism which instead of erasing differences makes them its own. As the protagonist of the novel Vina Apsara says:

> However, you get through your day in New York City, well then that's a New York kind of day, and if you're a Bombay singer singing the Bombay bop or a voodoo cab driver with

> zombies on the brain or a bomber from Montana or an Islamist bear do from Queen's then whatever's going through your head?, well that's New York stat of mind. (331)

This presents American in general and New York in particular as a cosmopolitan haven. However, as love matures the faults of the beloved became visible and thus in *Fury*, Rushdie presents a scathing critique of the American culture exposing the dark alleys underneath the scintillating bright sun. As critically acclaimed Fury is an insightful novel of New York, and of the frantic globalised culture for which that city stands as a symbol and sponsor.

To summarize, which is quite difficult with Rushdie, the protagonist of the novel is Malik Solanka, a historian by profession and a dollmaker by passion—a passion that earns him millions. He is consumed with such fury that it makes him dangerous to the ones he love and to avoid hurting them he flees to New York thinking it to be a panacea for all ills. This is the time when the city is at the peak if unprecedented plenty, wealth and power. But fury is all around him. Cab drivers are full of invectives and the sinister face of the city is seen in the serial killer murdering women with a lump of concrete. The petty spats and bone-deep resentment of the cosmopolitan metropolis engulf him. New York, supposedly the most cosmopolitan city of all appears differently under the sun. Thus, the question one is forced to ask is that can an erasure if differences usher in a cosmopolitan society. Far from the earlier passage where differences are adopted, I found the following passage where differences are homogenized:

> Everybody in the *same* accommodation, gettin' the *same* education doin' the *same* recreation lookin' for the *same*...ploymentation. Check it out. We gettin' the *same* bills, datin' the *same* girls goin' to the *same* jails.... (59)

Thus, the writer discovers how everyone is being forced into the 'same' culture. This sameness or homogenizing is Americanism, but this Americanism is not the cosmopolitanism we desire. Being citizens of the world is a noble concept but this nowhere implies that the world should turn into America. Thus in *Fury*, Rushdie presents with coruscating virtuosity how the glamour of America is attractive and blinding but how when one rips apart the surface there is a lot of ugliness lurking beneath. Rushdie presents the prejudice behind the façade of cosmopolitanism through the character of Jack Rhinehart for whom the glamour of the city proves to be fatal. Even the cosmopolitanism of Malik Solanka (as mentioned above) is critiqued as being sustained by his affluence.

The Oxford Dictionary defines cosmopolitanism as "of or knowing all parts of the world" or "unprejudiced" or "free from national limitations". Atwood and Rushdie advocate a cosmopolitanism which is coloured by multiculturalism. But they resist the multiculturalism of the 'hot pot' theory of America where all the differences are homogenized. A multiculturalism which respects and retains differences is the only form desirable and by this the only idea and practice of cosmopolitanism to be embraced should be guided by only one amongst all its definitions, that is "unprejudiced".

WORKS CITED

Anderson, Benedict. "Long Live the Nation!" *Cosmopolitanism and the Nation-State*. Biblio: A Review of Books. New Delhi, March-April 2002.

Appiah, Kwame Anthony. *Cosmopolitanism: Ethics in a World of Strangers*. London: Penguin Books, 2006.

Atwood, Margaret. *Surfacing*. Toronto: General Publishing Co. Limited, 1972.

Dev, Jai. A Study of Margaret Atwood's *Surfacing*. Patiala: Punjabi University, 1990.

Hierocles, Fragment excerpted in Eclogas IV, 671ff; Long and Sedley, 1987.

Nussabaum, Martha C. "Kant and Stoic Cosmopolitanism", *The Journal of Political Philosophy*, Vol. 5, No. 1, 1997.

Pathania, Sucheta. "From Consumerism to Globalisation: Perspective of Colonial Civilization in the Novels of Margaret Atwood", *The Atlantic Critical Review*, Vol. 4, No. 1, Jan-Mar 2005.

Rushdie, Salman. *The Ground Beneath Her Feet*. London: Jonathan Cape, 1999.

——. *Fury*. New York: Random House, 2002.

Tobin, Mary and Clare, Oh. "The Growing Urbanization of the World." Earth Institute News. Online: http://www.earth.columbia.edu/news/2005/story03-07-05.html

The Terrorist in the Text: The Deictic Construction of Otherness

6

Esterino Adami

> 'It's strange', said Urmila. 'Just the other day, I was reading a book of Phulboni's essays—you know, the writer who was given the award at Rabindra Sadan yesterday? What you were saying reminded me of something he wrote a long time ago. I remember the passage almost by heart. "I have never known", it begins, "whether life lies in words or in images, in speech or sight. Does a story come to be in the words that I conjure out of my mind or does it live already, somewhere, enshrined in mud and clay—in an image, that is, in the crafted mimicry of life?"'
>
> Amitav Ghosh, *The Calcutta Chromosome*

The thorny question of diasporic identity in its double dimension pre- and post-9/11 on the global stage constitutes the core of Mohsin Hamid's *The Reluctant Fundamentalist* (2007), a skilful novel grounded upon the literary strategy of the dramatic monologue. To approach the technical complexities of this text we need to adopt a linguistic/stylistic perspective and deconstruct the literary mechanisms employed by the astute author. Thus, I shall concentrate upon the narrative techniques that subtly inform the novel as a cutting-edge work of diasporic literature. The main model of reference on which Hamid's text revolves can be identified in the poem "My Last Duchess" by Robert Browning (1842), a significant example of language manipulation in the attempt to represent a speech situation by means of a printed text. A witty and eloquent writer, Hamid adopts this tactic and updates the diasporic condition in the 21st century globalised world. The entire novel is built as kind of long monologue: the narrator, a young man from Lahore who has lived for some time in the US, approaches a silent American tourist in the galleys of his native city and tells him about his eventful life. This single-voiced representation draws on Changez's memories, expectations, tensions and illuminates the conflicting and disturbing attitudes of the wondering migrant, after the rise of global fear of terrorism.

As a main tool of analysis, I would like to introduce here the notion of the double pattern, namely the interconnection of literary and non-literary aspects of discourse: by constructing his novel as a sort of monologue that insistently attracts the attention of the unnamed listener, and of the reader as well, as if it were an obsessive war bulletin or news broadcast on the terror campaign of fundamentalists, the author plays up with the territories of fiction on the margin of non-fiction in an engrossing narrative operation. Albeit the absence of turn-taking that characterises the monological form, the narrator's voice is crafted with the purpose of suggesting a dynamic interaction between Changez and the mysterious American, and therefore, we can perceive a speech event at work that moves away from a statically descriptive situation. Indeed, through a rich variety of devices, the writer grants vivacity and allusions to his text, a literary work that can also function as a site of diaspora. Originally, the critical category of the double pattern derived from the stylistic approach to poetry, but we can also apply it to other genres, such as narrative texts.

Indeed, as Richard Bradford states, "the novel will organize and situate non-literary modes and registers in a way that is particular to fiction writing: again their relationship involves the double pattern. The double pattern outside the text reflects the attention given by the interpreter to one or other pole of the double pattern within it". Hamid exploits to the full the involving power of the speech acts pertaining to the dramatic monologue and substitutes the neutrality of statements and narrative reports with loaded meanings. Through a carefully constructed textual architecture, the author expands and redefines the key themes of difference (the eastern migrant depicted as a perilous terrorist), and its perception from a western point of view. As a matter of fact, the migrant is culturally imagined as a pernicious enemy and grotesquely represented as a rough, bearded man, thus following a cliché of physical and symbolical otherness spanning over a variety of cultural, social and historical references. A product of orientalism in its attempt to categorise and control the eastern forms of alterity, the Pakistani subject is now identified as the alien breaking the social (textual) order, and as a consequence "the undiluted migrant looming in archaic menace in-between the disjointed boards of the global frame evokes the time-honoured colonial bogeyman, the concealing savage or the absconding deceiver serving us with fretful and uncanny devotion". Thus, he eventually becomes the (potential) terrorist in the text.

In order to articulate his exploration of such intricate issues, Mohsin Hamid ambitiously works out a peculiar focalization through the mellifluous voice of the narrator, that is the orientating viewpoint. It is worth pointing out that I am here concerned with the creation of textual discourse, that is "the whole complicated process of linguistic interaction between people uttering and comprehending texts", rather than the critical evaluation of a fictional work. Deixis is of paramount in this sense as it operates via a tripartite scheme, viz. with personal, temporal and spatial reference. Indeed, the astute choice of vocal gestures, rhetorical questions, indirect commands phrased with sham politeness, and exclamations aims at building up a complex deictic network. The author compels the American listener and implicitly the reader, to face and, to a certain extent, accept the intricate developing of Changez' storytelling, with its apparently "natural" digressions. The following quotations exemplify the attempt to create a (fictional) interaction between the imagined social actors:

> Your ears must be exhausted; the time has come to employ your tongue—for taste, if nothing more, although I hope you can be persuaded to speak! (*RF*, 76)

> It is impossible to tell, sir, given the gloom about us and the unexpressive cast of your face, but I suspect you are looking at me with a degree of revulsion; certainly I would look at

> you in such a manner if you had just told me what I have told you. But I hope your disgust has not banished your appetite, for I am summoning our waiter to take our order. Tonight, I can assure you, our mean will be anything but tasteless—and here he come. Good man! (*RF*, 107; Author's emphasis)

Throughout the two excerpts, indicators of time and place strive to anchor the speech event to a dynamic linguistic, and also intercultural, contact, camouflaged as a solo narration. Moreover, the incidence of interpersonal features (personal pronouns, possessive adjectives) contributes to the dramatization and characterization of the protagonist, by ingeniously alternating social deixicals, with the use of exclusive subjects (speaker plus others, excluding addresse: in our case the authorial 'I/eye' of Changez, the Pakistani people, and the migrant community) and inclusive subjects (speaker and addresse included, namely the narrator and the speechless American and the readership).

Let us now consider the node of focalization, that is "the literary-critical version of the general linguistic concept of ideational meaning". Since the novel branches out through a first-person narration, the narratee (addresse) is obliged to follow Changez's point of view and mood, although at times the narrator seems to indulge towards a certain degree of unreliability, provoking and eliciting a response from the reader, and simultaneously casting doubts upon his own act of narration:

> But your expression, sir, tells me that you think something is amiss. Did this conversation really happen, you ask? For that matter, did this so-called Juan Bautista even exist? I assure you, sir: you can trust me. I am not in the habit of inventing untruths! And moreover, even if I were, there is no reason why this incident would be more likely to be false than any of the others I have related to you. Come, come, I believe we have passed through too much together to begin to raise questions of this nature at so late a stage. (*RF*, 152)

Intentionally, Hamid creates his protagonist as a Janus-like figure, and collocates his storytelling in a liminal position, so as to make the writing a good deal more porous. The ambiguity that this type of focalization generates is instrumental in endorsing a multiple perspective concerning the split self of the eastern migrant, deemed as a brilliant Ivy League student before the Twin Towers attack, and suspiciously observed as an ambiguous and possibly dangerous subject afterwards.

Two other recent diasporic novels, *Londonstani* by Gautam Malkani and *Psychoraag* by Suhayl Saadi, present an idiosyncratic use of focalization. In the latter, for example, the omniscient narrator frequently gives way to the voice of Zaf, a Glasgow-based DJ of Pakistani origins, broadcasting his last playlist mixed with memories, feelings, and thoughts. The unreliability of the narrator lies not in the recollection of past events but rather in the re-elaboration of past experiences and connected lives: "The Colour of Memory. The substance of things which no longer existed. But what about the things that were in-between—where did they fit in?". In narrative terms, the notion of memory is always mediated by the author, and can be manipulated on purpose: with *The Reluctant Fundamentalist* Hamid seems to be more interested in asking provocative questions rather than providing reassuring answers. And perhaps, the same peculiar position dominates Londonstani: although the nature of the unreliable narrator is signalled by some minor clues, the whole textual construction is designed to climax in the final coup de theatre, as Jas, the narrating protagonist, drops his mask and reveals his real identity when he is treated in hospital after a violent fight. The painful confrontation with the order of things functions as a cathartic experience. We should also point out that unreliable narrators do not constitute an innovation per se, as they frequently feature in postmodern and contemporary literature, from Salman Rushdie's *The Midnight's Children* (1981) to Hanif Kureishi's stories. In a narratological perspective, readers have to side with texts, which to misquote Umberto Eco are essentially lazy machines that require much collaboration in order to work properly.

I would like to underscore the evocative power of time and space deixis that the novelist cunningly deploys in the text. The story regards an uncertain present, with the September 11 catastrophe functioning as a sort of catalysing divide, which bisects the perception of the world before and after the outburst of global terror. In the novel, the narrator's unclear reaction to the devastating event mirrors the Pakistani migrant's vision and confusion, a sense of being split and lost in an undecipherable world: "And yet...No, I ought to pause here, for I think you will find rather unpalatable what I intend to say next, and I wish to warn you before I proceed" (*RF*, 71-72). By describing the circumstance when he watched the Twin Towers destruction on television, he actually activates a strategy of psychological distance and invests with meaning and connotations words and phrases. This concerns a pragmatic event taking place, in so far as "more" is being communicated than is "said", although we need to decode the inner mechanisms of discourse. The timeline too, is marked by reference of past events that celebrate the rich heritage of the East through the appropriation of a binary vision ("we" versus "you/they"):

> For we were not always burdened by debt, dependent on foreign aid and handouts; in the stories we tell of ourselves we were not the crazed and destitute radicals you see on your television channels but rather saints and poets and—yes—conquering kings. We built the Royal Mosque and the Shalimar Gardens in this city, and we built the Lahore Fort with its mighty walls and wide ramp for our battle-elephants. And we did these things when your country was still a collection of thirteen small colonies, gnawing away at the edge of a continent. (*RF*, 102; Author's emphasis)

As Charles Fillmore states, the temporal organisation in the linguistic (and cultural) code needs to set up a fixed point through a sociocultural and sociolinguistic operation of selection, rooted in the hierarchical construction of perceptions: "once a temporal reference point has been established, it is then possible to speak of any point in time as being at a measurable distance earlier or later than, or coinciding with the accepted reference point". Here the narrator appears to upturn the time reference point by moving it backwards into a historical past, and so emphasis is laid upon not chaotic modernity, but rather the comparison of histories, back to a time when Pakistani culture fruitfully developed a rich heritage and body of arts and practices.

Another stylistic tool that contributes to the balanced tension that characterises Hamid's writing is represented by modality, a linguistic area that densely surfaces through the voice of Changez from the very opening of the novel. Traditionally modality "is the term for a cluster of meanings centred on the notions of necessity and possibility" and is realised by a variety of forms, in particular modal verbs, as in the formal incipit of the text when the narrator nears the American tourist: "Excuse me, sir, but may I be of assistance?" (*RF*, 1). The urge to contact the perplexed westerner coincides with a kind of Scheherazade's syndrome, that is the will to narrate a story, to disclose an entire world of words, and at the same time maybe hides some more sinister intentions: "What? Is somebody following us? I cannot see anyone—no, wait, now that you mention it there are a few figures there, in the gloom [...]. What do you mean, sir, did I give them a signal? Of course not! I have as little insight into their motivations and identities as you do" (*RF*, 176). The mesmerising effect that intentionally the author attributes to his speaking character is also originated by a sophisticated use of modal items which express the degree of commitment, evaluation, possibility, necessity or obligation. The riveting power of narration, which derives from the eastern tradition of orality, allows Changez to play up with unrealised conditions and possible states, so that the addresse is led to trust his point of view. Two types of modality operate in the text: deontic and epistemic. The former case deals with notions of duty and obligation, sometimes refined through polite construction, for instance when the narrator persuades, or rather forces, the American man to walk with him into the bazaar, to eat a tasty meal in the restaurant, or drink spiced tea. In all these circumstances, the principle of politeness actually conceals a performative function since Changez, in a very subtle way, instructs the silent interlocutor: he acts as a puppeteer and morbidly holds the man spellbound. Epistemic modality brings to light the speaker's viewpoint and his opinions and evaluations: it thus coincides with the way the narrator presents his vision and knowledge of the world.

The monological progress of the story is set as a one-voiced clash of cultures and histories on the edge, evoked by anaphoric and cataphoric references. Changez in his apt storytelling looks back on the past (the episodes of his life, the impact of world changes) and simultaneously calls on the near future, as if he could foresee dramatic consequences:

> Most of all, I must avoid doing what you are doing in this instant, namely constantly looking over my shoulder. It seems to me that you have ceased to listen to my chatter; perhaps you are convinced that I am an inveterate liar, or perhaps you are under the impression that we are being pursued. Really, sir, you would do well to relax. Yes, those men are now rather close, and yes, the expression on the face of that one—what a coincidence; it is our waiter; he has offered me a nod of recognition—is rather grim. But they mean no harm, I assure you. It seems an obvious thing to say, but you should not imagine that we Pakistanis are all potential terrorists, just as we should not imagine that you Americans are all undercover assassins. (*RF*, 183)

The sense of suspense that surrounds this passage and dots many other sections of the text seems to suggest or even anticipate a dramatic ending. Hamid masterfully makes use of implicature, viz. additional conveyed meaning to surprise the reader (and implicitly the gullible American) by blurring the outlines of the plot. Apparently neutral, the statements, provocations and questions that Changez intertwines on the double pattern are, in reality, barbed remarks against the imposition of a certain world vision, and evolve into a looming danger. As a matter of fact, the Pakistani's idiosyncratic revenge takes the form of words, and probably actions too, exactly following the wilful example of Robert Browning's Duke who, while praising the portrait of her late wife, confesses unsaid truths: "I gave commands;/Then all smiles stopped together. There she stands/As if alive".

Character and Fantasy in Mahesh Dattani's *Bravely Fought the Queen*

7

Subir Dhar

If some of the most significant plays written by Mahesh Dattani are anything to go by, this Indian playwright who deals insightfully and often incisively with contemporary issues of social relevance such as patriarchy, communalism, gender and sexual identity could very well have succeeded and flourished as a writer of whodunits. At least three of Dattani's early plays—viz., *Where There's a Will*, *Final Solutions*, and *Bravely Fought the Queen* pivot tellingly on the revelation of a secret which is hinted at or clued throughout the unfolding action, but is disclosed only in a climactic episode towards the end of each play. Thus, in Dattani's first performed play, *Where There's a Will*, the secret of Preeti, the daughter-in-law's hastening of Hasmukh Mehta's death comes out a little before its ending, and *Final Solutions* actually closes with Ramnik Gandhi's disclosure that his grandfather and father had been responsible for setting fire to a Muslim family's shop under cover of a post-Partition communal riot so that they could buy out the business at less than half its real value. Somewhat similarly, *Bravely Fought the Queen* turns on the revelation that Dolly and Jiten Trivedi's daughter Daksha is no talented child-dancer but a spastic child who has to attend a special school and to whom a 'dance' is actually "a spastic's uncoordinated arm and neck movement" (Dattani, 312).

Of course the unexpected uncovering of a fact that had been kept hidden from the knowledge or perception of the audience is an ancient bit of theatrical business to be found variously in classical Greek tragedy (cf. Aristotle's *Anagnorosis*) as well as in the professional practice of such late nineteenth-century playwrights as Eugene Scribe and Victorien Sardou.[1] A little like these dramatists who innovated the *la piece bien* faite or well-made play with its *scene a faire* or discovery scene, and more perhaps like thesis-playwrights like Ibsen and Shaw who were not above utilizing these strategies for their own ideational ends, Dattani too, in his plays clearly harnesses some of the theatrical energy of the sudden revelation to make a point or to highlight an issue. However, and more to the argument of this paper, it is well to remember that in *Bravely Fought the Queen* at least the revelation made is not a mechanical plot-contrivance but a far more plausible (and meaningful) psychologically propelled discovery. To put it simply, everything in the mental life of Dolly Trivedi, the play's protagonist, leads up to this. For her, the confession before the two outsiders Lalitha and Sridhar that her daughter had been born abnormal because of the violence her husband had inflicted on her even when she had been pregnant, is the final rending of the curtain of lies, self-delusions and illusions that she had carefully built up around her to try and live a life with a semblance of normalcy.

Theatre director Jeremy Mortimer has noted that Dattani's "plays often feature characters who are questioning their identity, and who feel isolated in some way," (Dattani, 4) and Erin Mee has observed that the dramatist's "characters struggle for some kind of freedom and happiness under the weight of tradition, cultural constructions of gender, and repressed desire" (Dattani, 319). These are sound observations, and even though they smack a little of generalizations, they can be well applied to the characters of Dolly and her sister Alka Trivedi in *Bravely Fought the Queen.* Certainly Dolly is an "isolated" figure as even the outsider Lalitha comments a few minutes into the play's opening, for not only is she emotionally estranged from her husband, but she has also to live in a house located in an isolated suburban part of the city, tellingly described as being built "in the middle of nowhere" (Dattani, 238). Alka too, is a study in alienation and repressed sexuality for she had been married off by her brother to a closet homosexual, and is also is childless by compulsion. At the same time, however, the two sisters have different personalities for while the elder sibling Dolly is apparently far more composed and self-possessed in public, Alka is an alcoholic and a clumsy liar who tries ineffectually hide the fact of her addiction. Thus, at one revealing moment in the first Act of the play immediately after pouring a stiff shot of rum into her glass of Pepsi, she reacts to Lalitha's comment: "You must do a bit of social drinking too," with a transparent untruth: "I don't. I don't drink at all" (Dattani, 244). Yet, it is important to note too that the two sisters are similar in that they both indulge in fantasizing, and it is specifically here that the two characters take on a life of their own both as unique dramatic personalities and as realistic representations of feminine selves.

It will be no exaggeration to say that some of the greatest women characters in theatre—the sleepwalking Lady Macbeth being a classic case in point—have been depicted as displaying or living out the deepest and most secret of their fears or fantasies on the stage. This is because even in real life, fantasizing is often a compelling psychological need in adults equally as in children, for as Freud indicated, fantasy is an essential means for the expression of repressed desire (Freud, 241). Or, as a more recent commentator has clarified, "Fantasy...not only promises ultimate jouissance for desire (either having or being the object *a*), it also protects the subject from being engulfed in the abyss of nonmeaning at the basis of human existence" (Bracher, 43). Embodied in action through the on-stage behaviour of one or more characters in a play, the psychological element of fantasizing depicted makes for a compelling realism in dramatic representation. In *Bravely Fought the Queen*, Dattani is as his usual practice working well within the frames of realistic theatre, but the depth of his realism in his portrayal of the characters of Dolly and Alka is evidenced through the fact that in either case the fantasies are related to both their unique personalities and their rather different situations as married women. And it is here that Dattani's maturity as a dramatist and skill as a creator of convincing and psychologically consistent *dramatis personae* stands revealed.

In his classic work on the concept of the fantastic, Tzvetan Todorov indicated that "[t]he fantastic is always a break in the acknowledged order, an irruption within the changeless everyday reality" (Todorov, 41), a recognition that Kathryn Hume has extended upon in her statement that fantasy is sourced in "the desire to change givens and alter reality—out of boredom, play, vision, [or] longing for something lacking" (Hume, 20). Both of the two major fantasies embodied in *Bravely Fought the Queen* clearly originate from a sense of lack. The second one, which is the less elaborately worked out of the two, though not the less complex for this, is that of Alka's dance in the rain outside in the open courtyard. What propels this fantasy and its physicalization is partly Alka's drunkenness and partly her internalization in her intoxicated state of Dolly's teasing suggestion: "You love getting wet and having your sari clinging to you. Your bra and choli showing.... And you love doing a filmi number in the rain." However, what is really at stake in this episode is Dolly's projection of Alka as a sort of Hindi film heroine as fixated by a typical male gaze. According to Laura Mulvey in her 1975 essay "Visual Pleasure and Narrative Cinema", "The determining male gaze projects its phantasy on to the female figure which is styled accordingly. In their traditionalist exhibitionist role women are simultaneously to be looked at and displayed, with their appearance coded for strong visual and erotic impact so that they can be said to connote *to-be-looked-at-ness*" (Mulvey, 750).

On one level it can be argued that it is because her husband is a homosexual that Alka acts upon Dolly's suggestion that she dance in the rain, for she would perhaps like to be perceived (and to think of herself) as a woman capable of arousing the erotic instincts of a heterosexual male. In other words, there is a strong possibility of the existence of an element of exhibitionism in Alka's living up to her fantasization of herself as a cinema heroine, an element that overrides her normal senses of both decorum and propriety in her drunken condition. In other word, this is a nar-classic instance of what psychoanalysts call (*pace* Lacan) "passive anaclitic fantasy", which according to Mark Bracher "involves embodying the object *that* the Other desires to possess as a means for jouissance". As Bracher adds,

> This type of fantasy is present in a...diverse array of cultural phenomena, most notably in passive sexual fantasies of being that something beyond image or signifier that gives the Other jouissance. The most striking instances of this are sadomasochistic fantasies, which play in complex ways with being the instrument of the Other's jouissance.... (Bracher, 44)

Yet, this is not all, for what is really significant here is not Alka's behaviour but Dolly's construction (or fantasy) of the figure of a sexually alluring Alka. Recent work in feminist criticism centered on the "gaze" have extended upon the pioneering theorization of phenemenologists like Maurice Merleau-Ponty and psychoanalysts like Jacques Lacan.[2] The Afro-American feminist bell hooks thus speaks of the possibility of the working of an "an oppositional gaze" on the part of the marginalized (black, in hook's essay) woman viewer of cinematic representations of women, a gaze that effectively deconstructs "the phallocentric gaze of desire and possession" (hooks, 213). Arguably at least, this is what Dolly does in this episode in *Bravely Fought the Queen.* A victim of patriarchal dominance and male violence herself, she has no illusions about the instincts of masculinistic desire and possession. And an added edge of irony to this comes in the form of the bathetic conclusion to Alka's performance of Dolly's original fantasy as she slips, twists an ankle and falls, and gets all covered in mud as a result.

But it is the second fantasy in *Bravely Fought the Queen* that relates more directly to the central issues of character and idea in the play. This fantasy which serves even as a compelling motive in the play's dramatic texture, is that of Kanhaiya who, as I have said elsewhere is "like Radha's eternally young lover in Indian mythology who is forever available to the believer whenever she wills him into existence and being" (Dhar, 224). The significance of the Kanhaiya episode has more than one dimension. In the first place it is like a secret shared in by and between the two sisters Dolly and Alka. This is hinted at when in Act I Dolly first "stiffens" at Lalitha's mentioning of "Kanhaiya, your cook", then reacts "sharply" and exclaims: "Alka had no business to mention...to mention Kanhaiya to you", and finally says "under her breath": "We shouldn't be talking about Kanhaiya to you" (Dattani, 258-59). As Alka explains a little later in the scene, the Kanhaiya fantasy is one of the sisters' "little distractions", comparable to the baseless malicious gossip she claims that she indulges in at the parties she attends.

For Dolly, however the Kanhaiya fantasy is no simple distraction. Both Alka and Lalitha who are tipsy by this time clearly perspectivize it as a sexual affair pure and simple. And this is clearly evident from Alka's evocation:

> Dolly comes to the door. In her pale blue nightie. The light behind her....
>
> He can't help but look at her. He can easily see the lines of her body, with the light behind her. Could it be? Or is it his imagination? He probably wonders.
>
> Perhaps he wishes he could see her face. For familiar signals.... He decides to find out. He flicks his beedi away, jumps off the parapet and slowly walks towards her. Head bent so as not to betray his intentions. He asks her something.... She moves a little to let him in. He strides in, very confident now. Dolly shuts the door. The kitchen light goes off. I can't hear the thumri anymore. (Dattani, 261-62)

For Dolly, but, the living out in imagination of the Kanhaiya fantasy is far more an emotional engagement than a physical encounter. Trapped in a loveless marriage with a lecherous and unfaithful husband who is prone to drink and violence, dominated over by a mother-in-law who unfeelingly imposes upon her, separated from a physically challenged daughter, Dolly's very soul yearns for communion with a man who would love, appreciate and have sympathy for her. All these desires she fantasizes in the image of Kanhaiya, the nineteen years old youth who represents for her all the innocence and tenderness of young and true love. And the dialogue of Dolly that holds out this feeling before us is a veritable masterpiece in the art of dramatic writing:

> The thumri plays. And it ends. Another one plays. I forget when that ends and a new one begins! All I'm aware of are two powerful black arms around me and the beautiful sound

> of the heartbeat of a warm gentle soul. The voice of Naina Devi comes back. It is the most beautiful song I've ever heard in my life! (Dattani, 262)

What is noticeable in this dialogue is not only the lyrical tone of the articulation, itself an indication of Dolly's ineffable emotion, but also the images of presence that lend the emotion a palpable and dramatic reality. The "two powerful black arms" may be abstractly or ideationally those of the God Krishna-Kanhaiya who according to Hindu mythology has a dark complexion. But more particularly, they may be the arms of Dolly's husband Jiten Trivedi who, as his mother says on one occasion, was born dark like his father. The power of the black arms, perhaps a sign of the kind of masochistic desire in married women that Simone de Beauvoir speaks of (Beauvoir, 470), is however offset in Dolly's imagination by the "warm gentle soul" of her fantasized lover. Significantly too, even the sound of the heartbeat of this loving soul is not left unparticularized by Dattani, but given a concrete dimension by its equation with the thumris of Naina Devi that the members of the audience are privileged to hear on several occasions during the play's enactment. And finally, the "most beautiful song" that Dolly speaks of is simultaneously a thumri and the inexpressibly beautiful voice of love that speaks and sings unarticulated in the innermost heart of the neglected and forsaken Dolly Trivedi.

Writing in her treatise *An Ethics of Sexual Difference*, Luce Irigary observes in two key paragraphs:

> For a woman, the question of *who loves whom*? in the love of self seems even more mysterious than for a man. Because a woman cannot place herself as an object for herself. And because, unsettled by this lack of a possible "position" she allows herself to be placed by the other—man or mother. She may try to love herself as innerness. But she cannot see herself. She has to succeed in loving the invisible and the memory of a touch that is never seen, that she often feels in pain because she is unable to perceive its place, its "substance", its qualities. A touch without tool or object, except for the test, the experience, of innerness. From within, and from her potential passage from inside to outside, and

> all this without the involvement of anything that moves from one place to another, but only a place of passage, and its movement.
>
> In psychoanalytic categories, this path has not been thought through. Nor even imagined? Except in its pathological symptoms. It is left in the shadow of the *pre-object*, and in the suffering and abandonment of the fusional state which fails to emerge as a subject. No space-time is available for experiencing it. Traditionally spacing is created, or occupied. By man, child, house-work, cooking. Not by the woman herself *for herself*. (Irigary, 60)

Irigary is here speaking specifically of a woman's *self-love*, but it is possible to apply her analysis of the feminine mind to a character like Dolly in *Bravely Fought the Queen* and to her self-realization in love. Indeed, several of Kristeva's conclusions have an uncanny applicability to the case of Dolly Trivedi. For in her fantasy of Kanhaiya, Dolly does "succeed in loving the invisible and the memory of a touch that is never seen". And by doing so, she enables herself to come out, even if only in fantasy, of the "position" of sister, daughter-in-law, dutiful mother and (house) wife and so on that she has been niched in, sacramentalized and confined, by man or the Other. Certainly, it cannot be asserted that Mahesh Dattani created the character of Dolly in the light of Kristeva's realizations, but it is a measure of the acuteness of this dramatist's insight that he gave form and substance to a woman whose psychology conforms to the model of the feminine mind proposed by one of the most distinguished feminist theoreticians of the twentieth century.

NOTES

1. For a brief but comprehensive account of both the well-made-play and the "obligatory scene" which Scribe confessed he thought up first before plotting the rest of the play, see J.L. Styan, *Modern Drama in Theory and Practice 1: Realism and Naturalism,* Cambridge: Cambridge University Press, 1981.
2. See in particular Maurice Merleau-Ponty, *The Primacy of Perception and Other Essays*, ed. James M. Edie, Northwestern University Press, 1964, esp. the essay "Eye and Mind", and Jacques Lacan, *The Four Fundamental Concepts of Psychoanalysis: The Seminar of*

Jacques Lacan, Book 11, ed. Jacques-Alain Miller, trans. Alan Sheridan, New York: W.W. Norton, 1978, esp. pp. 101-11.

WORKS CITED

Beauvoir, Simone (1949). *The Second Sex*, trans. and ed. by H.M. Parshley, London: Everyman's Library, 1993.

Bracher, Mark (1993). *Lacan, Discourse, and Social Change: A Psychoanalytic Cultural Criticism*. Ithaca: Cornell University Press.

Dattani, Mahesh (2000). *Bravely Fought the Queen*, in *Collected Plays*, New Delhi: Penguin. All quotations from Dattani's plays have been taken from this edition.

Dhar, Subir (2002). "Where There's a Will and Bravely Fought the Queen" in *Drama: Literature and Performance*, eds. Srobona Munshi and Jharna Sanyal, Kolkata: University of Calcutta, 2002. This essay is also reprinted in *The Plays of Mahesh Dattani: A Critical Response*, eds. R.K. Dhawan and Tanu Pant, New Delhi: Prestige, 2005. Sadly though, the original *Notes and References* to the essay have not been rightly published in the reprinted version.

Freud, Sigmund (1955). *The Standard Edition of the Complete Psychological Works of Sigmund Freud*, Vol. XVII, eds. James Strachey and Anna Freud. London: Hogarth Press.

Hooks, Bell (1992). "The Oppositional Gaze: Black Female Spectators", in *Feminist Postcolonial Theory: A Reader*, eds. Reina Lewis and Sara Mills, Edinburgh: Edinburgh University Press, 2003.

Hume, Kathryn (1984). *Fantasy and Mimesis: Responses to Reality in Western Literature*. London: Methuen.

Irigaray, Luce (1984). *An Ethics of Sexual Difference*, trans. Carolyn Burke and Gillian C. Gill, London: Continuum, (2004) 2005 (First South Asian Edition).

Mulvey, Laura (1975). "Visual Pleasure and Narrative Cinema", in Gerald Mast, Marshall Cohen, Leo Braudy (eds.) *Film Theory and Criticism: Introductory Readings*, New York: Oxford University Press, 1992.

Todorov, Tztevan (1975). *The Fantastic: A Structural Approach to a Literary Genre*. Trans. R. Howard, Ithaca, New York: Cornell University Press.

8

The Fashion of Postcolonialism and Karnad's *Hayavadana*

Gauri Shankar Jha

I

At present talking of postcolonialism and assessing any piece of art with this particular yardstick has become a fashion, particularly of literary critics. It has replaced the conservative terms like *Third World Literature* and *Commonwealth Literature*. Edward Said's book *Orientalism* (1978), Frantz Fanon's work *The Wretched of the Earth* (1961), Ashcroft, Griffith and Tiffin's *The Empire Writes Back* (1989), Homi Bhabha's *Nation and Narration* (1990) and *Location and Culture* (1994), Gayatri Spivak's *Outside in the Teaching Machine* (1993) and Aijaz Ahmad's *In Theory, Classes, Nations, Literature* (1994) are some books that discuss this term extensively. Basically, this term came as an offshoot of colonialism, as a reaction against the colonizing forces, yet it elaborates the contemporary status of literature comprising a variety of literature. The present paper is intended to discuss the ethics of postcolonialism in the world of literature, particularly, Indian English writing.

In fact, the study of postcolonialism includes a diverse body of cultures and literatures. As mentioned in *The Empire Writes Back*, it comprises literatures of African countries, Australia, Bangladesh, Canada, Caribbean countries, India, Malaysia, Malta, New Zealand, Pakistan, Singapore, South Pacific Island countries and Sri Lanka. From this geographical area we have literature that have certain common ingredients that may be identified as literature of resistance and subversion of the imperial centre and share common psychic and historical conditions and in *The Empire Writes Back*, the writers claim that they share three common features, namely, the silencing and marginalizing of the postcolonial voice by the imperial centre, the abrogation of this imperial centre within the text and the active appropriation of the language and culture of that centre. This literature of resistance or subversion of the centre or the colonizer that is otherwise also known as the dominating hegemonic power of the West from the point of view of hybridized subject. Obviously it is the voice of the oppressed or the colonized people, it is the discourse of liberation, identity and indigenous unison. No doubt, it is less allied to the Western taste or patronage: the identity known as 'hybridity' in the postcolonialist's dictionary. It is also surprising to note that only the European encounter matters as formative influence and not that of other invaders or settlers, particularly in case of India. Yet there are other ingredients too that are available in the postcolonial literature of India, such as, caste oppression, fundamentalism and women anguish; these are our own indigenous cultivation. In Indian writing there is distinct reflection of the colonial period (if at all we may call it so) of different lengths and severity, rather a complex one, the British being the last or top layer of all. However, the colonial period is not only the distorting period rather it transformed the entire set up to a great extent and Indian writing of the postcolonial period talks of fundamentalism, casteism and patriarchy which cannot be claimed to be the sole contribution of European imperialism.

According to Edward Said, the central preoccupation of the postcolonial theory is the opposition between the colonizers and the colonized and critics have been busy revising and expanding the category of the colonized. This is the most familiar connotation of this concept and it would be relevant to cite Helen Tiffin's opinion in this regard that talks of the writings that came up out of subordination to European colonialism and out of resistance to colonial ideology and legacy. On the other hand, we have instances of postcolonialists taking myth and history as discourses sediment in political and cultural hegemonies otherwise treated as opposition between the past and the present that leads to greater justice towards peace and progress and a purposeful life. According to McClintock, this term has outdistanced the terms like postmodernism, post-structuralism, post-coldwar, post-Marxism, post-apartheid, post-Souiet, post-Ford, post-feminism, post-national, post-historical, even post-contemporary. In postcolonial Indian writing, we find the thematization of the cultural history of India challenging and subverting the Western paradigms of historiography and narrative, also known as Eurocentric theories that fail to articulate the complexities, cultural provenance and ethos of a postcolonial society. We have our indigenous enduring tradition and metaphysical system and so we may suggest alternative ontological system.

II

If we examine the colonization of India by the British, we find it as a major insalubrious episode that pilot to the most awful sort of cultural subservience and coercion. The Orientalists' assessment of India as a land of snakecharmers, superstitious and illiterate bums, criminals and petty thugs who are basically uncivilized, was a part of tactic to vanquish and make the most of the nation. As Said points out the Orient has been observed as an illustration of a particular form of eccentricity and as a reservoir of infinite peculiarity and as a living tableau of queerness. The Indian writers convey the pluralism, heterogeneity and openness of the vast cultural, philosophical and spiritual heritage of India. Precisely, the postcolonial literature focuses on the social, cultural, economic and political practices which are concomitant with response and resistance to colonialism. However, the postcolonialists aptly question the epistemologies and social models that claim to be universal in its application throughout the globe. Tiffin is of the view that the postcolonial literature rediscovers indigenous theories of epistemology and language and in the process subverts the political and textual authority of the imperial European perspective. It is relevant to note that the formulations of hybridity, sycretization and pastiche as imminent ingredient of postcolonial literature is not plausible concern though it is found in most of them for the simple reason that it has its own local issues of greater significance. It gives rise to cultural reclaimation and metaphoric parallelism attaching prominence to ontological and epistemological underpinnings of a nation by revisiting the past that is also known as historiography as figurative and imagined and not as mimetic or empirical by employing plotting strategies and linguistic tropes, and thus correct the Orientalist discourse of disregard and disrespect to another culture. In postcolonial literature we also find the writers adopting a narrative strategy against the realism prevalent in the nineteenth century and the dreaded fragmentation of Modernism which talks of a sense of loss, divided self, and social disintigeration; however the postcolonialists treat it with a self-reflexive celebration. The question is that of the postcolonial identity. Salman Rushdie maintains that:

> Our identity is at once plural and partial. Sometimes we feel that we straddle two cultures; at other times, that we fall between two stools...but however ambiguous and shifting this ground may be, it is not an infertile territory for a writer to occupy. If literature is in part the business of finding new angles at which to enter reality, then once again our distance, our long geographical perspective, may provide us with such angles. Or, it may be that is what we must think in order to do our work. (1982: 18)

When we talk of Indian writing in English, we find a good assortment of writers involved in this practice. Rushdic's expression is simply a reflection of a diasporiac anxiety that is a victim of severe doubt and suspicion who feel to be marginalised and alienated. Here, we find Rushdie celebrating his status of cultural hybridity as a stage of fertile territory which also provides resistance to cultural authoritarianism and its claim to speak the absolute truth, absolute form of knowledge and western style of historiography. It is remarkable to note that almost all postcolonial literary critics have decried the stereotype portrayal of the formerly colonized world. It is pertinent to quote the definition of the term as in the book *The Empire Writes Back*:

> The term...suggests a concern only with the national culture after the departure of the imperial power.... We have used the term to cover all the culture affected by the imperial process from the moment of colonization to the present day. This is because there is a continuity of preoccupations

> throughout the historical process initiated by European imperial aggression. (1989: 1-2)

Obviously, historical, linguistic and locational factors have delimited such discourse. To have a clearer picture of the trends of postcolonialism in Indian English writing, we may examine a few writers. To start with, the first big three writers may not be exempted, that is, Anand, Rao and Narayan. From the present scenario we may take Salman Rushdie, Girish Karnad, and Sashi Tharoor who more or less represent the class that we are concerned with. Tiffin's assertion that postcolonial writing establish or rehabilitate self against either European appropriation or rejection, realized through a number of strartegies including consciousness towards use and abuse of history by using archetypal figures, situations, and relationships, as in Raja Rao's *Kanthapura* Sashi Tharoor's *The Great Indian Novel* and Karnad's several plays. *Kanthapura* is deeply rooted in the history of the time in which it was written whether it is the talk of the freedom struggle, the social structure/evil, or the impact of Gandhi—all comes out of the contemporary world it is in order to correct our concept of history. Here the postcolonial is created as an antithesis of colonial, as a voice of protest, or as a voice of resistance. Tharoor's *The Great Indian Novel* is also a kind of glorification of history based on the facts remembered, imagined and experienced. It is both the retelling of modern Indian history as the *Mahabharta* and the selective recasting of the epic by using contemporary historical characters; it also interperates the entire tradition of English fiction in India, disenchantment with the present to reflect the past its values and otherwise; it is a self-apprehension of the colonial past and a minute perception of the present. Surprisingly, to the Western mind history is simply a recordable and rational construct whereas myth is something prehistoric and hence fictional or irrational construct and in this sense Tharoor's attempt is to challenge the Western paradigms of history and myth. M.F. Salat maintains that Tharoor contradicts the Western dichotomy and asserts the unitary concept of Indian historiography which helps in developing a specific national consciousness and reclaiming the past, this metaphoric parallelism of the modern with the ancient is an indigenous device of propagating message collected from the past.

III

Postcoloniality, despite all controversies, includes the question of identity, alienation, moral code, fulfilment, mythological orientation, gender placement, metaphysical dualism, neo-colonial dialectic, etc. In almost all the plays of Girish Karnad we find the extensive use of themes borrowed from various sources of history and mythology to prove his perception of postcolonial tenets. Karnad plays with historical and mythological episodes to prove his typical postcolonial stature. As he says in the "Introduction" of the *Three Plays*:

> ...tension between the cultural past of the country and its colonial past, between the attractions of Western modes of thought and our own traditions, and finally between the various visions of the future that opened up once the common cause of political freedom was achieved. This is the historical context that gave rise to my plays.... (Karnad, 1995, 1)

As a true postcolonialist, Karnad perceives myth and history as discourses, sedimented in political and cultural hegemonies; the empiricist equation of myth with its primitiveness is enmeshed in race for power; it is only a myth that may offer the simultaneity of past, present and future; it is a hint at our 'national-culture after the departure of imperial power'.

The publication of *Midnight's Children* brought Rushdie to international scenario as a prominent postcolonial writer whereas Gayatri Spivak established as a postcolonial critic. Besides, migrancy is also a factor that influences such writers as an ontological condition engendering a counter-canon adopted as a narrative strategy. Rushdie's heritage is that of a displaced writer who includes both a British born Indian and that of as a member of postdiaspora community as we know the genesis of *Midnight's Children* lies in his visit to Bombay to reclaim history.

Thus goes the fashion of postcolonialism as a dormant inevitable current in the Indian English writing as a literature of a verity refuting the Orientalist's approach defining Indians as 'underdeveloped', though I am least concerned with other Oriental attitude claiming Chinese as 'perfidious'and Muslims as 'passive'.

On the Indian English drama scenario, Girish Karnad is the only playwright with substantial postcolonial reverberations. My present paper intends to overhaul his work in this context with particular reference to *Hayavadana*.

Postcoloniality, despite all controversies, includes the question of identity, alienation, moral code, fulfilment, mythological orientation, gender placement, metaphysical dualism, neo-colonial dialectic, etc. Karnad plays with historical and mythological episodes to prove his typical postcolonial stature. As he says in the "Introduction" of the *Three Plays*:

> ...tension between the cultural past of the country and its colonial past, between the attractions of Western modes of thought and our own traditions, and finally between the various visions of the future that opened up once the common cause of political freedom was achieved. This is the historical context that gave rise to my plays.... (Karnad, 1995, 1)

Hayavadana is, originally, one of the stories of *Kathasaritsagar*, though Karnad admits to have borrowed from Thomas Mann's *The Transposed Heads*, and provides a new rendering to make it more congenial to our soil. The most striking point is the element of Indianness, that is, the seed of post-coloniality; it is in abundance, for instance, the opening verse in praise of Lord Ganesha, introduction of Bhagwata, inclusion of several Hindu deities, singing of National Anthem, etc. Karnad's *Hayavadana* is different from the original story of *Kathasaritsagar* or from Thomas Mann's *The Transposed Heads*. The original story raises the moral problem and Mann 'uses it to ridicule the mechanical conception of life which differentiates between body and soul', ridiculing the philosophy of head being superior to body. On the other hand, Karnad raises 'the problem of human identity in a world of tangled relationships'. Besides the question of identity, the play also indulges in the issue of subaltern, call it subservient or the other. It is not to be taken on the surfacial value as an issue of moral erosion or physical gratification, rather an effort of symbiotic relationship. My analysis centres on Karnad's holistic approach to quantify his progression in empirical terms.

IV

The play opens with an invocation to Vighneshwara (Lord Ganesha), 'the destroyer of obstacles', 'Lord and Master of Success and Perfection' who 'removes all hurdles and crowns all endeavours with success. Yet there is a note of pessimism as the same deity is also described as the 'embodiment of imperfection, of incompleteness', 'with his crooked face and distorted body'. By the end of the play, Bhagwata is thoroughly transformed and finds Ganesha as that of 'unfathomable mercy' that 'fulfils the desire of all' and finds himself unable to describe His glory in 'poor disabled words'. The main plot and the sub-plot are interlinked. Princess of Karnatka and Padmini are not destined to face the ultimate rather they are the consequences of their own options, not imposed from any external agency. Hayavadana, having a man's body and a horse's head wants to be a complete man; instead he becomes a complete horse by the end of the play. The transformation of Hayavadana and Padmini's child is identical. Now let us come to the central characters, Devdatta and Kapila, "Two friends there were/one mind, one heart", like "Lava and Kusha, Ram and Lakshman, Krishna and Baldeva", "burned, lived, fought, embraced and died". Bhagwata's initiative is that of a traditional one: "Each one to his own fate. Each one to his own desire" (11), and then a prominent query by the Female Chorus, "why should love stick to the sap of a single body" (11).

Devdatta and Kapila are poles apart and yet close together. Devdatta is 'a slender, delicate-looking person' whereas Kpila is 'powerfully built' representing, above all, the two different classes of society, not at war with each other but somehow unable to accept each other. One is 'lost in thought' another in wrestling'; for one Kalidas is important, for another Nanda (a wrestler) is important. They are close but Kapila prefers to sit down on the floor insists Devdatta to be in chair. The conversation between the two exposes this relationship which is astonishing in the sense that most of the time Kapila is ready to follow Devdatta's request/order only as an obedient slave; more as a servent less a friend; more an oppressed less an equal. The concept of friendship here is that of between the colonizers and colonized, between two completely different classes of society, completely artificial, laboured and concocted. Though borrowed from mythology it appears to be post-colonial in taste and nature to reconcile/ negotiate the two classes. Kapila is ready to sacrifice himself but nowhere in the whole play Devdatta exhibits his inclination to that extent; most often Kapila surrenders before him, rather we should admit that he surrenders at every juncture. Kapila's search for Padmini, the most beautiful character of the play, "Yakshini, Shakuntala, Urvasi, Indumati—all rolled into one", is not out of nothing; it is his endeavour to please Devdatta, and so he cites:

> A poet. A pundit. Knows the Vedas backwards. Writes the grandest poetry ever. Long, dark hair. Delicate, fair face. Age twenty.... (19)

After the marriage, the old friendship flourishes and the citizens of Dharampura call them a team of three like—'Ram, Sita Lakshman'. For Padmini Devdatta is a 'fragile', 'a baby', 'saffron', 'marriage thread', 'deity' and Kapila 'an innocent', 'a proper devil', 'an ethereal shape', 'a Celestial Being'. The difference between the two is very clear. Kapila's dedication is very emphatic in his several utterances where he calls him 'my brother, my father, my friend...'but after the Kali temple episode, the scenario is completely changed; Devdatta rejects him completely and Kapila's submissive subaltern self accepts it humbly though 'broken hearted'—'so the road diverged'. In the last phase of the play Kapila realizes his place and so he says, "I have no place there, no peace, no salvation; I am an outcast" (57). Devdatta, too, realises this thing when he says, "I wanted your power, but not your wildness. You lived in hate—I in fear (60). This is how we discover Karnad's subaltern issue unconsciously discussed in the play.

The ethics of human identity and its confusing status is something that is torturous in this play. Almost all characters of the play, Devdatta, Kapila, Hayavadana, Padmini and Princess of Karnataka suffer from identity crisis. The astonishing desire of Padmini and Princess of Karnataka along with the mixed identity of Kapila, Hayavadana and Devdatta baffle the audience. It is simply incredible. Hayavadana wants to be a complete man and for this he runs from one place to another:

> Banaras, Rameshwar, Gokram, Haridwar, Gaya, Kedarnath,—not only those but the Dargah of Khwaja Yusuf Baba. The Grotto of Our Virgin Mary—I've tried them all. Magicians, mendicants, maharishis, fakirs, saints and sadhus with short hair, sadhus with beards—sadhus in saffron, sadhus in the altogether—hanging, singing, rotating, gyrating—on the spikes, in the air, under water, under the ground...I've covered them all. (9-10)

Bhagwata advises him to go to the temple of the Kali of Mount Chitrakoot. By the end of the play, Hayavadana reappears but not with the body of a complete man, rather with the body of a complete horse and human voice which is further corrected in playing with Padmini's child. The audience is awestruck to find this meaningless exercise of the Almighty. It is the humanistic dimension of Karnad's dramatic art that acts as demystification of superstitious religious beliefs and practices. Though prayer is an integral part of the world of Hayavadana, it fails to move any God or Goddess; even Lord Ganesha who is worshipped in the opening and closing scene conventionally.

The audience can perceive Devdatta's fascination towards books and his feminine physical being and Kapil's fascination towards wrestling and his stout physique; but the mixed identity after the Kali temple episode cannot be explained in simple words—it is a romantic concept and cannot be justified. To change the whole scenario just for the physical gratification of Padmini is not rationale. Bhagwata apprehends everything in advance, "And the head is bidding good bye to the heart" (25). Kapila has the right answer by the end of the First Act, "I know what you want, Padmini, Devdatta's clever head and Kapila's strong body..." (38). This mixed body is welcomed by Padmini, "My celestial bodied Gandharva.... My sun faced Indira.... My Devdatta comes like a bridegroom with the ornament of a new body.... It's my duty to go with Devdatta. But remember I'm going with your body" (41).

The play continues for a few days but Padmini's 'fabulous body—fabulous brain—fabulous Devdatta' fades with the passage of time. Devdatta is puzzled,

> I'd always thought one had to use one's brain while wrestling or fencing or swimming. But the body just does not wait for thoughts—it acts. (43)

The physical pleasure does not last for long; the defiguration of the physique occurs; Devadatta's body turns delicate and Kapila's stout. Padmini is in trouble again. She rushes to Kapila again. It is not the race for completeness but for fulfilment only. This mixed or confused identity meets its disastrous end. Karnad does not provide any answer. Identity crisis is a deliberate construction and everything remains inconclusive by the end of the play. Perhaps Hayavadana has an answer to all such emotional game,

> I firmly believe—that it's this sort of sentimentality which has been the bane of our literature and national life. It has kept us from accepting Reality and encouraged escapism.

V

One ridiculous juncture can be noticed in *Hayavadana* where we find Hayavadana singing patriotic song including the National Anthem. The relevance of this episode cannot be explained and when it is explained by Hayavadana, it appears to be quiet misleading:

> That's why I sing all these patriotic songs—and the National Anthem! That particularly! I have noticed that the people singing the National Anthem always seem to have ruined their voices—so I try. But – but – it – it doesn't seem to work ...what should I do? (69)

Such an explanation is completely absurd. One plausible reason is the playwright's probable intention to provide postcolonial colour to the old mythical legend; perhaps it is as per Salman Rushdie's assertion "that literature is an expression of nationality".

We have a sub-plot of the mythical story of a Gandharva and the shape—shifting to a stallion due to a curse, a device often used by Karnad in his plays. The celestial shape of Gandharva is shifted into the shape of a horse and reconverted to Gandharva. The horse turned Gandharva asks his wife to accompany him to his heavenly abode, she refuses to comply; the same sort of shape shifting appears in case of Devdatta and Kapil. Hayavadana's visit to Kali temple and his narration of the incident is noteworthy, "I fell at her feet and said, 'Mother, make me complete'. She said, 'So be it' and disappeared—even before I could say, 'Make me complete man!' I became a horse." How ridiculous it is! Perhaps the search for completeness is a meaningless concept in the postcolonial era.

In *Hayavadana*, we find diametric shift in Karnad's critical strategy that we know as 'subjugation, domination, diaspora, displacement' (Bhabha); as a result Kapila is marginalised and his marginality is valorised. If mode of postcolonialism is 'the operation of hearing oneself speak' (Derrida) it happens with almost all the characters of the play. As a true postcolonialist Karnad perceives myth and history as discourses, sedimented in political and cultural hegemonies; the empiricist equation of myth with its primitiveness is enmeshed in race for power; it is only a myth that may offer the simultaneity of past, present and future; it is a hint at our 'national-culture' 'after the departure of imperial power'.

On the sociological plane, the play manifests two faceted relationships, that of a failing Brahmanical potential and a subaltern hijacking on the pretext of quest for completeness or fulfilment. It has multilayered enigmatic implication that interrogates the basic human relationships against the awesome backdrop of both physical gratification and intellectual starvation. Tuntun Mukherjee in her paper titled "The Unravelling of the Self: Broken Images, Karnad's Post-modern Project" (JSL, Autumn, 2006) opines,

> A consistent preoccupation of Karnad's has been to explore the hidden depths of human mind. Whether it is the drama of the king who takes away his son's youth (Yayati); or, the tragic history of the ruler considered at once brilliant and mad (Tughlaq); or, the narrative of the unhappy beings in

> perpetual search for completeness (Hayavadana); or, the tale of the woman who must identify her real husband (Nagamandala); or any other—Karnad's plays invariably demonstrate the playwright's enduring interest in and sensitive enquiry into the causality of human behaviour. Karnad's latest play continues his study of the human psyche. (97-98)

In his other plays, too, we find similar snags, for instance, in *The Fire and the Rain, Bali: The Sacrifice* and *Yayati.* In all these plays we find Karnad's interrogation on the moral order of the world that can be achieved only through righteous and virtuous way of life which, in turn, provides meaningful stature to life. We find that a common mind is dominated by selfish motives, evil desires and undue passions and he submits to them inviting miseries and wretchedness. It is nothing but delusion or deception and even the godly characters resort to demonic tactics to crush evil minded wicked characters proving evil as inherent corruption and deceit as finite existence. Our minds remain disturbed by various sensuous and worldly passions that compel us for irresponsible exercise of power and utter forgetfulness of the imperishable values of life. Taken as a whole, Karnad's plays hover around the theme of betrayal, bloodshed, violence, impersonation, treachery, deceit, adultery, hatred, jealousy, infidelity, lust, wrath, and revenge—all hijacked from different episodes of mythology. In the dark recesses of human mind, these instincts lie as basic trait and disturb Karnad all the time. Karnad's characters are available in history, myth and legend with the same attitude, motives, ambitions and purpose. Karnad has woven out a magnificent texture of love, betrayal, passion, jealousy and sacrifice besides the rising voice of women characters.

Obviously, Karnad's *Hayavadana* is a postcolonial offshoot of a matured postcolonial mind highlighting social and psychological problems, interrogating human ideas and ideals. *Hayavadana* represents everyman's predicament more authentically, and tries to access the definition of his place in this indifferent universe.

REFERENCES

Ashcroft, Bill, G. Griffiths and H. Tiffins, 1989, *The Empire Writes Back,* London: Routledge.

Karnad, G., 1995, *Three Plays*, New Delhi: O.U.P.

McClintock, A., 1992, "The Angel of Progress", Baker, Hulme and Iverson (ed.) *Colonial Discourse/postcolonial Theory,* Machester University Press.

Rushdie, S., *Imaginary Homelands,* London Review of Books, 7-20 Oct. 1982, 1980, *Midnight's Children,* New York: Avon.

Rao, Raja, 1974, *Kanthapura,* Delhi: O.U.P.

Salat, M.F., 1993, "Making the Past Present: Sashi Tharoor's The Great Indian Novel", *Native Responses to Contemporary Indian Novel,* ed., R. Bhongle, New Delhi.

Said, Edward, "Representing the Colonized: Anthropology's Interlocusters Critical Inquiry", 15.2 (Winter 1989).

Tharoor, Sashi, 1989, *The Great Indian Novel*, New Delhi: Penguine.

Tiffin, Helen, "Post Colonialism, Post Modernism—Rehabilation of Post Colonial History", *Journal of Commonwealth Literature,* 23.1 (1988).

9

"Borders don't Really Apply": A Note on Diasporic Dimensions in Amitav Ghosh's *The Circle of Reason* and *The Shadow Lines*

K. Mishra

Indisputably, Amitav Ghosh holds a distinguished position among the avant-garde Indian writers in English. His works have earned him lots of national and international awards as well as admiration. His enviable recognition is due to his unusual power of depicting the postcolonial human predicament, distinctive narrative technique and considerable artistic potential. His oeuvre in fact represents one of those significant voices of diasporic Indians who have provided honour and stature to Indian writings in English.

We know that the fictional world of expatriate Indian writers reflects a wide and varied range. Alienation from the roots, cultural dislocation, seeking an identity in the adopted land, conflicts between the values of the motherland and those of the western society, problems of assimilation in the new social milieu, nostalgic memories, racial discrimination, hybridity, nationalism and the sense of being a marginalized community in the adopted homeland are the dominant issues in the novels of Indian immigrants, such as Salman Rushdie, Vikram Seth, Vikram Chandra, Meena Alexander, Shoma Ramaya, Bharati Mukherjee, Shashi Tharoor, Bharti Kirchner, Amitav Ghosh, Kiran Narayan, Chitra Bannerjee Divakaruni and Jhumpa Lahiri, to quote a few best-known names. Ghosh's novels, broadly speaking, reflect, besides the colonial as well as postcolonial society, patterns of history, subaltern consciousness, issues of crossing national boundaries, the meaning of political freedom, impacts of globalization and dynamics of displacement in his own distinctive style. The present paper attempts to examine his portrayal of diasporic situations and the impacts of the forces of globalization in *The Circle of Reason* and *The Shadow Lines*, the writer's first two novels, for it seems that national boundaries and diasporic thoughts have assumed a central importance in the constructions of these novels.

Migration and dislocation, indubitably, are strikingly significant phenomena of the present time. They truly and effectively depict the postcolonial society as well as people's post-modern predicament. In his essay, "The Diaspora in Indian Culture", Amitav Ghosh observes:

> The modern Indian diaspora—the huge migration from the subcontinent that began in the mid-nineteenth century—is not merely one of the most important demographic dislocations of modern times: it now represents important force in world-culture.[1]

As a matter of fact, Ghosh's personal life itself has been a fascinating story of shifting locations—crossing boundaries. He was born in Calcutta (West Bengal), and grew up in Bangladesh, Sri Lanka, Iran and several other parts of India. In pursuit of his higher education and research objectives, he travelled down to Egypt and England. In addition, Ghosh has worked at several leading universities in the United States of America. But then, this reference to the facts of the writer's personal life by no means intends to suggest that his novels are autobiographical. Actually, it tends to imply that the experience of the writer's immigrant background has perhaps gone into shaping his diasporic thoughts, sensibility, art and vision. To reiterate, Amitav Ghosh's novels are woven around diasporic discourse. Displacement, relocation, transition, shifting, journeys, alienation and migration are found pivotal to his narrative world and do inform significantly the other aspects of their plots. Robert Dixon as such appears right when he maintains,

> Ghosh's writing reflects the recent concern of anthropologists with the porosity of cultural boundaries.[2]

Like many of his contemporaries, Amitav Ghosh perhaps believes that no culture is self-contained. Nor can any culture exist in isolation. His stories as such move over countries and continents. The characters go beyond their national boundaries and incidents extend across several locations. *The Circle of Reason*, *The Shadow Lines*, *The Calcutta Chromosome* and *The Glass Palace*—all represent life in crisscross cultural spaces. Both *The Circle of Reason* and *The Shadow Lines* start and end with migrations. As for *The Circle of Reason*, the novel may be described as a story of flights and adventures of its chief protagonist—Alu. Balaram Bose, Alu's foster father, is obsessed with phrenology, scientific reasons, western ideas and books of Louis Pastur. In his strong belief and exciting campaign to clean his settlement of dirt and squalor, diseases and ignorance, myth and superstition, he makes use of drums of Carbolic acid and thus destroys the whole village. Bhudeo Roy too, sets afire Rakhal's explosive following his plan to take revenge on Balaram. In this process of purification and retaliation, Balaram, Toru Devi, Maya and Rakhal all are burnt to death and finally there is left heaps of ashes and debris. Alu then is charged with sedition and extremism by the police. To evade police, subsequent arrest and punishment Alu runs away from Lalpukur to Calcutta, from Calcutta to Kerala, from Kerala to the imaginary gulf-country al-Ghazira and from al-Ghazira finally to Algeria through Alexandria, Egypt, Lisbon, Tunis and El Oued. Moreover, on his voyage, the hero encounters so many diasporic men and women, events and situations. A few of them influence his fortune in a significant way as well.

This outline truly exhibits how the narrative design of *The Circle of Reason* is made of changing locations and settings as the hero goes on travelling across borders of various regions. He actually lives in many places. By this, the novelist perhaps intends to suggest that constant movement is a reality of human life and crossing borders is a kind of primordial human desire for quest and exploration. Alu's journey across borders is full of changes and eventful experiences. It is life-like indeed. The implication is that it is all futile to draw lines of demarcation between two cultures or two national identities or peoples. 'The Shadow Lines', Ghosh's next novel (after *The Circle of Reason*) appears an extended and emphatic representation of the same concern in a new way. It betrays the fact that borderlines between two societies and cultures are insubstantial. Lalpukur, the locale in the first part of *The Circle of Reason*, is a village in West Bengal. It is very close to Bangladesh border. The place itself is a product of diaspora. It is a settlement of refugees from Bangladesh:

> Most of the people of Lalpukur belonged originally to the remote district of Noakhali, in the far east of Bengal, close to Burma. They had immigrated to India in a slow, steady trickle in the year after East Bengal became East Pakistan.[3]

Besides, Ghosh's fictional world shows his deep interest in and preoccupation with national history. References to past events as well as conditions appear a marked feature in him. This might be a means of commenting on the bygone times, a technique of assessing comparatively the contemporary situations or a metaphor for the writer's philosophy. The important point, nevertheless, is that the tradition of diaspora is rooted to human history and culture. Dixon notes:

> For Ghosh even societies that appear to be static and traditional are always already diasporic.

Lalpukur too has such a history.

> Long before the world had sniffed genocide in Bangladesh, Lalpukur began to swell. It grew and grew. First, it was brothers with burnt backs and balls cut off at the roots. Then it was cousins and cousins of cousins. Then it did not matter; borders dissolved under the weight of millions of people in panic-stricken flight from an army of animals.[4]

The second part of the novel is set against the background of an oil town, al-Ghazira, the Middle East. The town is crowded with migrant labourers and foreign settlers from various parts of the world:

> It was a merchant's paradise, right in the centre of the world, conceived and nourished by the flow of centuries of trade. Persians, Iraqis, Zanzibari Arabs, Omanis and Indians flattened upon it and grew rich....[5]

Zindi al-Tiffaha, for instance, is an Egyptian prostitute and owns a house in The Seven Head area. All sorts of migrant workers, refugees and traders live in her house. Jeevanbhai Patel presents yet another very interesting example of a real diasporic man. He is a Gujrati Hindu who comes from Durban in South Africa and finally settles in this oil town after a long course of continuous flight as his marriage was not acceptable to his parents. Prof. Samuel, Kulfi, Karthamma, Rakesh, Abu Fahl, Florid Mian, Hiji Fahmi and Mast Ram—are all settlers here. Not only in al-Ghazira but also in the small town of El Oued, Algeria, in Part Three, where Zindi and Alu, finally decide to migrate, with Kulfi and baby Boss, we see many emigrant Indians such as Mr. and Mrs. Verma, Dr. and Mrs. Mishra, and Miss Krishnaswamy. It is interesting to note that Jyoti Das, the Police Inspector, too tracks Alu all along India .and the gulf country and finally to the African country. *The Circle of Reason* can thus appropriately be described as a novel of migration. It weaves together the various strands of diasporic phenomena. In an interview with Sheela Reddy, Amitav Ghosh clearly said:

> The whole system of nation-states is coming under increasing strain. The rich countries are essentially more and more a single unit: Borders don't really apply.[6]

The fact that 'borders don't really apply' has been expressed emphatically and metaphorically by the image of weaving which recurs throughout the novel and appears integrated to the plot. In the beginning of the story we see how one day, after much deliberation, Balaram decides to make Alu, his nephew, a weaver. He takes Alu to Shombhu Debnath to learn the skill, technology and patterns of weaving. Weaving consists in joining and uniting separate threads. It doesn't allow any separation or division. Moreover, it depends basically on borrowing and lending across borders. Diaspora too, is involved with transcendences across regional borders. Justifying his decision of selecting Alu as an apprentice weaver, Balaram thinks of weaving:

> It has created not separate worlds but one; for it has never permitted the division of the world. The loom recognizes no continents and no countries. It has tied the world together with its bloody ironies from the beginning of human time.[7]

Weaving, thus, does not have one single root or fixed borders. It is inclusive and all embracing.

> All through those centuries cloth, in its richness and variety, bound the Mediterranean to Asia, India to Africa, the Arab world to Europe in equal, bountiful trade.[8]

This feature of inclusion and homogenization is reflected in the subtitles of the three sections in which the novel has been divided. The three parts of the novel are named—Satwa: Reason, Rajas: Passion and Tamas: Death. Satwa, Rajas and Tamas actually refer to the well-known Sankhya system of thought of the ancient Indian Philosophy. Adherents of the philosophy believe that the doctrine has its roots in the Upanisads and Kapila rsi is the father of the principle. According to this school of thought Satwa, Rajas, and Tamas are the three Gunas—the three constituent powers of Prakriti, the fundamental substance from which this world has evolved. For development, goodness and happiness these three Gunas have to be in the state of equilibrium. The predominance of one over the other produces disturbances in individuals and the world. The respective functions of Satwa, Rajas and Tamas are manifestation, activity and restraint. The three Gunas are never separate. They support each other and produce pleasure, pain and sloth respectively. The world as a matter of fact is composed of these elements. By referring to these three Gunas perhaps the novelist tends to suggest that across the geographical, economical and political boundaries as well as divergent cultures a world of global human culture can possibly be established.

As we see, *The Circle of Reason* relates globalisation too—its condition, impact and failures. The portrayal of the crumbling of boundaries appears suggestive of a universal humanity and homogenized culture. It insists on a culture of accommodation and inclusion. The novel, nevertheless, depicts the bleak and grim realities of the global economy and migrancy as well. Balaram is obsessed with phrenology, carbolic acid and Louis Pasteur. It shows his enormous fascination with the western thoughts and scientific reasoning across borders. Nonetheless, all his efforts result in disastrous consequences. He loses every time.

Life of immigrant workers and diasporic traders at al-Ghazira (a global market place) depicts the realities of this international system (globalization) such as, economic inequalities, slavery, miseries, helplessness and exploitation. In the novel, most of the people are victims and sufferers and it is the desire to earn money, gain economic security and gets rid of the miserable life at home that has driven both men and women from their homes. Alu is a victim to the meaningless war between his uncle Balaram and the dishonest landlord, Bhudeb Roy. He is on the run because of them. Zindi is forced to cross the national border and take up prostitution as her business for living because she is tortured at home for not being able to produce any child. Her displacement is, thus caused by the patriarchal oppression, violence and the loss of home. Her thoughts and style of working too are formulated by her own conditions and the global theory of consumerism. She provides shelter and opportunity to the oppressed, the deprived and the exploited women. There is no sense of morality or conscience involved in her business. Her trade is as good or bad as any other trade. Moreover, she knows the art and skill of marketing her product: "But I don't take them all. I take only good girls." To her, prostitution is "work" and women are hard workers. She believes that sex-work and her "entrepreneurship" are legitimate. Zindi's thinking thus, presents prostitution as a productive labour. She tries to dignify her business as such. Evidently, her ideas are in conformity with the principles of global economy and western consumer capitalism.

Karthamma, another migrant worker, undergoes a pathetic and tortuous experience of pregnancy and delivery. Her story really presents an abject picture of how the forces of globalisation are operating in social life. She is not ready to deliver her child on board without signing the delivery form. She thinks that her child will be deprived of a lawful birth certificate and thus the right to get admission to a school and obtain a job in absence of the right form. Prof. Samuel describes to Alu:

> She says that she knows that the child won't be given a house or a car or anything at all if she doesn't sign the forms. It'll be sent back to India, she says, and she would rather kill it than allow that to happen; kill it right now with a bottle while it's still in her womb.[9]

Karthamma is enormously fearful of the identity, future and alienation of her unborn child. There is apprehension that if the child is born in the ship, it will not become al-Ghazira. It will then remain economically insecured. This acute feelings of economically insecured future as well as fear of national identity for emigrants are postmodern features. The situation becomes more pathetic as she does not want to go back to India. The examples of Zindi, Karthamma and Kulfi clearly underline the consumer culture in the wake of globalized capitalism. All these women suffer exploitation as subprolitarian female workers. Their stories show the plight of marginalized women in their own countries as well as across their countries. They exhibit the failures of globalization—the increasingly transnational world culture.

As for *The Shadow Lines*, in his essay "A Reading of the Shadow Lines", Prof. A.N. Kaul observes:

> Crossing of frontiers—especially those of nationality, culture and language—has increased the world over, including India. Of this tendency *The Shadow Lines* is an extreme example.[10]

True, *The Shadow Lines* depicts incidents, experiences, conflicts and people of two diasporic families that belong to three countries—India, Bangladesh and England. The lives of three generations are the subjects of exploration here. Throughout, the locations go on shifting, realistically and imaginatively, between Calcutta, Dhaka and London. It is important to note that all the incidents of crucial importance emanate from crossing national borders and the men and women undergo pleasures and pains as a result of this transition. Mr. Lionel Tresawsen leaves his home in north London and comes to Calcutta, after Malaysia, Fiji and Ceylone, establishes his business and finally settles into life here. He is a man who has travelled a large part of the globe. In Calcutta, Mr. Tresawsen becomes a friend to Datta-Chaudhuri, a high court judge. The friendship grows deep and transforms into an enduring relationship of blood between the two families. Tresawsen's grandson, Nick Price is married to Datta-Chaudhuri's granddaughter, Ila, and Datta-Chaudhuri's grandson, Tridib, gets married to May Price, Tresawsen's granddaughter. Thus, the two families of different cultures—of the East and the West—get united. The political and national frontiers construct no barrier.

The diasporic subjects such as crossing boundaries, nationalism, freedom, and rootlessness have been brought up and described at several points in the story. Nevertheless, they get focused prominently in the perspectives and character of the narrator's grandmother, Tha'mma, and her journey to Dhaka—her ancestral homeland, where she goes to bring her Jethamoshai back to Calcutta. In fact, the grandmother has her own ideas on nationality and border lines. Ghosh has portrayed in her a common woman of conventional ideas and ideology. She has revolutionary patriotic fervour. She thinks that a nation is built on plenty of sacrifices and wars and blood of its people. She feels utterly confused to think that her own place of birth, education and forefathers has become a foreign land. She wonders how she can become an alien in her own home. Ila stands as a perfect foil to her as she does not feel rooted to one culture or confined to the borders of one nation, or to home for that matter. Once she even tells the narrator that she does not like his culture and wants to be "Free of your bloody culture and free of all of you". She really shows a major characteristic of the 20th century diasporic mind and behaviour as she loves freedom. She has travelled abroad so constantly and extensively (her father is a diplomat at the U.N.) that new places and cultures do not excite her impervious mind. Quite contrary to this, the grandmother is a firm believer in the concept of nationality. The narrator notes:

> All she wanted was a middle-class life in which, like the middle classes the world over, she would thrive believing in the unity of nationhood and territory, of self-respect and national power: that was all she wanted—a modern middle class life, a small thing that history had denied her in its fullness and for which she could never forgive it.[11]

It seems that forced mainly by this outlook that one evening when she is lying in bed in hospital and the narrator tells her about Ila's tensed married life and racist treatment at school in London, where she was not defended by her philandering husband, she bursts out furiously. She does not accuse her husband for all those happenings but blames Ila for her choice of selecting a home outside her own country and decision of living in the Western culture. She says that Ila should not live in London as she is not culturally and nationally rooted there:

> Ila has no right to live there, she said hoarsely. She doesn't belong there. It took those people a long time to build that country; hundreds of years, years and years of war and bloodshed. Everyone who lives there has earned his right to be there with blood: with their brother's blood and their father's blood and their son's blood. They know they're a nation because they have drawn their borders with blood.[12]

But then, the grandmother's long faith in nationality, culture and borders get dashed to pieces when confronted with realities. Her family, it seems important to note here, lived in East Pakistan (Bangladesh) but came to Calcutta (India) after the partition of India. She was married to an engineer in Burma, lived there for about twelve years and did not visit her house in Dhaka. But when she decides to go to Dhaka after so many years, the prospect of crossing the national borderlines of India excites her wildly. The partition of India has not reduced her love for her birthplace. She wants to know from her son if "she will be able to see the border between India and East Pakistan from the plane" (151). She thinks that perhaps there are trenches, or soldiers or guns pointed at each other or barren strips of land—at the borders of the two nations. But when her son tells her that "she won't be able to see anything except clouds and perhaps, if you're lucky, some green fields", she is disappointed. A significant realization of her mistakes dawns on her,

> My grandmother thought this over for a while, and then she said: But if there aren't any trenches or anything, how are people to know? I mean, where's the difference then? And if there's no difference both sides will be the same; it'll be just like it used to be before, when we used to catch a train in Dhaka and get off in Calcutta the next day without anybody stopping us. What were it all for then—partition and all the killing and everything—if there isn't something in-between?[13]

The grandmother's changed outlook gets reinforced and by her Jethamoshai in Dhaka when he outrightly refuses her proposal of going to Calcutta:

> Once you start moving you never stop. That's what I told my sons when they took the trains. I said: I don't believe in this India-Shindia. It's all very well, you're going away now, but suppose when you get there they decide to draw another line somewhere? What will you do then? No one will have you anywhere. As for me, I was born here, and I'll die here.[14]

All this shows how the novelist paints a global canvas here. The narrator's voice appears to be the author's voice and suggest that these issues of boundaries and national culture are illusory and flimsy. There cannot be any divisions of universal humanity. And if there is any dividing line, it is the invisible line of humanity. The concept of time in the story can be taken as a metaphor for the national borders. It seems to suggest that as there is no division or wall between past and present, the separating lines between nations also cannot stand. When the narrator hero discovers at last the realities of his cousin, Tridib's death, he realizes how wrong he was in his belief,

> I was a child, and like all the children around me, I grew up believing in the truth of the precepts that were available to me: I believed in the reality of space; I believed that distance separates, that it a corporeal substance; I believed in the reality of nations and borders; I believed that across the borders existed another reality. The only relationship my vocabulary permitted between those separate realities was war or friendship.[15]

"Ghosh's novels, in sum, depict some significant aspects of the contemporary life. Long before migrancy and globalization became household words, the writer attempted to explore their features and examine how they could shape our future. He can thus, be described as a predictive novelist who loves to travel between varied cultures to understand, in his own words, "individuals and their specific predicament". To the readers of our times, as such, the novel has become more engaging and enlightening.

NOTES

1. Ghosh, Amitav. "The Diaspora in Indian Culture". *The Imam and the Indian: Prose Pieces*. Delhi: Ravi Dayal/Permanent Black, 2002, p. 243.
2. Dixon, Robert. "Travelling in the West: The Writing of Amitav Ghosh". Ed. Tabish Khair. *Amitav Ghosh: A Critical Companion.* Delhi: Permanent Black, 2003, p. 10.
3. Ghosh, Amitav. *The Circle of Reason.* New Delhi: Ravi Dayal/ Permanent Black, 1986, pp. 26-27.
4. *Ibid.*, p. 13.
5. *Ibid.*, pp. 59-60.
6. *Ibid.*, p. 221.
7. Hawley, John C. *Amitav Ghosh.* New Delhi: Foundation Books, 2005, p. 5.
8. *Ibid.*, p. 55.
9. *Ibid.*, p. 59.
10. Ghosh, Amitav. *The Shadow Lines.* With Critical Essays by A.N. Kaul, Suvir Kaul, Meenakshi Mukherjee, R.S. Rajan. Ed. New Delhi: Oxford University Press, 1995, p. 299. .
11. Ghosh, Amitav. *The Shadow Lines.* New Delhi: Ravi Dayal Publisher, 1988, p. 78.
12. *Ibid.*, pp. 77-78.
13. *Ibid.*, p. 151.
14. *Ibid.*, p. 215.
15. *Ibid.*, pp. 218-19.

Theme of Cosmic Loneliness as an Extension of Individual Loneliness as Delineated in the Science Fiction Writings of Arthur C. Clarke

10

Geetha B.

> Nowhere in all space or on a thousand worlds will there be men to share our loneliness. There may be wisdom; there may be power; somewhere across space great instruments...may stare vainly at our floating cloud wrack, their owners yearning as we yearn. Nevertheless in the nature of life and in the principles of evolution we have had our answer. Of men elsewhere, and beyond, there will be none forever. (Eiseley, in *The Immense Journey*)

A large chunk of mainstream literature of the twentieth century has focused on the existential questions, the perennial anguish or the angst that individuals have been suffering from. The themes of fragmentation, sense of alienation and loneliness have been given an expression in much of the literature of the times. While literary giants handled these themes in all kinds of mainstream literature with aplomb—be it short fiction, novel or drama—a parallel fiction called science fiction (SF) was being written and consumed in a large scale in the west. Being a different genre of literature from the one that gave an expression to the post-war disillusionment, sense of alienation engulfing the modern man, fragmentation of the self, SF of that period was a literature that dealt with the concerns of an 'alternative' or 'parallel' reality. Science fiction is a 'literature of change' and it vigorously focuses on 'ideas'. What has now come to be also known as 'mainstream literature of alternative reality', SF, often handles issues of cosmic scale, paying more attention to the 'collective' than the 'individual'. For more than a century, it has been exhibiting great potential for extrapolation, for drawing futuristic scenarios and for philosophizing.

Science fiction being a literature about 'thought experiments', thinks beyond the immediate. It involves different frames of reference, discusses technological innovations and futuristic visions; yet, it has its central concern in the relationship between man and the universe he is a part of. Even when discussions related to science and technology take the fore-front of SF, it tries to locate humanity's place in the ever changing universe. Apart from being everything else, SF at its best, is also a philosophical discussion about the nature of our existence and our place in the universe. However, it has largely been ignored in the academic circles in India. Regarded as somewhat of an 'alien' entity in academic circles, SF—particularly British—has quite a lot to offer for serious scrutiny. In this article, I am looking at the theme of cosmic loneliness as delineated in one of the most celebrated British SF writers—Arthur C. Clarke.

A discussions related to the chosen theme here necessitates some information about other recurring themes handled in the SF writings of the writer. Known as the prophet of space age, he uses the medium of SF to engage in discussions of technological extrapolations, projections of futuristic scenarios, space explorations, first contact, human colonization, post-human universe and conquest of other worlds, etc. There is a philosophical expansiveness in his works as he uses certain tropes and asks bigger questions related to humanity and the universe. His awareness of the grandeur of the universe against which humanity seems to be in its infancy gives a different perspective to the earth-bound problems—whether be of individuals, groups or nations. It calls for a serious thought about man's hierarchy in the universe.

Clarke uses the motif of space exploration to constantly place man against the grandeur of the universe and ponder over the questions of man's relative value in the cosmos. From the early novels on, space voyage works as a technological threshold for humanity to step out of the cradle Earth. The idea that man is an adolescent trying to grapple with a universe that is mysterious, beautiful and sometimes indifferent is oft repeated in Clarke's works. The recurring motif of space exploration works at various levels in his SF. If at one level it is a means to connect Man with the universe, at another it is a means of mapping humanity's position in the cosmos. Yet, it is the 'stage' for confrontations with the 'otherness', what in SF is referred to as the 'first contact'.

Having given a brief outline on Clarke's thematic concerns, we now take up the theme of cosmic loneliness in greater detail. Though the theme keeps manifesting throughout the large body of his SF, this paper focuses on the works that deal with the theme with more rigour: novels *Childhood's End, 2001: A Space Odyssey, Odyssey 2010, Rendezvous with Rama*, 'Songs of Distant Earth' and the short story 'Sentinel'.

Cosmic Loneliness, one of the dominating themes of Clarke, is often related to the sense of the vastness of space that Man experiences as he explores the universe. Clarke adeptly handles the question of humanity's loneliness and correlates it with the eventuality of finding equals across the gulfs of time and space. In Rendezvous with Rama and the first two novels of the Odyssey series Clarke exhibits this approach. In works like Songs of Distant Earth, he uses a slightly different approach: cosmic loneliness is seen as an extension of the perennial metaphysical anguish that man has felt for long.

Many of Clarke's protagonists experience a sense of loneliness and insignificance when faced by the cold apathy of the vast space. When acute, it is almost similar to the existential questions that fazed the twentieth century existentialist writers. In Clarke's fiction, these have their genesis in the unfathomable nature of the universe, its vastness and its indifference towards Man. However, Clarke approaches these queries at a different plane: he imagines that the sense of loneliness would be experienced by any intelligent being, not only Man. The focus is not only on individual characters but also on humanity as a whole. Most of his works speak of possibility of other intelligent beings and he conceives that such intelligences quarantined by the great gulfs of space and time, too would experience the same acute sense of loneliness. This idea finds an expression in his short story *Sentinel* for the first time. In this short story, he posits that long ago other races on other worlds must have scaled and passed the heights that we human beings have reached now. He considers if there were such beings they too must have experienced a sense of loneliness: "theirs would have been a loneliness we cannot imagine, the loneliness of gods looking out across infinity and finding none to share their thoughts" (160). He develops this idea in *2001: A Space Odyssey*, and suggests it is this sense of loneliness that leads 'intelligent' beings to explore the space in search of 'fellow travelers'. In this context, the search of the external universe, though very fundamental to human nature, is to find an answer to the overriding emotion of loneliness. And it is not just a human trait, but an 'intelligent' trait! In the short story *Sentinel*, Clarke spells it out clearly:

> They must have searched the star clusters as we have searched the planets. Everywhere there would be worlds, but they would be empty or peopled with crawling, mindless things. It passed the frozen outer worlds, knowing that life could play no part in their destinies. It came to rest among the inner planets, warming themselves around the fire of the Sun and waiting for their stories to begin. (54)

The first Odyssey novel, in which Clarke envisions a manned space voyage, examines the theme of loneliness in detail. Here while describing the voyage of space ship 'Discovery' and its crew, Clarke speaks how space flight makes Frank Poole—one of the crew members of Discovery—into 'a new dimension of remoteness' (73). Almost all his emotional links are said to have been stretched beyond the yield-point. Similar experience is felt by his fellow traveler Bowman too. The sense of isolation is heightened in deep space:

> David Bowman sometimes found it hard to believe that he had ever known any other existence than the closed little world of discovery. All his years of training, all his earlier missions...seemed to belong to another life...Frank Poole admitted to the same feelings.... But this sense of isolation and estrangement was easy enough to understand. (54)

2010: Odyssey Two also examines the issue. In a somewhat similar instance, Heywood Floyd the immensity of space and the challenges it throws intensify the sense of loneliness that he felt after his estrangement from wife Catherine. And yet, the 'space' that became the reason for his wife Catherine's estrangement, diverts him from his personal loss and the sorrow. The remoteness that he feels from everything that is 'earthly' is an escape from his worries and loss that he has suffered. Even the weightlessness in space removes many earthly worries and the heaviness of emotions: "With loss of weight went many of the cares and worries of Earth. Heywood Floyd had not forgotten his sorrow, but it was more bearable there" (Clarke, 1983: 200). The distance and the vastness seem to make the personal loss appear less real and hence less painful. Clarke, quite interestingly, uses the same immensity of space to evoke a sense of loneliness at one level and at another uses it as an escape too.

Songs of Distant Earth, a novel set in Thalassa—a colony of human beings who manage to find a home outside the solar system before the sun goes Nova—speaks of a voyage of a grand scale. Here humanity crosses gulfs of time and space by crossing technological thresholds. Even when the novel is visionary in its technological innovations, Clarke pays a great deal of attention to the human elements as well. Here the theme of loneliness figures with more intensity as Clarke develops individual characters sufficiently and moves from the particular to the universal. By quoting Loren Eiseley early in the book, Clarke brings the theme of cosmic loneliness to focus from the very beginning:

> Nowhere in all space or on a thousand worlds will there be men to share our loneliness. There may be wisdom; there may be power; somewhere across space great instruments...may stare vainly at our floating cloud wrack, their owners yearning as we yearn. Nevertheless, in the nature of life and in the principles of evolution we have had our answer. Of men elsewhere, and beyond, there will be none forever (Eiseley, as quoted in Clarke, 1986: i).

The novel has many references to the immensity of time and space, to the coldness and the indifference that 'freezes' one's heart. The love story that unfolds in the astronomical stage has tragic elements from the very beginning. The cold indifference of the cosmos is juxtaposed with the very human need for warmth, for companionship: "Clarke meant to use the love between a spaceship officer and an island maiden, a love that most of his readers would recognize as probably doomed, to represent nothing less than the insufficiency of the universe".

Through the character of Thalassan Mirissa, Clarke examines the theme closely. Though she is caught between her immediate reality in which she is married to Brant and her 'doomed' love for the space farer Loren, she understands that the lives of people, all their loves, hopes and fears, are very little when seen against the inconceivable gulf between the stars that space travelers have dared to challenge.

Apart from framing Mirissa and Loren in a relationship—beautiful in its present and yet without a future—Clarke highlights the theme of loneliness in a powerful way. Thalassans who have never been exposed to the melancholic beauty of the songs of Earth are given a treat to the songs of distant earth: songs that have the dominant theme of loneliness that engulfs humans; it was the music that had been composed on Earth, and to Earth alone:

> The slow beat of mighty bells, climbing like invisible smoke from old cathedral spires; the chant of patient boatmen, in tongues lost forever, rowing home against the tide in the last light of day; the songs of armies marching into battles that Time had robbed of all their pain and evil; the merged murmur of the ten million voices as man's greatest cities woke to meet the dawn; the cold dance of the aurora over endless seas of ice; the roar of mighty engines climbing upward on the highway to the stars (288) a dirge for all loves lost in the loneliness of space.

All these songs of distant Earth had the dominant theme of loneliness that results in the face of an immense and finally deadly universe. Human beings can only embrace each other; they can 'only cling to the other changeable and mortal selves'. The lovers in the story seek warmth and comfort beside the fire of love. The need for individuals to have a companion, to have something to cling on to remains fundamental to human nature even when they have found a new home far in the wilderness of space. As Clarke scholar John Hollow points out:

> While that fire burned they were safe from the shadows that prowled the night; and all of the universe of stars and planets shrunk to a toy that they could hold within their hands. (Hollow, 1986: 195-96)

This idea of human relationship as the only solace to individuals who are bound to have to confront the 'loneliness' finds an expression in the novel Rendezvous with Rama. The novel speaks of humanity's exploration of the mysterious spaceship of some unknown origin and it ends with a sense of futility. Clarke conveys a sense of loneliness and inadequacy experienced by the protagonist commander Norton and fellow astronaut Laura; it is a loneliness that stems from the monumental indifference of the universe towards humanity. To overcome it, the two individuals seek companionship through lovemaking. We are told they had done so once earlier too: "on Earth, long ago, in a moment of mutual loneliness and depression".

Again, in the second Odyssey novel, same idea recurs: human love is the only solace that individuals can seek for in a vast and indifferent universe. When the Russian-American spaceship Lenova is rounding Jupiter in order to use its atmosphere to brake, Sasha—the young Russian woman seeks out Floyd in a moment of crisis. Here too human contact becomes a matter of exchanging vulnerabilities of seeking solace.

Imperial Earth, one of the later works of Clarke, set in 2276 A.D. too brings the theme of cosmic loneliness into the fore from the very beginning. The book conceives of a colonized Titan—the planet of Saturn—and of chartered interplanetary space flights. In this work, references to the sense of isolation triggered by experiencing the immensity of space abound. One such example is the reference to the acute sense of estrangement that is experienced by the protagonist Duncan as he leaves Titan on a tour to Earth:

> It lay only there seconds away, yet that was enough. He had traveled a mere million kilometers in less then half a day, but the sense of separation was already complete. The

> experience brought to him, as nothing else had yet done, the sheer immensity of space. The solar system, he began to suspect, was not designed for the convenience of Man, and that presumptuous creature's attempts to use it for his own advantage would often be failed by laws beyond his control. (86)

The discussion so far has looked at how Clarke's theme of 'cosmic loneliness' is akin to or an extension of the 'loneliness' individuals experience; how the indifference of the external universe triggers or accentuates the feeling of loneliness in individuals. However, what needs to be examined is Clarke's ambivalent approach to the question of cosmic loneliness. It is an interesting proposition too, because of the way in which Clarke intertwines the question with possible answers through the suggestion of other intelligences. The following discussion attempts to see the scenarios that Clarke draws as possible answers to this question.

Even as, much of Clarke's fiction raises the question of loneliness, a great deal of his SF speaks of 'other' intelligences in the universe. He uses the motif of 'first contact' (a generic term to refer to the first meeting between humanity and some extraterrestrial intelligence) as an answer to the age old question of man's loneliness. Often, instead of giving a form to the extra terrestrial beings, what Clarke does is to use artefacts like space vessels and monoliths that serve to counteract the questions related to cosmic loneliness. Childhood's End, Odyssey novels and Rendezvous with Rama are the major works that use this tactic.

In *Childhood's End*, one of Clarke's early works, he first asks the question 'are we alone in the universe?' The question is followed up by one of the elaborately worked out scenarios of 'first contact'. As humanity is made to witness and experience the 'first contact', Clarke puts many important thoughts into the work which later become some of the recurring ideas in Clarke's large body of work. As human beings witness the great ships of the overlords descend in their overwhelming majesty there is an understanding that dawns upon humanity:

> There had been no warning when the great ships came pouring out of the unknown depths of space.... Now it had dawned at last: the gleaming silent shapes hanging over every land were the symbol of science Man could not hope to match for centuries.... All that the past ages had achieved was as nothing now: only one thought echoed and re-echoed through Reinhold's brain: The human race was no longer alone. (5)

The arrival of these 'Overlords' again is a reminder that man is not lonely. It is a thought that Clarke could decisively put across in his science fiction. It is interesting that in his non-fiction, he could only suggest possibilities of life elsewhere in spite of the fact that the thought has been deeply entrenched in him. As he put it in his essay *Life Beyond the Earth*:

> Despite disappointments and false alarms, the search will continue; surely, someday, it will succeed.... Perhaps there is only one thing of which we can be sure. The universe is infinitely surprising, and our knowledge still very limited. As the past history of science has so often shown, one cannot outguess nature. The most unlikely possibility of all is that we are completely alone in this galaxy of a hundred billion suns, this cosmos of a hundred billion galaxies. It is far more probable that the universe is crawling with life. (Clarke, 1974: 174)

In the first Odyssey novel, very early in the book, we are introduced to the monolith—a symbol of an intelligent, much advanced alien intelligence. The first thought that seems to come to Heywood Floyd as he stands in front of the monolith discovered on moon is that of finally found an answer to the question of humanity's cosmic loneliness. The fact that the monolith was buried deliberately by some other intelligence that passed by the solar system and the monolith withstood all the three million years with all the moonquakes and other natural catastrophes immediately bring issues related to man's loneliness and man's relative insignificance to the fore:

> At last, one of man's oldest questions has been answered; here was the proof, beyond all shadow of doubt, that his was

> not the only intelligence that the universe had brought forth. But with that knowledge, there came again an aching awareness of the immensity of Time. Whatever had passed this way had missed mankind by a hundred thousand generations. (46)

Another related thought in Clarke's SF is about the need for humanity to possess a technological threshold to be taken seriously by any other intelligent beings in the universe. In that sense, a race would experience 'loneliness' until it is intelligent enough to equip itself with a means to communicate with other beings. The best example in this context is the novel Rendezvous with Rama in which humanity comes in touch with the huge spaceship of the aliens, but is ignored by them for reasons unknown to humanity. The suggestion, however, is that the superiorly intelligent aliens find humanity in its present stage of evolution as 'nothing'!

This paper has discussed how the theme of cosmic loneliness is manifested in much of Clarke's SF, how it is an extension of individual loneliness, and how the idea of first contact becomes an antithesis to questions related to the 'loneliness'. From the discussion, it is clear that Clarke uses the same immensity of space to evoke the sense of loneliness at one level and uses it as an escape at another level. What Clarke said in one of the interviews places his approach to the whole issue in context:

> If in fact we are alone, it means that we're not only the heirs to the Cosmos, but its guardians, which is a portentous thought.... Either alternative is amazing: whether we're alone or not alone. (Clarke, 1993)

REFERENCES

Clarke, Arthur C. *Childhood's End*. London: Pan Books, Macmillan Publishers Ltd. (1953) 2000.

——. *2001: A Space Odyssey*. London: Inner Circle. (1968) 1984.

——. *Rendezvous with Rama*. New York: Ballantine Books. 1972.

——. *Imperial Earth*. London: Gollancz. (1975) 2001.

——. *2010: Space Odyssey Two*. London: Granada. (1982) 1997.

——. *The Songs of Distant Earth*. New York: Ballantine Books. 1986.

——. *The Sentinel*. London: Harper Collins Publishers. 2000 (1948).

Eiseley, Loren. *The Immense Journey*. New York: Vintage Books. 1993 (1957).

Greenwald, Jeff. Interview with Arthur C. Clarke. On Life (and Death). July-August 1993. 15 August 2003. http://www.wired.com/wired/archive/1.03/clarke.html

Hollow, John. *Against the Night, the Stars: The Science Fiction of Arthur C. Clarke*. London: Harcourt. 1983.

Manlove, C.N. *Science Fiction: Ten Explorations*. Kent: Kent State University Press. 1986.

11

De-Africanising Womanhood and the Dilemma of Africanity: Mariama Bâ's *So Long a Letter* and Buchi Emecheta's *Second Class Citizen*

Mbuh Mbuh Tennu

Introduction

In her poem 'Phenomenal Woman', Maya Angelou draws on a tradition of the counter colonial/slavery discourse and suggests a 'universality' that sutures gender to race myths.[1] Within these categories woman harbours divergent identities, and expresses parallel levels of consciousness that are both complex and illuminating as she strives for liberation from her normative 'place'. When she succeeds, her personality as daughter/wife/mother is an evolution that is dependent on how woman challenges the 'roles of daughter, wife, and mother [that] are rigidly defined and [...] expected to [be] fulfil[led] [...] according to custom.'[2] This is the basis of a destabilising self-assertiveness in the works of African female writers, which celebrates acquired cultural deficiencies as trump cards of a revolutionary conquest. While these writers demystify inhibiting barriers of cultured otherness, the amorphous world of such consciousness is always a battle ground where woman's image is again interrogated.

My analysis of Mariama Bâ's *So Long a Letter* and Buchi Emecheta's *Second Class Citizen* will contend that in what Carole Boyce Davies describes as 'the activity of exploring and defining African womanhood',[3] the woman's challenge coincides with her 'globalised' status and that her self-apprehensions become manifestations of a different consciousness. As she moves into, and tries to relate with more differentiating categories of race and other forms of cultural awareness, her perception of life tends to be both comparative and qualitative. Inasmuch as her 'culture' dissolves into alien and more dominant ones, it still retains certain characteristics that either facilitate or resist attempts to de-Africanise the 'traditionally' framed image of the African woman. In her 'identification of African values', Gay Wilentz 'distinguish[es] African societal norms from Western values and mores', by signalling 'variants in how human existence is culturally evoked' in terms of Western individualism and African communality.[4] Aware of the danger of cultural homogeneity especially in feminist discourse, my concern is with '(de-)Africanising' utterances which represent views in which 'contact zones' of 'peoples geographically and historically separated come into contact with each other and establish ongoing relations, usually involving conditions of coercion, radical inequality, and intractable conflict'. Colonial insinuations apart, Bâ and Emecheta's works also 'invoke the spatial and temporal copresence of subjects previously separated by [religious and cultural] disjunctures, and whose trajectories now intersect'.[5]

One way of addressing the issue is Florence Stratton's suggestion for the 're-placement' of the female writers in a cross-cultural validation in which African women's writing will complement, or be complemented by, that of their male counterparts.[6] Bâ and Emecheta engage the possibility of such complementarity through characters who enact the rhythms of personal and social maturity across borders. Their adjustment allows the novels to address the configuring of identity in a postcolonial context where re-drawing boundaries from a traditionally uncontested way of life reclaims spaces and resists attempts to trivialise the image of woman. Such *re-boundarying* whether as the 'interpretive movement across putatively fixed biological, cultural, or ideological lines in order explore [...] difference'[7] or 'in cross-cultural, trans-national, diasporic contexts',[8] challenges categorizations that stymie womanhood into a silenced conspiracy against its own ideals.

The writers face a dilemma of how to negotiate the transition at complex levels whether in woman's traditional constituency or as tentative voyagers through a culturally fluid space. Davies comments on the latter option as 'fundamental to migration' and notes that '[i]t is the convergence of multiple places and cultures that re-negotiates the terms of Black women's experience that in turn negotiates and re-negotiates their identities'.[9] On her part, Laura Charlotte Kempen describes this as the 'heroine's trajectory from a victim of reductive patriarchal and postcolonial violence, to her self-reinvention as an active agent'.[10] This occurs at the level of education, religion/law, and attempted reconciliation of a relative African worldview with an Anglo-American phase, thus qualifying the works as 'Diaspora' literature, 'which transcends national boundaries and reflects a cultural lineage beyond that of even familial ancestry'.[11] My application of a gendered argument for Africanity thus opposes the ironies of the Negritude romanticists whose nostalgia particularly associated woman to a ripe fruit with firm flesh. This metaphor supports the masculinist assumptions that Bâ and Emecheta question, and accounts in part too for why Negritude representations today associated with 'race abandonment'.[12]

So Long a Letter and the Dilemma of Motherhood

Bâ's novel is the confession of an abused woman-in-mourning, Ramatoulaye, to her friend, Aïssatou, in which she also reassesses her as well as the African woman's identity. The story describes Ramatoulaye's state of frustrated loyalty and indecision and her fluctuating recollection of hopes reduced to servitude. Recounting it, Ramatoulaye is purged of her willing sufferer's guilt, and juxtaposes this with a more rebellious female self in others through what Mineke Schipper describes as an 'embedded narrative'. In that mode, '[a] real dialogue is not possible, since the addressee is not on the spot'.[13] It is, therefore, significant that the novel opens by describing a solid communal past of shared feelings and relationships enhanced by the desire to ensure that 'the past begets the present' (*SLL* 1). Evidence of that present exposes the ironies of woman's commitment, and leaves her almost personally devastated and socially rootless and makes Ramatoulaye the 'archetypal image of female experience'.[14]

That experience poses a dilemma within the changing phases of social life, especially when, for Bâ, African women 'do not imitate men' but instead feel 'fulfilled *as women*',[15] even if she was also to concede to 'a fundamental unity in all of [women's] sufferings'.[16] When, for instance, she recalls her first encounter with Modou Fall at a dance, Ramatoulaye does so with the nostalgia of equality that she earned through education but which was never accorded her in the practicalities of matrimony. Modou's stay in France transforms his conservatism into the Negritudinist expression of Ramatoulaye as a Senghorian refuge for the gratification of his fancies: 'It's you whom I carry within me. You are my protecting black angel. Would I could quickly find you, if only to hold your hand tightly so that I may forget hunger and thirst and loneliness' (*SLL* 14). Bâ rejects this fantasy as insufficient, insisting that '[t]he black woman in African literature must be given a dimension that matches her proven involvement next to the man in the battles for liberation'.[17]

A parasitic pattern, which camouflages as love, helps Ramatoulaye to identify man's symbolism of her with the religious demands of her traditional set-up. According to Kenneth W. Harrow, the Prophet Mohamed gave the following definition of marriage: 'The best of your women [...] is one who rejoices when her husband looks at her, who obeys him when he commands her, and who guards preciously his memory and his possessions when he is absent'.[18] Without any significant sphere of influence by Islam personal and social disharmony are inevitable, since woman as Simone de Beauvoir argues bitterly, 'is defined and differentiated with reference to man and not he with reference to her; she is the incidental, the inessential as opposed to the essential'.[19] Religion compromises the emancipatory dream of education through which Ramatoulaye's generation hoped to abandon 'the bog of tradition, superstition, and custom' and instead 'appreciate a multitude of civilisations without renouncing our own, to raise our vision of the world, cultivate our personalities, strengthen our qualities, to make up for our inadequacies, to develop universal moral values in us' (*SLL* 15). Eventually condemned to either share a husband without complaining, or divorce him and be branded as a prostitute, institutionalised widowhood thus subjugates Ramatoulaye in a mêlée of urban affluence and selective religious intolerance and hinders her self-awareness. Otherwise, her independent self threatens the man's centrality and he then brands her as 'scatter-brained' (*SLL* 15).

Marriage, thus, becomes a prison where, as 'breeder', Ramatoulaye is destituted by various loyalties, not least to her victimiser; and 'beyond her possessions she gives up her personality, her dignity, becoming a thing in the service of the man who has married her' and his entire family (*SLL* 4). Such a patrilocal tradition which dispossesses Ramatoulaye is at the core of Bâ's representation and censure of widowhood. Yet, Ramatoulaye's complicity to such injustice argues against her introspective faith in the 'grandiose verses from the *Qur'an*' (*SLL* 2), whose vested interpretation 'proclaims the partnership of men and women and the equal rights' and yet is vulnerable to 'local custom and male ascendancy in society' and inevitably 'put women under men's control' (*SLL* 91). By 'hold[ing] tightly to [her] prayer beads', Ramatoulaye inadvertently assists a tyranny which distorts her personality and confirms the claim that 'it is primarily writings *about* the *Qur'an*, which relegate women to an inferior position of servitude'.[20] The woman is not to be seen as 'violent or subversive but [as a] true [heroine], unknown in the mainstream of history, never upsetting the established order, despite [her] miserable condition' (*SLL* 11).

The problem, which Ramatoulaye faces, is how to reconcile the traditional exclusionism she endorses with the individualistic modernity she admires. This is problematic to a generation that was 'full of nostalgia' and 'resolutely progressive' (*SLL* 18-19) and as Hitchcott remarks, '[f]emininity is the virtue of the traditionalist; feminism, the veneer of the progressive striving to become a man'.[21] Analysing her complex position, Angelita Reyes remarks that Ramatoulaye's 'perspectives encapsulate the difficult position of the contemporary non-[W]estern feminist caught between a valuable heritage that she will not forfeit and an opposing need to express herself as a progressive woman'.[22] To dismantle the past, be nostalgic about it and yet press ahead with progressive reforms is a (re)construction that is hampered by Ramatoulaye's hesitant acknowledgment of her own stimulus for change. Her inhibiting loyalty to tradition, like her potential and motivations, is determined by the demands of motherhood, which as Davies argues, defines womanhood in African societies.[23] How then is she to be a self-conscious, assertive woman, blurring invented and/or obsolete boundaries, and yet nurture her children within an enabling, contemporary consciousness? A shadow of her former self, weighed down by successive maternity, and resigned to her fate as co-*épouse* Ramatoulaye's 'traditional' responsibilities surpass those of the rebellious ego. Constrained by a wayward tradition-empowered husband, the abiding responsibility of motherhood, and the desire for an independent life, Ramatoulaye expresses the need for some form of stability, but also realises that such balance is actually established in her own household, with herself as the *queenpin*. As already suggested, the institutions, which Ramatoulaye respects are the very pillars of her alienation and she is unable to define convincingly her position against them. Harrow again points out that '[t]he clause in the *Qur'an* which gives permission to contract four concurrent marriages is immediately followed by a restriction [that] "If you cannot treat them with perfect equality in material things as in love and affection, then, marry only one."' Contrary to this, however, 'the older male members of the community create their own set of beliefs and moral values [so that] their given interpretations and applications [...] will overshadow the principles and ideals of Islam.'[24]

Ramatoulaye's slavish compromise contrasts respectively with the views of her friend and daughter, Aïssatou and Daba. In a similar situation, Aïssatou not only left Mawdo Bâ, but also abandoned her country, moved across continents, and challenged the sex-defined restrictions to her professional development. By extending her psychological and physical spaces, Aïssatou challenges previous appropriations in which she was a mere appendage. She dares to 'work, outside the home[,] [...] the key to liberation' and thereby 'break[s] the bonds of economic dependency on men, which would in turn enable them to resist sexist domination' (*SLL* 95). Aïssatou understands 'the internal ordering of [...] society with its absurd divisions' (*SLL* 31) and denounces Mawdo's polygamous logic 'for reasons of duty' and declares: 'I am stripping myself of your love, your name'. Aïssatou embodies what Giyatri Spivak refers to as 'inversions and counterinversions' of postcolonial identity, rejecting '[e]ntitling nicknames' that foster a 'patronymic' culture since '[t]he proper name is more unilateral, [and] can claim locationist identity with assurance'.[25] Pacesetter to a disrupting feminism, Aïssatou's self-preservation against the male-forged identity celebrates her *dangerously* rebellious 'dignity, the only worthy garment' in which multiple 'locations' suits her option to 'go my way' (*SLL* 32). She wrestles herself from Ramatoulaye's cushioning tolerance and fits into Filomina Chioma Steady's definition of feminism as the 'abnegation of male protection and a determination to be resourceful and self-reliant'.[26] As Obioma Nnaemeka points out, in addition, '[b]y walking out on her husband, Aïssatou demonstrates that the initiation of divorce can also be the woman's prerogative'.[27]Aïssatou's transformed personality thus rejects Ramatoulaye's words 'to be an ally to polygamic instincts' and renders her 'the courageous pioneer of a new life' (*SLL* 34).

Daba is even more militant in her inheritance of the Aïssatou initiative, confronting her father in the night club where he feels clumsily out of place. Her matrimonial situation opposes the mother's, rehabilitates Aïssatou's estrangement with the possibility of a reformed man, and sheds light on what the older generation initiated. 'Daba does not find household work a burden, because the task is shared with her husband; and the latter also sees her as 'wife [...] not my slave nor my servant' (*SLL* 73). Even then, Daba is prepared for any eventualities since marriage is 'not a chain', but a 'mutual agreement over a life's programme' (*SLL* 74) and thus exposes Ramatoulaye's 'stay put-*ness*' and philosophy of 'eternal compromise' (*SLL* 72); and endorses Aïssatou's decision for the road only as a possibility in the event when all else fails. This attitude highlights the generation gap that characterizes the narrative between the mother's defeatism and the daughter's assertiveness. Although Nnaemeka describes Bâ's revolutionary approach as 'less a rebellion than the quest for truth' since she 'subver[ts] [...] myths and distortions',[28] it is clear that rebellion and truth complement the rejection of a cheapened, male-elected mode of physical and functional utility. Ramatoulaye's compromise is significantly 'all-encompassing' as 'it moves from a heightened awareness of herself, of the family, of the nation/society, and then of her position in the global and feminist arena;'[29] and provokes

Aïssatou's self-quest, which Daba seizes as the base for her security. Where Ramatoulaye rationalises her 'misfortune' and assigns herself the task of a woman's spokesperson in terms of what is acceptable, conventionally, Daba the practical individualist like Aïssatou, is concerned with the self before relating to others and institutions. By the end of the narrative, therefore, the story is no longer that of Ramatoulaye's abused matrimonial life and widowhood, but an opening into 'we' generalities that attempt, but fail to resolve the problems associated with the notion of an archetypal motherhood. The story's narration of how motherhood relates to wife and widow therefore underscores individual fulfilment as central to the transgression of various boundaries, natural and imposed.

Second Class Citizen and the Challenge of Africanity

If Bâ portrays the plight of woman constrained by tradition, Emecheta's *Second Class Citizen* depicts woman's substitution of cultural conservatism with a disturbing elitism. Resisting Francis who is psychologically stunted by patriarchy, the change which Adah expects is not so much the difference between Lagos/Africa and London/England as it is her (in) consistency at self-affirmation to the extent that she even participates in her own momentary and fairly regular defeats. The determination to prove her new consciousness grows out of accumulated frustrations with cultural habits and in this way, the novel replicates Bâ's *Letter* in its representation of woman's embodiment of a consciousness that is no longer 'traditionally' African, nor purely 'Western'. Owing to this mixed provenance, Adah's interest in an African moral aesthetic is peripheral to her desire for a quasi-first class citizen westernisation, and also accounts for the contradictions that characterise her priorities.

Unwanted at birth because of her sex, Adah struggles to change her 'very low opinion of her own sex' (*SCC* 5) beyond 'the bigger [...] dowry' resulting from her educated status (*SCC* 10). When she meets Francis, 'an African through and through' (*SCC* 19), conflict is already predictable from her own reflections, before now, against 'any man, rich or poor, to whom she would have to serve his food on bended knee: she would not consent to live with a husband whom she would have to treat as a master and refer to as 'Sir' even behind his back' (*SCC* 12). Nor is she critical of her own vulnerable aspirations against the African race-solidarity in London, while Francis, the child of his ancestral culture, is a willing victim whose condition does not prevent him from victimising Adah. Even London does not moderate his chauvinistic disposition; he is so 'fixed' that even the environment in which his family finds him is the same squeezed-in contingency of his upbringing. Adah's sense of social dignity and self-esteem is infringed upon and begins to crumble, and her efforts to discriminate against the Nigerian community only isolate her more.

London, thus, provides the ambiguous setting for cultural identification in which Francis' role is displaced as a replaceable central figure, and gender and racial difference becomes a confused category for Adah's identification. In the first case, as a single parent, she also compromises her role as a domestic pillar by eliciting the reader's understanding and possible sympathy without acknowledging the disadvantages of single parenting as a consequence of her 'ambition'. On the other hand, Adah's assertive entrance into the new culture and her learning process leads to a conceit in exploding Western myths of superiority. This seems to be the means for her to justify her conceptions of racial difference, which will also ensure her rapid integration into the new culture. Self-knowledge widens her understanding of the 'new' world in which she can no longer take things for granted, and her 'discovery' about white fallibility (they too tell lies) gives her a sense of confidence that challenges both gender/matrimonial and race representations. Whether we consider Adah's position in terms of gender or race, her goal as independent woman introduces a confusion that her propagandistic tone fails to resolve. While Francis had symbolised her hopes in a new world, and now personifies her doubts of those very possibilities, she seems to treasure his blunders for self-vindication.

The duplicity of London fits Adah's attempt at double identity., when for instance, she 'press[es] her wide, tunnel-like nostrils together as if to keep out a nasty smell' (*SCC* 62). In search of a house she becomes a poor alternative for Wole

Soyinka's persona in 'Telephone Conversation'. While sympathy for Soyinka's character stems from his being an arrogant, race-conscious survivalist, Adah seems to stage-manage a need for sympathy. She becomes one of Homi Bhabha's 'figures of a doubling' consciousness who assists in 'the repetition of *partial presence*' in spheres that undermine her true identity.[30] Unlike Bâ's Aïssatou, Adah justifies de Beauvoir's observation that, '[t]o decline to be the other, to refuse to be party to the deal—this would be for women to renounce all the advantages conferred upon them by their alliance with the superior caste.'[31] Adah often gives the impression that discrimination actually facilitates a willed antagonism with paternalistic domesticity in which she is breadwinner.

Adah's ambiguous stance betrays her fight for a genuine selfhood that defies artificial barriers since she herself is guilty of inventing such barriers. Suspecting Francis' entrenched doubts about her suffering, and in order to 'get the sympathy she want[s]' and also to give Francis 'the most terrible proof he ha[s] ever seen'—we are not told of what—she entreats God to 'give Francis a sign, any proof to make him believe me' (*SCC* 82). Adah thus minimises genuine birth pains she is going through, and is afraid of Francis' reaction on learning of her situation, in order to uphold his callous inhumanity. Her self-pitying image (when Francis '[will] accuse her of laziness and [will] remind her that they needed her money' (*SCC* 82) is that of a faithful, dedicated wife who is still to be accorded due recognition by a wayward, undeserving husband. True to the enslaving part of the tradition she challenges, Adah wants to make it believable that she hands over her pay to Francis as testimony to her state of imprisonment. The patriarchal argument is rather overstretched here, and selectively substantiated against Francis. This is a consequence of the 'displacement' resulting from the third-person narrative voice, which as Joya Uraizee remarks, 'tries to explain all the cultural customs and taboos of the community, but ends up erasing its own authority'.[32] Although the book is not only an indictment but also a celebration of her home culture, casting Francis unfavourably suggests an inscrutable patriarchy that resists cultural changes (both spatial and temporal) to which it is exposed. While Theodora Ezeigbo does not agree completely that the traditional [Ibo] system was democratic and egalitarian, she affirms that 'there is some truth in the claim' that [Ibo] traditional society had ingrained in its socio-political and economic structures a system of 'checks and balances' which enabled women to *manipulate* situations to their advantage.'[33] Adah's overall attitude toward Francis, whether to accuse or reclaim, is therefore a strategy to foreground her vulnerability.

At times Adah's contradictory indecisions are inexplicable, even as evidence against Francis. This is the case when she hesitates to inform him of the possibility of them having lodging at Mr. Noble's (*SCC* 72). Bearing in mind Francis' joy the last time there was such a possibility—she even thought then that he was in love with her, and hoped that 'surprises like this once in a while' will sustain their relationship (*SCC* 64)—it is now surprising that she hesitates. Given the pressure from their landlord, and the fact that she is the one to pay the bills, Adah's decision to wait for 'the right moment' to inform him is a tactic to enhance the dehumanisation of Francis. In her self-defence, she casts a spell on Francis, reduces him to the instinctive depravity that readjusts to colonial categorisation and at the same time uplifts—or hopes to uplift—her own imagined image of the abused liberator, even as she is in a stronger position than she will want us to believe. When she claims to have been 'banned' by Francis from going to the Nobles for fear of 'a bad influence on her' (*SCC* 81), it only recalls her insinuation of a developing intimacy between Francis and Mrs. Noble the first time they go there for a room.

Adah, therefore, paints the picture of a trapped and culturally deracinated African woman in Europe who identifies with Ibo cultural values as condescending afterthoughts. Even *In the Ditch* which attempts 'to paint rosy pictures of Nigeria' is implied acknowledgement of cultural entrapment, and therefore rejected by Adah's children (*Ditch* 80). As an alternative, she savours English Spring and 'feel[s] so happy [she] could burst' (*Ditch* 17). She had earlier doubted the protection from the goddess Oboshi, on behalf of her husband, because of her 'being a Christian' (*SCC* 21). 'At home in Nigeria' is subsequently a recurrent refrain of hers in London, often modified in her impatience with being treated 'like a native woman'. She unconsciously associates with the racial exclusionism which also imposes its own aesthetics of judgement on her and from which she adopts a Wordworthian romanticism 'to train herself to admire the songs of the birds however riotous, to appreciate the beauty of the flowers however extravagant their scent' (*SCC* 121). Her passionate desire for flowers and cards, in the hospital, imposes itself as a culture-determined love from which Francis withdraws into his cocoon manhood.

The doubtful direction of Adah's identity transforms the Africa of her nostalgia into a cultural crossroads of what Katherine Fishburn cautiously describes as a 'false universalism'.[34] Such universalism raises the question of how we can probe the feminist theme in the novel, viewed as 'dangerous' if focused upon 'almost exclusively' as suggested by Abioseh Michael Porter.[35] On the other hand, Umeh insists that 'Emecheta's treatment of sexual politics [...] is grounded in [Ibo] women's protest against retrogressive cultural norms such as clitoridectomy,[36] women as baby-machines, the prioritising of boys at the expense of girls and widow inheritance.'[37] In her analysis of sexual/textual politics in Emecheta, Fishburn concludes that although the 'worldview' of Emecheta's childhood 'does not elevate women to the co-equal status demanded by Western (liberal) feminists, it does [...] express feminist ideals of cooperation, community, and oneness with nature.'[38] While this is true of the later Emecheta, evidence in both *The Ditch* and *Second Class Citizen* proves the contrary as Adah consciously aspires for westernised definitions. Thus, when she questions Francis' feminism, which is based on the English word 'woman' and as justified by Christian mythology, her intention is to juxtapose it with the Ibo 'opoho' (*SCC* 24-25) and claim a cultural cognisance that is absent in Francis. Regardless of her attempts at narrative objectivity, Adah betrays a pro-Western attitude that gradually dissolves her African credentials.

The sense of rootlessness also implicates her children whose education in 'English schools and, if possible, English universities' (*SCC* 25) will transform them into 'different people' (*SCC* 104) who will 'enjoy being black, be proud of being black, a black of a different breed' (*SCC* 121). Adah's vacillation between the quest for a new elitist self and the need to hold onto the previous identity is influenced by a selective subjectivity that renders its goal of a new womanhood suspect to the very vision it seeks. Consequently, she insists on 'Francis' family' in a way that excludes her and perhaps the children. Such familial and cultural distantiation is fuelled by Francis' naive claims that the children 'won't learn good English' if they do not have foster parents. He seems to echo the later Emecheta who distances herself and her writing linguistically from 'plodding' African writers: 'using the [English] language every day and staying in the culture my Africanness is, in a way, being diluted'. Reacting to this condescending tone, Chinua Achebe's remarks that '[t]he psychology of the dispossessed can be truly frightful'.[39] The sarcasm apart, it is necessary to note that a linguistic complex becomes one variable of identity and acceptability in the aspired-for society. The new voice which describes changing identities is a self-conscious denial of a limiting cultural medium, and meant to be understood as the distance between the ordinary but traditionally 'conscripted' self and the imagined liberty in the West.

Porter has suggested that environmental deprivation accounts for Adah's problems,[40] although such forces are external and contribute only minimally to her indecisions. Adah's perceptiveness endears her initially to the father-in-law as 'a woman who would think before she acts' (*SCC* 20). Unfortunately, he and the son prey upon her and by the time she arrives London, Adah is not, as Porter claims, so 'ignorant of the culture of a foreign country'[41] following her professional experience in Nigeria. The relative ease with which she finds employment, the beginning of her literary career, and the legal and institutional support she benefits from against Francis, all argue for an environmental solidarity. If in this way 'we begin to see a rupture of socialisation and psychological dispositions that stand in opposition'[42] it is important to point out that the 'rupture' had already occurred in Nigeria, and only becomes dramatic in London. Rooted in the paternalistic marriage arrangements, estrangement is most noticeable at the airport scene when they see off Francis to England. Contrary to expectations, Adah is 'dry-eyed', and internalises her reaction to the moment 'like an outcast' whose aloofness only earns her 'a pat on the shoulder' from Francis (*SCC* 22). Adah's detachment, echoed in a letter from England in which Francis accuses her of not weeping for him at departure, and of being 'very happy to see [him] go' (*SCC* 23) anticipates the senseless beatings she receives from him in London.

Part of Adah's problem in narrating her story and that of the reader in following her, is the schematic articulation of her plight. The very chapter titles and Adah's reflections against 'random' writing, instead preferring 'a purpose [...] a pattern' (*SCC* 144), offer a neat textbook format for the narrative that hypothesizes her clinical argument about gender relations. However, everything about *this* new woman remains almost experimental, always on the verge of discovery and re-invention, up to chapter twelve when it becomes clear that she is wiser and more aware of herself and her changing environment than is apparent. In the last chapter therefore, she finally snaps back at Francis, over his abominable destruction of her manuscript: 'Bill called that story my brainchild. Do you hate me so much, that you could kill my child?' (*SCC* 147). This long-awaited response to what Nancy Topping Bazin has described as 'grim' and 'painful to read'[43] should have consolidated her esteem and identity as it embodies both the literary and biological mother-identity, and accounts for why the rift with Francis comes with such finality soon after. Hankering after cultural adaptation and Englishness, Adah fails to understand her *self* and to reassess her priorities in life. For instance, she juxtaposes her destitution with the apparent affluence of English women, and then condemns Francis for this. Such parallels culminate at the moment of birth pangs when her hitherto casual imaging of Francis crystallises into Lucifer whose voice, 'like the persistent bells of death', insisted 'that she was being punished for not waiting to read *The Truth Shall Make You Free*' (*SCC* 91).

With all his weaknesses, this is Adah's unconscious wish so that in her declamatory against Francis can be justified. In this functional imaging of Francis and the change she expects of him, the reader is never allowed into his consciousness; what seems habitual of him is filtered through Adah's discriminatory emotions. Consequently, his opposition to blood transfusion is given sporadically in arrears, probably to prove the point that 'Francis was not a bad man, just a man who could no longer cope with the over-demanding society he found himself in' (*SCC* 86). But comparing her misfortunes with the blessings of other (white) women, Adah clouds her own irresponsibility in the relationship. Rejecting 'implicit or understood love' in preference for that which is 'explicit and dramatised'[44] there is evidence in the text that Francis is not irredeemable, and that African cultural values can still cohabit with western influence. Yet, in stating her case, Adah freezes time and other possibilities, and gauges the happiness of others from a momentary semblance of her fancies.

Conclusion

Jessie Chambers, D.H. Lawrence's girlfriend and heroine of his most popular novel, *Sons and Lovers*, claims that Lawrence could only realise in fiction what he failed to achieve in real life; that is, a supremacy over her/woman.[45] Reading Bâ and Emecheta's novels from the perspectives of gender and autobiography, Chambers' claim raises questions that implicate authorial responsibility in their responses to gender equality and how this is achievable or not. Nnaemeka's context of exposing and challenging the validity of myths, whereby the 'writers rescue their protagonists from the quagmire of objectification, impotence, and lifelessness'[46] threatens male centrality in an attempt to overcome previous parameters of identity. Consequently, the African male in the two novels is presented as blundering from an ill-weaned mother/culture-fixation into unstable manhood just as mother/child parallels reveal an affirmative motherhood (with a slight qualification in Emecheta) that is also aware of the liberal space for which the child is destined. Once out of his previous hegemonic culture, she/he is exposed as selfless and handicapped.

The same applies to religion, whether Islam, whose interpretation incapacitates Ramatoulaye or Christianity/

tradition's duplicity, which authenticates Francis' sadistic 'love'. While Ramatoulaye is condemned to a religion-ordained state of polygamy poorly managed, Adah has to confront Francis and his one-man-one-woman ideology. Recourse by both writers to positive traditional African values suggests a confluence point for the reconciliation of ideologies. Emecheta's success in subverting patriarchal models in identical ways like Bâ, is meant to 'shock', but to do this, as in Ramatoulaye's post-mourning excursions into modernity, woman has to beware of the 'arrogance' of independence which may be detrimental to her purposeful struggle. This is important because while the females re-visualise their world, they still wish for an enabling past that must be substantiated as changeable and not idealised as trouble-free. In the words of Mr. Okpara, whose brief appearance represents the desired gender mutuality, 'a husband and his wife always build their home for many things but particularly for quarrels' (*SCC* 134). This is also what Daba's freethinking husband implicitly articulates in *So Long a Letter*, and reverses the representation of these men from what has been perceived as 'a self-perpetuating phallocentric society'.[47]

The problem is how to manage this fluctuating atmosphere without overreaching actions of which the man has been accused. Ezeigbo proposes a conglomerate of 'elders, priests, priestesses, wealthy and titled men of integrity, articulate and respected members of the society, age-grade groups, association of daughters and association of wives',[48] that provided leadership in traditional Igbo/African society. If postcolonial posturing disrupted the apparent balance, the expectations of a new leadership reconfiguration from Bâ and Emecheta become all the more significant and will necessarily consider characterisation in male writings like those of Achebe and the Cameroonian playwright Bole Butake, who mythologize woman as the context for a radicalised new vision for society.[49] This is appropriate in appreciating fully the new perspectives opened by the younger generation of women in the novels represented by Dada, in order to see how their vision coheres with the meeting-point masculinity of the 'reformed' men.

NOTES

1. Maya Angelou, 'Phenomenal Woman', *Collected Poems The Complete Collected Poems* (New York: Random House, 1994).
2. Nancy Topping Bazin, 'Venturing into Feminist Consciousness: Two Protagonists from the Fiction of Buchi Emecheta and Bessie Head', in Marie Umeh, (ed.), *Emerging Perspectives on Buchi Emecheta* (Trenton, NJ: Africa World Press, Inc., 1996), 144.
3. Carole Boyce Davies, 'Motherhood in the Works of Male and Female Igbo Writers: Achebe, Emecheta, Nwapa and Nzekwu,' in Carole Boyce Davies and Anne Adams Graves, eds., *Ngambika: Studies of Women in African Literature* (Trenton, NJ: Africa World Press, Inc., 1990), 242.
4. Gay Wilentz, *Black Women Writers in Africa and the Diaspora* (Bloomington: Indiana University Press, 1992), xviii.
5. Mary Louise Pratt, *Imperial Eyes: Travel Writing and Transculturation* (London: Routledge, 1993), 6-7.
6. Florence Stratton, *Contemporary African Literature and the Politics of Gender* (London: Routledge, 1994), 12.
7. Michael Awkward, *Negotiating Difference: Race, Gender, and the Politics of Positionality* (Chicago: The University of Chicago Press, 1995), 4.
8. Carole Boyce Davies, 'Introduction: Black Women Writing Worlds: Textual Production, Dominance, and the Critical Voice', *Moving Beyond Boundaries,* 1.
9. Carole Boyce Davies, *Black Women, Writing and Identity: Migrations of the Subject* (London: Routledge, 1994), 3.
10. Laura Charlotte Kempen, *Mariama Bâ, Rigoberta Menchú, and Postcolonial Feminism* (New York: Peter Lang, 2001), 3.
11. Wilentz, *Black Women Writers,* xv.
12. See especially Wole Soyinka, 'The External Encounter: Ambivalence in African Arts and Literature', *Art, Dialogue and Outrage* (Ibadan: New Horn Press, 1988), 236-37.
13. Mineke Schipper, *Beyond the Boundaries: African Literature and Literary Theory* (London: Allison and Busby: 1989), 105.
14. Stratton, 'Shallow Graves: Archetypes of Female Experience in African Fiction', in Umeh, 114.
15. Barbara Harrell-Bond, 'Mariama Bâ, Winner of the First Noma Award for Publishing in Africa: An Interview', *African Book*

Publishing Record, quoted in Nicki Hitchcott, *Women Writers in Francophone Africa* (Oxford: Berg, 2000), 71.

16. Mariama Bâ, *Scarlet Song* (Dakar: NEA, 1981), quoted in Irène Assiba d'Almeida, *Francophone African Women Writers: Destroying the Emptiness of Silence* (Gainesville: University Press of Florida, 1994), 122.
17. Mariama Bâ, 'La function politique des littérature africaines écrites', *Ecriture française* 3, no. 5 (1981), quoted in Renée Larrier, *Francophone Women Writers in Africa and the Caribbean* (Gainesville: University Press of Florida, 2000), 48.
18. Kenneth W. Harrow, *Faces of Islam in African Literature* (Portsmouth, NH: Heinemann, 1991), 91-92.
19. Simone de Beauvoir, *The Second Sex* (London: Vintage, 1997), 16.
20. Laura Charlotte Kempen, *Mariama Bâ, Rigoberta Menchú, and Postcolonial Feminism* (New York: Peter Lang, 2001), 31.
21. Hitchcott, *Women Writers in Francophone Africa*, 71.
22. Angelita Reyes, 'The Epistolary Voice and Voices of Indigenous Feminism in Mariama Ba's *Une si longue letter*,' in Davies, *Moving Beyond Boundaries,* 196.
23. Davies, 'Motherhood in the Works of Male and Female Igbo Writers', 243.
24. Harrow, *Faces of Islam in African Literature,* 92, 98.
25. Giyatri Spivak, 'Resident Alien,' in David Theo Goldberg and Ato Quayson eds. *Relocating Postcolonialism* (Oxford: Blackwell Publishers Ltd., 2002), 48, 50.
26. Filomina Chioma Steady, *The Black Woman Crossculturally* (Cambridge, Mass.: Schenkman, 1981), quoted in Davies, 'Motherhood in the Works of Male and Female Igbo Writers: Achebe, Emecheta, Nwapa and Nzekwu', in Davies and Graves, eds., *Ngambika,* 241.
27. Obioma Nnaemeka, 'Mariama Bâ: Parallel Convergence and Interior Space', in Edris Makward, et al., *The Growth of African Literature: Twenty-Five Years after Dakar and Fourah Bay* (Trenton, NJ: Africa World Press, Inc., 1998), 201.
28. Nnaemeka, 'Mariama Bâ: Parallel Convergence and Interior Space', 199.
29. Reyes, 'The Epistolary Voice', 196.
30. Homi K. Bhabha, 'Of Mimicry and Man: The Ambivalence of Colonial Discourse', *The Location of Culture* (London: Routledge, 2002), 88.

31. Simone de Beauvoir, *The Second Sex,* 21.
32. Joya Uraizee, *This is no Place for Woman: Nadine Gordimer, Nayantara Saghal, Buchi Emecheta, and the Politics of Gender* (Trenton, NJ: Africa World Press Inc., 2000), 72.
33. Theodora Akachi Ezeigbo, 'Tradition and the African Female Writer: The Example of Buchi Emecheta.' Umeh, 9 (my emphasis).
34. Katherine Fishburn, *Reading Buchi Emecheta: Cross-Cultural Conversations* (Westport, CT: Greenwood Press, 1995), 22.
35. Abioseh Michael Porter, '*Second-Class Citizen*: The Point of Departure for Understanding Buchi Emecheta's Major Fiction.' Umeh, (268). Porter prefers a reading of the novel as a *bildungsroman*, which will render understandable some of its 'seeming inconsistencies' (268). But this ignores the fact that as a genre the novel of development transforms inconsistencies into a thematic reservoir. These are usually realised from hindsight by the main character as an unconscious boost into self-awareness; but Adah's are mostly conscious foresights of her prospecting, and therefore suspicious, intelligence.
36. Emecheta however passionately denounces Alice Walker on the basis of the latter's treatment of this theme which she claims to be a 'dying' and 'no longer relevant' practice in Africa; (quoted in Oladipo Joseph Ogundele, 'A Conversation with Dr Buchi Emecheta' Umeh, 454-55).
37. Umeh, *Emerging Perspectives on Buchi Emecheta*, xxvi.
38. Fishburn, *Reading Buchi Emecheta*, 136.
39. Chinua Achebe, *Home and Exil* (Oxford: Oxford University Press, 2000), 72. Achebe quotes Emecheta's words from Adeola James' interview with Emecheta *In Their Own Voices: African Women Writers Talk* (London: James Currey Ltd., 1990), 39.
40. Porter, 'Point of Departure', 270.
41. *Ibid.*
42. *Ibid.*, 293.
43. Nancy Topping Bazin, 'Feminist Perspectives in African Fiction: Bessie Head and Buchi Emecheta', *The Black Scholar,* 17(2): 35.
44. Joseph Okpaku, 'Culture and Criticism: African Critical Standards for African Literature and the Arts', quoted in *Fishburn*, 65.
45. Jessie Chambers, *D.H. Lawrence: A Personal Record* (Cambridge: Cambridge University Press, 1980), 202.
46. Nnaemeka, 'Mariama Bâ: Parallel Convergence and Interior Space', 198.

47. Hitchcott, *Women Writers in Francophone Africa*, 73.
48. Ezeigbo, 'Tradition in the African Female Writer', 7.
49. I think obviously, of Beatrice in Achebe's *Anthills of the Savannah* and Butake's attempt to weave myth and revolution into female cults in his plays, notably *Lake God* (1986), and *And Palm-wine will Flow* (1990).

Decolonization and the Politics of Language

12

Vandana Datta

Decolonization is a major theme in post-colonial discourse. Taking the cue from Salman Rushdie's statement that the English language which was the 'instrument of subservience' has now become a 'weapon of liberation' this paper proposes to study the way the writers from the colonies have appropriated the English language to fight the cultural imperialism of the British. The countries that come under this umbrella are Australia, Canada, New Zealand, India, Pakistan, Bangladesh, Malaysia, Malta, Singapore and the African, Caribbean and South Pacific Island countries. The literatures of these countries have one thing in common that they have all emerged from the experience of colonization. To all these countries English came as the language of the colonizers but in the hands of the natives it acquired a local flavour and name and became a marker of identity. These countries, however, fall under two categories, to use the terms of Maxwell, they are: settler colonies and invaded colonies. In the settler colonies like Canada, Australia and New Zealand, the European colonizers dispossessed the indigenous population, occupied the land and transplanted their own civilization and language. In the case of invaded colonies like India and Africa, the indigenous population was colonized on its own land and dispossessed of their faith and pride in their own ancient culture and civilization by the imposition of English. In both cases the relationship between language and place suffers due to a sense of alienation. To take the words of Maxwell once again—

> ...In the first, the writer brings his own language—English— to an alien environment and a fresh set of experiences:

Australia, Canada, New Zealand. In the other, the writer brings an alien language—English—to his own social and cultural inheritance: India, West Africa.[1]

It is this conflict between language and experience that sets apart the writings of post-colonial countries from the British tradition.

History is evidence that the poets who pulled out English Literature from the decadence of the Edwardians and the Georgians were not from England. It was for the Irish Yeats and the American Eliot and Pound to inaugurate the modern movement in English poetry. As the countries of the Commonwealth gained political freedom one by one vibrant voices started coming from them compared to which writings in England continued to sound complacent. The empire started writing back and it wrote back with a vengeance. They turned the English language upon the imperial masters, appropriating it to suit their needs, thereby launching a struggle against cultural imperialism. And it was only in English that this struggle could be fought for though the political hegemony of England was lost, their cultural hegemony was still to be broken. Standards of judgment continued to remain Euro centric. The post-colonial literatures of each of the Commonwealth countries carried on its struggle in its own way. Since it is not possible to look into each of them in this paper, I choose to concentrate on African and Indian Literatures.

'Abrogation' and 'appropriation' of language acquire wider ramifications in the literatures of Africa and India. In fact, here the politics of language offers an interesting study in post-colonial literature. In many ways, the two are similar—they have a rich cultural heritage of their own and the imposition of the English language in both these places has caused a conflict between language and experience. Till quite recently African Literature meant South African Literature, but now it has almost exclusively come to mean Black Literature and Chinua Achebe, Ngugi, Wole Soyinka, Amos Tutuola are some of the well known names. The choice of English as the medium of creative writing was a conscious decision on the part of these writers. A very important reason was the fact that most of the African languages did not have a script of their own. But there were other reasons too. And the primary objective was to aid and assist their respective national liberation struggles. Such writings were also aimed at what Ngugi wa Thiong'o has called 'decolonizing the mind' of the African educated middle class. One of the first novels to come out of Nigeria was *The Palm Wine Drinkard* by Amos Tutuola in 1952. What immediately attracted attention was the irregular English of Tutuola as this small excerpt amply demonstrates:

> I was a palm wine drinkard since I was a boy of ten years of age. I had no other work more than to drink palm wine in my life.... My father got eight children and I was the eldest among them, all of the rest were hard working, but I myself was an expert palm wine drinkard....[2]

Such bad English was a source of embarrassment for Tutuola's colleagues most of whom had been to English schools and the university. The western critics, however, hailed it as a novel use of the English language. Dylan Thomas referred to it as 'young English by a West African' and Anthony West saw in it 'the very beginnings of literature'. Still, it was considered a freak. But matters came to a head when Tutuola repeated the freak five times with his other novels. There was more to Tutuola's novels than just bad English. It was the Yoruba folk material that Tutuola had so cleverly built into it, bending the structure of the English language as well as of the novel form to carry the burden of his narrative. This was the strength of Tutuola's form which was soon adopted not only in Nigeria but all over Africa.

Chinua Achebe was perhaps among the first to notice the immense possibility of such 'hybridization'. But he took care to avoid the irregular English of Tutuola. In his first novel *Things Fall Apart* Achebe replaced Tutuola's incorrect English with simple, crisp, short and correct structures and the Yoruba folk material with his own Ibo myths, customs, superstitions and sayings. The result—hailed as a modern classic *Things Fall Apart* has been translated into scores of modern major languages of the world. Besides Africanizing the language Achebe also Africanizes the political theme of the novel by taking up the colonized versus colonizer agenda and universalizing it. It is by foregrounding the colonization of Africa on the agenda of African fiction that Achebe became the trend-setter and many novelists across the continent began to write similar novels. Ngugi wa Thiong'o from Kenya modeled his first novel *The River Between* on *Things Fall Apart*. But Ngugi is more radical in his views than the mild-mannered Achebe. Protest became the main political agenda in most of the novels from East as well as South Africa in the writings of Meja Mwangi, Godwin Wachira, Nadine Gordimer, Alan Paton or Alex La Guma. In another novel *Devil on the Cross* Ngugi builds the story around the worsening living conditions of ordinary Kenyans and blends it with generous use of technical terms of political analysis based on class. But the most significant feature about this novel is its original publication in Gikuyu, Ngugi's mother tongue. Ngugi had already decided to give up the use of English for his creative writing and the reasons he cited were political. Continued use of English in free Kenya, he had said, symbolized the colonized mind and had also alienated him from the Kenyan masses with whom he needed to interact in order to reach his political message to them. He was of the view that literature written in colonial languages is not African literature since it involves a 'dissociation, divorce or alienation from the immediate environment', an idea which becomes clearer when the colonial language is seen as 'a carrier of culture':

> Language carries culture, and culture carries, particularly through orature and literature, the entire body of values by which we come to perceive ourselves and our place in the world.[3]

Apparently, Ngugi is not satisfied by mere portrayal of the socio-political-cultural situation in Kenya during and after the national struggle for independence. He suggests, in a book of the same title, 'decolonizing the mind'. By this he means a kind of 'dialectical negation of the colonial process', dismantling, as it were, the various psychological structures that had been in the minds of men as a result of sustained colonial propaganda during the period of colonization. He, therefore, pleads with the

African writers to write in their own languages rather than in European languages. He assigns a very radical role to the writer:

> ...literature cannot escape from the class power structures that shape our everyday life. Here a writer has no choice. Whether or not he is aware of it, his works reflect one or more aspects of the intense economic, political, cultural and ideological struggles in a society. What he can choose is one or the other side in the battlefield: the side of the people or the side of those social forces and classes that try to keep the people down. What he or she cannot do is to remain neutral. Every writer is a writer in politics. The only question is what and whose politics....[4]

Of course, Ngugi drew considerable flak for giving up the use of English for creative writing. Nurudin Farah, for instance, criticized him bitterly for becoming a 'backwater fish'. Even Chinua Achebe had reservations about this decision of his. Achebe is not against the use of English, though he certainly advocates the use of a different English, one that would be 'still in its full communion with its ancestral home but altered to suit its new African surroundings'.[5] This comes close to Raja Rao's famous words in his Foreword to *Kanthapura:*

> ...One has to convey in a language that is not one's own the spirit that is one's own. One has to convey the various shades and impressions of a certain thought-movement that looks ill treated in an alien language, I use the word 'alien', but English is not really an alien language to us. It is the language of our intellectual make-up—like Sanskrit or Persian was before—but not of our emotional make-up. We are all instinctively bilingual, many of us are writing in our own language and in English. We cannot write like the English. We should not. We cannot write only as Indians....[6]

Raja Rao himself has made experiments of considerable value. Besides adapting the novel form to the ancient Pauranic tradition of storytelling, he has also paid attention to the smaller details—expressions like 'little mother' 'nose-scratching Nanjamma of Satamma', 'corner-house Moorthy', 'fig-tree-house-people', 'front-house-Akkamma' are all typical Indian usages and would never occur in proper English. But if a language has to come out of the books and become a living language it has to be one in which people don't only speak but breathe, feel, think, dream, cry and shout. In short, it has to be Indianized. Poets and writers have made a number of experiments in this direction. G.V. Desani, Joseph Furtado and Ezekiel have been bold enough to write some poems in pidgin English, imitating the typical features of English used by Indians:

> If you are coming again this side by chance, Visit please my humble residence also. I am living just on opposite house's backside.[7]

Parthasarthy rightly points out that pidgin English is not part of the spoken idiom in India as it is in Nigeria.[8] Hence, here the attempts of Furtado and Ezekiel cannot go beyond parody. There have also been attempts to retain the original word rather than replace them with their English equivalents. The Nigerian writer Wole Soyinka has done it, so has Daruwalla. Words like *ghat*, *panda*, *amavasya*, *banjaras*, *Chaitra*, *salagram*, *ashram*, *bhog*, *semul*, *yakshas*, and many more occur frequently in his poems. More often they are not even italicized. In fact they are used like English words—an 's' is added to denote the plural in banjaras and yakshas. That this is not just a matter of 'certain tricks and gimmicks'[9] would be clear from the poem quoted below:

> I tire of superstitions:
> the *asoka* blossoms only
> at the touch of the beloved's feet;
> the *babula* must be splashed
> with rinsed wine from her mouth;
> the *tilaka* must be hugged
> and the *amaranth* should get a glance from her
> before leaf turns green
> or the *petals* colour.
> I quicken into flower
> at the memory of your touch.[10]

Had Daruwalla used the English names for the trees the Indian superstitions would have lost their original flavour and tone.

All these are strategies of subversion and appropriation. These smaller details go to prove the fact that language is a marker of identity and a carrier of culture. This is what Raja Rao meant when he said that 'we cannot write like the English' and also that 'we cannot write only as Indians'. It is true that there was a lot of politics behind introducing English education in India. It was part of the imperialists' design to justify colonialism and pose as humanists. Macaulay's infamous minute of 1835 defended the introduction of English education at the cost of indigenous literatures saying that 'a single shelf of a good European library was worth the whole native literature of India and Arabia'. Naturally, then the Indians who started writing in English began with daffodilizing their landscapes after the English models. But literature cannot remain alienated from reality for long. As the sense of nationalist self-assertion took root, the power and self-esteem could be read in the language which rejected the colonial culture. Raja Rao, while carving out a place for himself which is relatively free from imperial dictates, does accept the presence of the English influence when he says that 'we cannot write only as Indians'. Kamala Das rejects the colonial presence outright when she says that '...the language I speak / Becomes mine'.[11] The next phase that followed was one of the development of the indigenous idiom when the colonized writer is able to appropriate the English language to communicate his/her own cultural experience. This is what the chutney—English of Salman Rushdie has achieved. He has been able to, in the words of Frantz Fanon, 'construct liberating narratives of decolonization'. *The Empire Writes Back* and writes back with a vehemence. *Midnight's Children* is considered the model post-colonial novel and has influenced a whole generation of writers and critics. This is what Meenakshi Mukherjee says about the impact of the novel:

> In retrospect, we see that Midnight's Children had a very important role to play in the reversal of the 'centre-periphery' paradigm in English literary culture, in dissolving the great

> tradition of F.R. Leavis into a plurality of traditions coming from many races, many regions, many cultures....[12]

This brings us to a very crucial subject, that of criticism. How are the New literatures to be judged? So far standards of judgment have been Euro centric. And with the spread of English education all over the globe the British Empire succeeded in establishing English Literature as the normative referent. Even today, the criteria for judgment are constructed and determined by the needs and demands of the receiving culture. But, I refer to the words of Kamala Das again, if the language is mine how can the standards of judgment be theirs? This much is clear that no single paradigm is adequate. It has already been established that the resources of a rich language like English are too varied to be exhausted by a single nation. It then follows that criticism too should be marked by a completeness of responses—Western as well as Oriental. Chinua Achebe, for instance, reacted strongly to Dylan Thomas's comment that *The Palm Wine Drunkard* is 'a tall, devilish story' and says:

> The reader may, of course, be so taken with Tutuola's vigorous and unusual prose style or beguiled by that felicitous coinage, 'drinkard' that he misses the social and ethical question being proposed: What happens when a man immerses himself in pleasure to the exclusion of all work; when he raises pleasure to the status of work and occupation and says in effect: 'Pleasure be thou my work!'?[13]

He, therefore, adds:

> Tutuola is weaving more than a tall, devilish story. He is speaking strongly and directly to our times. For what could be more relevant than a celebration of work today for the benefit of a generation and a people whose heroes are no longer makers of things and ideas but spectacular and insatiable consumers?[14]

An important poser in both Africa and India has been regarding the use of English for creative purposes. Why English at all? This question has been asked again and again. In Africa, Ngugi has gone so far as to switch over to writing in Gikuyu and abandon English altogether and has even proposed the abolition of the Department of English. But is English any longer the language of the English alone. It has risen to the stature of a world language. And can there be any animosity towards any language? One may be averse to a people and their ways, certainly not to a language. In R.K. Narayan's *The English Teacher* the hero Krishna rebels against the methods of English teaching calling it a 'whole century of false education', but venerates English Literature: 'What fool could be insensible to Shakespeare's sonnets or 'The Ode to the West Wind'?'[15] Besides, there are many in India who due to their English upbringing and education could not have written in any language but English. So it is not just a question of the man choosing the language but also the language choosing the man.

It is, however, true that post-colonial studies ignore the indigenous literatures. In India, for instance, the writings in the Indian languages may prove to be more than a match to the writings in English, both in quantity and quality. To this, the writers of *The Empire Writes Back* respond in a typical imperialist manner:

> This may well be the case, though until much more extensive translations into english from these languages have been produced it is difficult for non-speakers of these languages to judge.[16]

To this, Leela Gandhi shoots back the question: 'but what does judgment refer to here—what is being judged and by whom?'[17] The centre stands to judge only because the empire writes back to it. It falls then on the post-colonial writers to shift the focus and stop writing back to the centre. In spite of writing in English—an indigenous English of course, an English with a small 'e', the writers need not write back to the centre and colonialism and nationhood need not remain the central issue any more. Other diverse and complex problems like the disintegration of older social orders and challenges to patriarchy posed by the women, the subalterns, and the themes of diaspora and migrancy need to be looked into. It is these and various other pressures that reorient the New Literatures—I deliberately use the term 'new literatures' in place of post-colonial literatures because it is high time we are done with the colonial hangover.

NOTES

1. Maxwell, D.E.S. Quoted in *The Empire Writes Back: Theory and Practice in Post-colonial Literatures* by Bill Ashcroft, Gareth Griffiths and Helen Tiffin, Routledge, London and New York, 1989, p. 24.
2. Tutuola, Amos. *The Palm Wine Drinkard*, Faber & Faber, London, 1990, p. 7.
3. Ngugi wa Thiong'o. *Decolonizing the Mind: The Politics of Language in African Literature,* James Currey, London, 1986, pp. 15-16.
4. Ngugi wa Thiong'o. 'Preface', *Writers in Politics*, Heinemann, London, 1981.
5. Achebe, Chinua. Quoted by C.D. Narasimhaiah, *Essays in Commonwealth Literature: Heirloom of Multiple Heritage*, Pencraft International, New Delhi, 2005, p. 38.
6. Rao, Raja. 'Foreword', *Kanthapura*, Orient Paperbacks, New Delhi, 1970.
7. Ezekiel. 'The Professor', *Latter Day Psalms*, O.U.P., New Delhi, 1982, p. 24.
8. Parthasarthy, R. (ed.), 'Introduction', *Ten Twentieth Century Indian Poets*, O.U.P., New Delhi, 1976, p. 9.
9. Naik, M.K. *A History of Indian English Literature*, Sahitya Akademi, New Delhi, 1982, p. 290
10. Daruwalla. 'The Round of the Seasons', *Landscapes*, O.U.P., New Delhi, 1987, p. 35.
11. Das, Kamala. 'An Introduction', Narasimhaiah, C.D. (ed.) *An Anthology of Commonwealth Poetry*, Macmillan India, 1990, p. 47.
12. Mukherjee, Meenakshi. 'The Perishable Empire', *Essays on Indian Writing English*, O.U.P., New Delhi, 2000, pp. 76-77.
13. Achebe, Chinua. *Hopes and Impediments*, Heinemann, London, 1990, p. 69.
14. *Ibid.*, p. 75.
15. Narayan, R.K. *The English Teacher*, Indian Thought Publication, Mysore, 1955, pp. 220-21.
16. *The Empire Writes Back*, p. 121.
17. Gandhi, Leela. *Postcolonial Theory: A Critical Introduction*, O.U.P., New Delhi, 1998, p. 163.

Anglophone Cameroon Poetry: Poetics and the Politics of the New Deal

13

John Nkemngong Nkengasong

Cameroon is a central African country which achieved independence in 1960 with a dual colonial heritage of the English and the French. Following the 1961 United Nation sponsored plebiscite in which the Anglophones of Southern Cameroon joined the Francophone Cameroon, the two colonies were supposed to be governed as two autonomous states within a federal system. But the influence of Ahmadou Ahidjo who ruled the country from independence to 1982, and later Paul Biya who has ruled the country from 1982 to the present, has been overwhelming in thwarting the conditions for the union between the Anglophone state and Francophone state. Thus, for over four decades Anglophone Cameroonians have been considered as the inferior other because of their 20% minority status, a situation which has raised a serious issue famously known in Cameroon as the "Anglophone problem". It is for this reason that Anglophone Cameroon writing, particularly its poetry is so radical, especially that which was written in the so-called "New Deal" era which succeeded the Ahidjo regime.

The circumstances surrounding Ahidjo's precipitated resignation in 1982 still remains a major puzzle not only to political analysts but also to literary enthusiasts. There was however, a general sense of relief at the time with the fact that Cameroon was moving from a reign of terror to what his successor termed the "New Deal". In applying the expression, "New Deal" Ahidjo's successor wanted to show a clear break from the tyrannical past masterminded by his predecessor. The

"New Deal" therefore, was baptized with political slogans like "Rigour and Moralization" which were expected to be the guiding principles for the thorough cleansing of the society which, according to the proponents of the New Deal, was rendered hopeless and inarticulate by the Ahidjo regime. With the assertive promises of the New Deal regime, Cameroonians hoped to find in the new dispensation positive reconstruction of the society and its politics.

The flourishing of literature within this period, especially Anglophone Cameroon literature is a demonstration of that zeal and hope to find in the new republic the freedom of expression that had been stifled in the regime before it. Anglophone Cameroon writers saw this not only as an opportunity to reconstruct the Cameroonian past and provide alternative visions for the future but also to reassert their colonial identity as an Anglophone state in a federal republic. Cameroon Anglophone poetry in particular offers a more distinctive perception of the new deal era than any other genre written within this period. The poets have expressed a lot of concern with regard to the historical moment and elaborated in their works the paradox of political propaganda and the demise of historical and social justice in the era.

This essay thus attempts a discussion of Anglophone Cameroon poetry, its preoccupations, obsessions and visions within the New Deal era. It is approached from the New Historicist perspective which according to Raman Selden and Peter Widdowson tries to establish the interconnections between literature and the general culture of a period. What Selden and Widdowson imply is that all history is foreground. Consequently, literary works should be regarded as texts amongst other texts, not just the "sublime and transcendent expression of the 'human spirit'" (162-63). This means that Anglophone Cameroon poetry can be better understood if its poetics, implying its textuality, meanings and effects are interpreted in relation to the socio-political, historical and cultural conditions of its production. From the perspective of John McLeod, the analysis attempts to situate the poems in history "by exposing how historical contexts influence the production of meaning within literary texts and how literary representations themselves have the power to influence their historical moment" (38).

Apart from enacting in poetic form the histo-political moment Anglophone Cameroon poetry also fits comfortably on the grounds of postcolonial discourse. A clearer conceptualization of postcolonial literatures which fits the context of this study is that by Alexandra Lewis who states that: "...postcolonial literatures and theories engage in unlocking unspoken, unheard or silenced pasts (of individuals, communities, genders, nations) thus expanding the scope of possibility for culturally and politically viable presents and futures" (93). Postcolonialism is built on the framework of discourse about those who inherited the colonialists.

Because of the oppression, the marginalisation and the attempts to suppress their colonial heritage by their majority Francophone counterparts, Anglophone Cameroon poets are more overt preceptors and critics of the regime and raise in addition antagonistic issues related to Cameroon's second leadership after independence in 1960. Anglophone Cameroon poets can comfortably be divided into two groups—the early and later poets. The first group of poets like Bole Butake, Bate Besong, Ngong Kum Ngong, Babila Mutia, Nol Alembong and John Nkemngong Nkengasong (including those who wrote in the Fonlonian era from 1955-82) were those who wrote some of their major poems from 1982 to 1990. The later poets who wrote from the 1990 were influenced either by the precipitating degeneration of the economy and social life of the Cameroonian people, the wave of democratic change that swept through Africa and the world or the intensive subjugation of Anglophones by the francophone compatriots.

The first group of Anglophone poets celebrated political renewal in Cameroon and joined the bandwagon, to use Abiola Irele's words, in "rejoicing the unmasking of the political legitimacy in post colonial Africa, the rupturing of an oppressive system, due to a profound movement of the collective unconscious" (302). Bate Besong is one of Anglophone Cameroon's most prolific and daring poets, was one of those poets who rejoiced the unmasking of Ahidjo's political legitimacy. His poem, "The Party's Over" for example, is a celebration of the end of that gruesome and horrifying past expressed with a great sense of relief:

> Long we have listened to the howl of human misery
> The dying voices from that human world below:
> Filling the gaps
> Of the distant exultations...
> Ah! In those days there was fear
> Booming loud and long in every skull
> We thought you and I;
> That it would always be like this.
> (*The Grain of Bobe Ngom Jua*, 15)

One notices in the lines an inherent expression of tragic relief in a poet who hoped (as most Cameroonians hoped) that the New Deal regime was going to provide the glories of independence absent in the long years of misery in the Ahidjo's reign.

But this was not going to be the case. It turned out that just within two years of the existence of the regime Anglophone Cameroon poets were actually celebrating the transition from tyranny to anarchy, political buffoonery, social insecurity, dictatorship, incarceration, torture, the marginalization and exploitation of Anglophone Cameroonians, the fleeing of the youths to Europe and America as a result of hardship (bushfalling), embezzlement and squandermania by government officials, and moral bankruptcy. The poets express their disillusionment with severe poetic indignation especially dictated by the searing irony of political propaganda against the background of its terrible practical contradictions.

Having discovered that he had been tricked by his postcolonial mentors to relinquish power to his successor, Ahidjo attempted to regain power through the diabolic resources of his most reliable aide, Captain Salatou. This was clearly the advent of a new era of horror and socio-political anarchy. Shortly after, the abortive coup d'état in the April of 1984, organized by some disgruntled followers of Ahidjo posed a new threat to the peace and freedom Cameroonians had for so long anticipated.

In the poems written after the events of April 1984, "April 1984" and "The Iron Swallows are Gathering" Bate Besong portrays the new threats in what he refers to as "vengeful massacre" and "pointless butchery", "bangs of mortar" and "outcries of woe", "the horrible anthems of everlasting cavalries". In "Facsimile of a Jackal", the poet penetrates the darkness through exquisite use of imagery suggesting death, misery and horror. Added to these "novel horrors" are the floating ridiculous promises masterminded by the authors of the New Deal. Their dexterity in embezzlement, capital flight and misappropriation of state revenue literally brought the nation to her knees and saddled Cameroonians with poverty which was going to be the new harbinger of untold hardship, wretchedness and languor for more than two decades after. Bate Besong attacks the authors of the New Deal in a rather satirical poem titled "Makers of a New Society" with the scurrility of Wole Soyinka:

They will exchange
Planes
In the midair
To further the exchequers of
Multinational corporations.
(*The Grain of Bobe Ngom Jua*, 20)

Besides Bate Besong, the other poet who clearly signals the end of the Age of Fonlon and who overtly criticizes the misdemeanour of the new regime is Nol Alembong in his collection of poems titled, *The Passing Wind*. His vision of the New Deal is that of rot, moral decadence, filth and poverty. From the viewpoint of Marxist dialectical materialism he projects in the poem titled "May Day" the lamentable gulf that exists between the "eagle-eyed manager" and the "tantalized serf" of the erstwhile estate that would have been referred in modern terms as a nation. While the "serf" who represents the labourer and who does enchant his "manager" by sinking into the "pit of serenade", while the "employee", the one hired to provide security for the "manager" parades the "scarlet balcony". The phenomenon, as explained by Paul Tiyambe Zeleza, is that elsewhere in Africa the rationality of the postcolonial state "rested in promoting and sustaining accumulation for the indigenous bourgeoisie as well as the ever present imperialist predator" (480-81).

The metaphors of the "serf" and "manager" are clearly representative of the New Deal postcolonial status. The "serfs" sing panegyric songs in spite of themselves. They love

To hear their coarse voices
Shower gold dust on the master's head
For having opened their eyes to
The beauty of squalor. (15)

The "beauty of squalor" expresses the very horrible paradox of new democracies. The paradox hinges on the metaphor—"squalor"—to demonstrate the excellence of putrefaction, filth, corruption and consequent poverty which is representative of the New Deal era.

John Nkemngong Nkengasong views the New Deal era from his own perspective. From the sustained languor and wretchedness imposed on the people by the unholy New Deal regime, the poet issues an indignant cry in a poem, "Wailing in the Jungle":

Will no one listen to the silent cries
from homesteads choked
with th'offending midnight breeze
of blood...?
Walk down the Mungo's shores
Nyieh! See the giant's silver coat
shimmering in the morning glare
and is want of drink
the humble's cry?
(*Cameroon Life*, 47)

This concern about scarcity and want is carried forward by the younger Anglophone poets in a more elaborate manner with a view to soliciting change in the degenerating society.

The 1990s and the first decade of the twenty-first century have produced in Anglophone Cameroon a series of angry poets who saw in the wake of the so-called democratic change not only the perpetration of embezzlement and political buffoonery but also a terrible betrayal of the honest citizens by the powers that be. Poets like Ebini Atems in his collection of verse *Partners in Prison*, Emmanuel Doh's *Wading in the Tide*, G.N. Gwangwa'a's *Cry of the Destitute*, and Mathew Takwi's *People Be Not Fooled*, John Ngong Kum Ngong's *Walls of Agony*, are committed poets who portray the socio-cultural and political predicament of their people with overwhelming poetic indignation. As the titles of the their poetry collections suggest, the society of the old decade as portrayed is horrifying, with the forces of oppression very much alive, with excesses of power abuse, harassment, beatings, looting and killing of innocent citizens against the background of hypocritical slogans and propaganda. In this kind of system, execution is rife. Merciless execution or incarceration awaits anyone who ventures to criticize the hollowness and buffoonery of leadership.

The theme of oppression is recurrent in Gwangwa'a, Atem, Doh and Ngong Kum Ngong. John Ngong Kum Ngong deviates to some extent from the poets who published after the 90s. The grandeur of his recent collection of poems titled Walls of Agony lies not in the raw and evocative feelings that characterise poets like Mathew Takwi but in the poet's subtle use of language and the veneration of the poetic image. The striking unity of Walls of Agony is reinforced by the recurrent metaphor—walls. The walls can be conceived as walls of infamy and dungeons, walls of desecration, walls of social, psychological and political agony within which the masses have been subdued for years.

Mathew Takwi, on the other hand, heaves an indignant cry against moral bankruptcy, filth, violence, exploitation and squandermania in poems like "Varsity Filth", "My People Be Not Fooled" and "When We Shall Dance". He demonstrates the emotional turbulence of the young daring angry poets through a series of poignant metaphors which reveal the disgusting situation of the masses against the background of the affluence and nonchalance of their leaders. In the poem, "Redress", the poet expresses a yearning to meet the President, the symbol of postcolonial anarchy and mass agony, to redress him:

Now, I stride to meet the President
And to hit his glittering glass table
And pour venom into his face....:

You toy with the life of the masses
While their hardship embraces your messes. (5)

Fale Wache stands in a category of his own. He carries this general concern about hopelessness further to the expression of the lamentable predicament of the Cameroonian youth whose future is clouded in oblivion, uncertainty and hopelessness. He re-enacts in a long reflective poem, Lament of a Mother, what may be described as the "bushfaller" theme. That is, the plight of the youths who have fled into obscurity from the misery, uncertainty and wretchedness dictated by the New Deal society; the mass exodus of talented Cameroonian youths into voluntary slavery in Europe and America as the only alternative for survival.

Lament of a Mother is definitely one of the longest poems in the English language. It is not a narrative epic or dramatic poem like 'Beowulf' or Pope's 'The Rape of the Lock'. It is a meditative poem, a poem of sorrow and lament expressed in the manner of Okot p'Bitek's 'Song of Lawino'. The story of Lament of a Mother portrays the misery of a mother whose son abandons her for ages and goes to Europe and never returns:

Ndikochong, my son, my husband
My father, my all,
Thirty long years since you left us
Thirty weary years you've been away from us
Your silence sends daggers through my heart
I am miserable...
Ndikochong, my son, is it you
Who has done this to me?
Thirty years and the tears have
Flowed like the Kibin river at the
Peak of the rainy season.... (1)

Through an excellent blend of Noni oral tradition and the conventional versification of the English language Wache reveals the excruciating poverty that causes the disappearance of the youth and which in consequence cuts the ties between parents and children and provides fresh waves of misery in the New Deal era.

Many New Deal poets, especially of the late 90s and the early 2000 decry the maltreatment of Anglophone Cameroonians by their Francophone counterparts who are segregationists, and who look on the Anglophone Cameroonians as pariahs. The poets regret the fact that Anglophone Cameroonians are given second place positions in the administration; the Anglophone part of the country is not developed; their resources—oil, forests and other valuable minerals—are tapped to develop the French speaking regions. Above all, the poets express the political strain involved in coping with the Francophone mentality which is quite estrange from their British colonial heritage. In brief, the poets express a fiery indignation against a series of other galling indignities to which the Anglophone Cameroonian has been subjected.

The galling indignities are poetically evoked in Ngong Kum's poem "Admit Us O Brethren" in an earnest yet cynical appeal to the Francophone Cameroonians:

> Admit us the homeless, the wretched
> knocking on your doors, happy brothers
> knocking for crunches of stale bread
> knocking for recognition, pleading
> knocking to be remembered, hungry
> our hearts swollen with disappointment.
> (*In Search of a New World*, 10)

Gahlia Gwangwa'a is one of those poets whose bitterness about the Anglophone problem is very revealing. Many poems in his collection *Cry of the Destitute* dwell on this theme. For example, "The Imperfect Blend", "If an Anglophone Must Die", "Frogs With Us", etc., demonstrate the agonizing circumstances under which the Anglophones survive in the experimental bilingual country—Cameroon. In the face of the gruesome exploitation, the marginalization, harassment, torture and imprisonment by their Francophone counterparts Anglophone Cameroon leaders who dared raise their voices have been ruthlessly dealt with. Gwangwa'a instils confidence and hope in the folks by asking them to work towards a unified consciousness of their being:

It's a must that we work in unison.
Together we can stink like a bee
And we can sing that we're free
"frogs", Ah! We shall be
No more to be watered
("Frogs With Us", 23)

Gwangwa'a evokes the passion for Anglophone freedom with the intensity of tone that distances him from Mathew Takwi's restrained portrayal of Anglophone marginalisation in poems like "Les Ennemies dans la Maison", and "Twin Streams".

Tanure Ojaide has remarked that, "African literature is traditionally didactic. The writer in the modern-day Africa has assumed the role of the conscience of the society, reminding readers and society of the high cultural ethos that must be upheld" (43). This is the objective of Anglophone poets, especially imbued with the radical spirit of the 1990's when Cameroonians witnessed not only incarceration and murder but the corruption of all the moral fabrics of the nation. They depart distinctively from the mellifluous verse and quasi romantic subject matter of their Francophone compatriots through their critical integrity with the aim of causing the transgressors of socio-political ethics to become useful agents in the construction of the society. The manner of expression or the poetic form especially from the 1990's is quite estranged from the gentle, meditative, uncommitted and didactic poetry of the earlier era. The poets of the 1990s are revolutionary, outspoken and often satirical. Their ideas are expressed in varied forms of poetic expressions, with the concordant effect of line and stanzaic patterns, sound and figurative devices. The poets therefore demonstrate an inherent zeal for experimentation and the expression of their turbulent and revolutionary minds.

Far from mere expression of anger against political deficiency that has governed the Cameroonian society for over four decades, Anglophone Cameroon poets fit appropriately in their role as the acknowledged legislators of mankind. In other words, they do not only lambaste, satirize, lampoon and meditate on the plight of his compatriots. They suggest solutions to a more meaningful and harmonious existence through the idolization of nationalists and patriots, the veneration of spiritual essence no matter what form it takes, and in the sublimation of art. Some of the poets see in the idolisation of patriots and nationalists a means towards the attainment of the glories anticipated in Cameroon. These are patriots and nationalists like Bobe Ngom Jua, Ernest Wanji, and others who sacrificed their lives in the fight for glory for the oppressed people whose example, the poets believe if emulated by Cameroonians will place the masses on the pedestal of anticipated glory. When for example, Bate Besong cries out with so ethical a mind in the last but one stanza of "The Beauty of Exile":

Who will convert the broodings
Of these people over the past
Into bouquets of a new dawn?
("The Grain of Bobe Ngom Jua", 17)

one finds in him the earnest desire to reconstruct society, to create a new harmonious society sustained by the metaphor: "bouquets of a new dawn". To the poet, this can be achieved if people incorporate the spirit of Bobe Augustine Ngom Jua, who, in the context of Bate Besong's poetry is the symbol of justice. Jua is the visionary precursor of freedom and the greatest of all human needs—happiness. He is the symbol of conscience and commitment of the society's sane course. Therefore, in order to live a harmonious existence Bate Besong thinks that his spirit should be emulated:

He left behind
In those days, (there was sadness
In your cheeks)—all that time!
The grain to you who plough the prairies
Dread;
("The Grain of Bobe Ngom Jua", 26)

Gwangwa'a like Bate Besong encourages and glorifies those who work unreservedly for their country; those who leave behind some great achievement for mankind and those who have the courage to die for the ideals they cherish especially in an era when the spirit of patriotism and nationalism has been stifled, when no one feels protected by the nation or is willing to protect the nation anymore. In Gwangwa'a's *Cry of the Destitute*, he portrays the nationalists with so philosophical a mind:

Patriots Um Nyobe, Moumie,
Kingue, and of course Wandji
Takala, Wambo le Courent, et al
In their brothers' paid the supreme
Sacrifice.
("In Search of My People", 22)

The "supreme sacrifice" by the patriots is the sacrifice of their lives to tyrants. It is supreme because it involves insurmountable courage, grandeur, and selfless commitment in the effort to save the people from all forms of oppression in the system. From the experience of the patriots, Gwangwa'a cautions that "The biggest mistake in living / Is the fear of dying." Thus the poets encourage the spirit of self-sacrifice and the deployment of individual resources for the salvation of the society.

For Ngong Kum Ngong, the solution to the hotchpotch of the New Deal politics and its demeanour on the masses lies in the consciences of those who wield power, the selfless deployment of the artistic and visionary resources of the poet whom he symbolizes, and in the spiritual consciousness symbolized by Kezeh and Zekembi. The poet therefore constantly appeals to the spiritual order to provide him with wisdom, courage and determination through poetic vision to rescue the despondent masses:

I have come, immutable father,
To master how to resuscitate
And nourish the despondent with hope.
I have come omnipotent jurist
My mind overwrought, my heart beating,
Weighing my people's crushing wretchedness.
Help me help them invisible warrior.
("Help Me Help Them", 21)

Few writers in the contemporary literary dispensation in Cameroon have so earnestly emphasised the significance of the artist in the reconstruction of a better society and providing visions for the redemption of mankind as John Ngong Kum Ngong has done.

Having considered the major trends and the different socio-political and cultural perspectives from which the Anglophone Cameroon poet views his society in the New Deal era, it can be concluded that he is not glued to a single area of experience. Above all, he demonstrates unflinching commitment for the problems that hamper development of the society especially those created by the vestiges of colonization. The Anglophone Cameroon poet has come to the realization like other postcolonial writers that he is a tool for prosperous society. Confronted with the challenges of a dual postcolonial predicament (that posed by the colonial predators and that of his Francophone compatriot) he comes to an understanding that a genuine Anglophone Cameroon writer must not be the kind of writer Chinua Achebe describes in Morning Yet on Creation Day:

The African creative writer who tries to avoid the big social and political issues of contemporary Africa will end up being completely irrelevant-like the absurd man in the proverb who leaves his burning house to pursue a rat fleeing from the flames (78).

Some Anglophone Cameroon poets, however, have a number of weaknesses which include their inability to distinguish between poetry and prose, inappropriate application of the image, excessive indulgence in formalistic experimentation, and plain cowardice in the face of excruciating socio-political circumstances. For example, Sankie Maimo's escapist tendencies are very revealing in many of his love poems and even poems that treat political subject matter. Bole Butake and Nalova Lyonga write of the poet:

He [Maimo], as the poet protagonist either bears the knowledge of treachery in painful silence or escapes in exile, or recoils in endless torture from unsuccessful amoral relationships (128).

These weaknesses do not, however, obliterate the fact that there exists a huge body of literature in Anglophone Cameroon that clearly depicts national image for over forty years. Its subject matter, themes, images and leitmotifs are largely drawn from within a geographical setup shaped by an interrelated set of historical circumstances. As Buma Kor confirms: "Our problems today were identified by our poets long ago, but were not given the benefit of proper hearing" (63).

One can conclude, therefore, that the Anglophone poet is the most silent solitary visionary of the currents of his society from the falsity of independence through the unification process to the New Deal era, an era of the battered National Integration dream. From his vision and experiences we can construct more meaningful panoply of realities fundamental to the reconstruction of the society which in his opinion is depraved, egotistical and banal. Anglophone Cameroon Literature, therefore, responds to the call by Bate Besong, for greater commitment to both the Anglophone and the national cause when he writes:

> The Anglophone Cameroonian writer must never forget his origins. His writings must depict the conditions of his people, expressing their spontaneous feelings of betrayal, protest and anger.... That Literature must be inspired by an historical myth informed consciousness. It must embody in bold relief the specific historic features of the entire Cameroonian society. (*Anglophone Cameroon Writing*, 18)

The Anglophone Cameroon poet, therefore, handles postcolonial issues, especially in the New Deal era with exuberant poetical ingenuity. For, the grandeur of his poetry is not only in what it communicates but how it communicates; not so much what feelings or thoughts overflow the banks of the poet's mind but the patterns of the rendition of the thoughts and feelings; not so much the mystery which the words evoke but the mystical patterns of the woven word.

REFERENCES

Achebe, Chinua. *Morning Yet on Creation Day*. London: Heinemann, 1975.

Alembong, Nol. "May Day." *The Passing Wind*. Lagos: Association of West Africa Young Writers, 1991.

Ambanasom, Shadrach A. *Education of the Deprived: A Study of Four Cameroonian Playwrights*. Yaoundé: Presses Universitaires de Yaoundé, 2003.

Atems, Ebini. *Partners in Prison*. Bamenda: Patron Publishing House, 1995.

Besong, Bate. "Literature in the Season of the Diaspora: Notes to the Anglophone Cameroon Writer." *Anglophone Cameroon Writing: WEKA*. Vol. 1. Eds. Britinger, Bole Butake, and Nalova Lyonga. Bayreuth: Bayreuth University, 1993.

——. "The Party's Over." *The Grain of Bobe Ngom Jua*. Yaounde: A Drapoe Publication, 1986.

Bjornson, Richard. "National Literature and National Identity: The Case Study of Cameroon." *Epasa Moto*, 1.2 (1995).

Fru, Emmanuel Doh. *Wading in the Tide*. Bamenda: Patron Publishing House, 1995.

Gwangwa'a, G.N. *Cry of the Destitute*. Limbe: Nooremac Press, 1995.

Irele, Abiola. *The African Experience in Literature and Ideology*. Bloomington: Indiana University Press, 1990.

Kor, Bumar. "The Literature of the Hunchback." *Anglophone Cameroon Writing: WEKA*, Vol. 1. Eds. Britinger, Bole Butake, and Nalova Lyonga. Bayreuth: Bayreuth University, 1993.

Lewis, Alexandra. "Postcolonial Literatures and the Ongoing Process of 'Writing Back'". *Journal of African Literature and Culture: Reimaging African Literature*, 2 (2006), 93-116.

Lyonga, Nalova and Bole Butake. "Cameroon Literature in English: An Appraisal." ABBIA (Special Issue 1982), 121-74.

McLeod, John. *Beginning Postcolonialism*. Manchester and New York: Manchester University Press, 2000.

Ngong, Kum Ngong. *In Search of a New World*. Yaounde, 1985.

——. *Walls of Agony*. Yaounde: Editions CLE, 2005.

Nkengasong, John Nkemngong. "Wailing in the Jungle." *Cameroon Life*, 1.10 (1991), 47.

Ojaide, Tenure. "Modern African Literature and Cultural Identity." *African Studies Review*, 35.3 (Dec. 1992), 43-57.

Selden, Raman and Peter Widdowson. *Contemporary Literary Theory*. Kentucky: The University Press of Kentucky, 1993.

Takwi, Mathew. "People Be Not Fooled." Limbe: Design House, 2004.

Tchého, Isaac Célestin. "La carte littéraire du Cameroun." *La littérature camerounaise depuis l'epoque colonial*. Yaounde: Presses Universitaires de Yaoundé, 2004.

Wache, Fale. *Lament of a Mother*. Calabar: Blue Print, 1995.

Zeleza, Paul Tiyambe. "The Democratic Transition in Africa and the Anglophone Writer." *Canadian Journal of African Studies*, 28.3 (1994), 472-97.

Women as Victims: Manju Kapur's *Difficult Daughters* and *A Married Woman*

14

Malti Agarwal

"India has not been able to make the lives of the majority of its women secure" comments a correspondent of the *Frontline* (January 4, 2008). To some extent it is true. From womb to tomb Indian women face violent forms of gender bias. There has been escalation in violence against women in the past two decades. Daily newspapers, whether local or national, abound with the news of bride burning, dowry deaths, gang rapes, molestations, eve-teasing, female foeticide and so on. As far as domestic violence against women is concerned, efforts are being made on government and also on non-government levels to resist it. The Indian government has recently passed a bill against domestic violence similarly many women organizations and NGOs are making ceaseless efforts to curb this violence. Moreover, one more change is visible in this present social scenario, i.e. for as many women who are beaten, there are an equal number of women who refuse to be beaten yet till today physical violence has been recognized as an only form of violence. This sort of violence is often seen in the economically vulnerable families. Apart from these forms of physical violence women not only in India but world over undergo some other newer forms of violence. In middle class or upper middle class families, women are subjected to mental and emotional violence also for various socio-economic and cultural reasons. They face multiple forms of discrimination. They are deprived of many amenities which their male counterparts enjoy. Despite of the provision of the equal rights which our constitution ensures, a girl child does not get her due in the tradition bound Indian society. She is not recognized as an individual and thus her life becomes an unending tale of woe and suffering, devoid of love of her parents or of her husband.

Indian writers writing in English have largely delineated the multiple aspects of this gender-discrimination. The writers like Kamala Markandaya, Anita Desai, Shashi Deshpande, Nayantara Sahgal, Manju Kapur and others have painted a kaleidoscopic picture of this suffering lot. How these women react to the oppressing agencies is worth considering. If Kamala Markandaya's Rukmani in *Nectar in a Sieve* tolerates all injustices meekly, staying within her loveless marriage, the heroines of Anita Desai walk out of the loveless wedlock either by suicidal or homicidal attempts. The female protagonists of Shashi Deshpande, on the other hand, wade through mud of conjugal relationship in order to ultimately come upon self-realization. Manju Kapur's heroines—Virmati, Astha and Nisha—all strive for love in their loveless lives. The present paper aims at studying Manju Kapur's heroines—Virmati and Astha—who, certainly, do not suffer from physical violence but fall victims to emotional, mental and sexual violence.

Manju Kapur, a professor of English at Miranda House, Delhi till date has three novels to her credit—*Difficult Daughters, A Married Woman and Home*. Her maiden novel *Difficult Daughters*, which is set around the time of partition, is the story of a woman who fought for her independence, who in her search for love falls in love with a Professor—a man who is already married. The seventeen-year-old Virmati is torn between her duty towards her family and her desire for education and love. Born in a family of a jeweller, she soon becomes the 'second mother' of her siblings and also an attendant of her ever-pregnant mother. She is brought up in an atmosphere where the duty of a girl is to live for the family and get married as Kasturi, her mother, remarks, "Still it is the duty of every girl to get married" (13). A woman in such traditional families is not supposed to work since "a woman's shaan is in her home" (13). Virmati's urge to get education draws her towards her cousin, Shakuntala who is a teacher at Lahore and whose responsibilities are beyond a husband and children. But Kasturi, the symbol of the patriarchal agency in the text, does not like the life-style of this 'new woman', Shakuntala. "She's become a mem", Kasturi said disapprovingly "Study means developing the mind for the benefit of the family. I studied too, but my mother would have killed me if I had dared even to want to dress in anything other than was brought for me" (14). Defying the authority of her mother (patriarchy), Virmati joins A.S. College "the bastion of male learning". And finally her desire to be independent and to be loved traps her in Professor Harish Chandra's mesh of illicit love-affair. The emotional security which she could not find in her home finally dragged her into a whirlpool of misplaced emotions and she fell a victim to Professor's lust who, despite of being the father of two little kids, misguides her. Had Virmati been loved and cared and been emotionally secured with her parents, she perhaps would not have taken such a disastrous step. She revolts against the patriarchal set-up of her family which eventually culminates into her unwed pregnancy and in her becoming the second wife of the Professor who gives her the status of a pariah. Virmati's life moves like a pendulum of a clock to and fro. She represents thousands of Indian girls who are not free to choose a life-style of their own choice. Such girls in their pursuit of defying the patriarchal norm and asserting their individuality are misled. The protagonist of *Difficult Daughters*, Virmati, is the girl, caught in the flux of customs and fashions, aspirations and compulsions and tradition and modernity. She is torn between the physical urge and ethical sense. Finally, her preference to her physical urges portrays her as a new woman but soon this new woman is disillusioned when she finds Professor's wife Ganga pregnant for the second time. She gets hurt yet she bears it patiently as if she was "strong to bear the pain silently, without anyone knowing" (101). Her battle for independence creates lines of pain around her and she always finds herself dependent upon her husband emotionally and intellectually. Seema Malik rightly sums up Virmati's efforts of compromising and adjusting and suffering uncomplainingly, "To some extent she even conveys a personal vision of womanhood by violating current social codes yet she lacks confidence, self-control and foresightedness and is physically imprisoned with an underlying need to be emotionally and intellectually dependent on a superior force" (135). She strives for her autonomy and more she tries to be free, more she is tied in chains of relationship whether legal or illegal. The novel, thus, turns out to be a tale not of the difficult daughters but the difficult mothers. The daughters groan under the burden of social conventions and crave for freedom. Virmati's urge for education seems to be a means to get freedom from the bondage of patriarchy as Veena Singh writes, "For Virmati herself education is an escape...an escape from the reproaches of her family and her mother's silent disapproval" (165).

Manju Kapur's second novel *A Married Woman* is the story of an educated married woman, Astha who lives happily with her engineer husband and two little kids. Astha was born and brought up in a middle class family, bound by traditional mode of living. Like Virmati's mother, Astha's mother also thinks that a girl is born to be married and the parents' duty is to get their daughters married. She often declared, "When you are married, our responsibilities will be over, Do you know the shastras say if parents die without getting their daughter married, they will be condemned to perpetual rebirth"(1). In her novels, Kapur introduces either a man or a woman who provides substantial support to the protagonist. In *Difficult Daughters*, Virmati found Shakuntala quite friendly and supportive. In *A Married Woman*, Astha's father rises to Astha's support. He wants his daughter to get good education, do well academically and finally get a good job. He knows that "with good job comes independence" (4). However, Astha's parents believe in imparting their daughter the knowledge of the cultural heritage of India since they know that "Our shastras teach us how to live. You will learn from the Gita, the Vedas, the Upanishads" (27-28). Astha is, thus, brought up in a family ingrained in noble human virtues. She is married to a USA returned engineer, Hemant. They were tied in this nuptial knot not because they loved each other but because Astha, an Indian girl, an ideal grahluxmi could take care of Hemant's old parents. Hemant tells Astha, "I had responsibilities to my parents, I am the only son, and I wanted someone who would fit in with our family life. American women are too demanding. Their men have to cater to all their whims and fancies" (40). For sometime Astha lived happily due to the sole fact that "She was now a homemaker in her own right, a grown woman..." (37). A few months passed and soon Astha began to feel dull. No doubt, Kapur's heroines whether Virmati or Astha or Nisha accept a passive existence, discharge their domestic duties sincerely and uncomplainingly and create comfort for their men-folk. But Astha—the female protagonist of *A Married Woman*—soon realized the loneliness and dreariness of her married life. She freed herself from the mundane routine of a housewife who keeps waiting for her husband all day. How can such loveless marriage be the source of happiness? The novelist writes, "Astha's desire receded. She felt cold, dreary and distanced from him. She had been waiting for him all day, thinking of their being together, but nothing of this was reciprocated. He was a criminal, destroying her anticipation, ruining her happiness" (50). Now she realized that she had no business kneeling and taking off her husband's shoes. She took a teaching job which helped her to dispel the boredom which surrounded her.

Manju Kapur has raised multiple feminine issues in her novels. She minutely studies the dynamics of love-relationships in the life of the married couple and demystifies the age-old concept of marriage. To Kapur's heroines, marriage is not merely the union of two bodies but it implies the union of two persons on physical, mental and emotional levels too. Astha soon came out of the hallucinatory experiences of marriage when she noticed the changes that took place in their conjugal relationship with the passage of time. Hemant who used to respect women, enjoyed every aspect of his wife's pregnancy and wished to become the father of a baby girl suddenly became crazy for a son. He sounds like a traditional Indian husband when he clearly expresses his wish, "I want to have my son soon, 'declared Hemant, looking emotional and manly at the same time'. I want to be as much a part of his life as Papa-ji is of mine" (61). At this Astha asked, "How do you know we will have a son?" (61) Hemant answered, "Of course we will have a son, and if we don't stop at two" (61).

Being the only son, Hemant considered it his duty to give a son and heir, the carrier of the line the seed, the name. Finally Astha gave birth to a boy whose naming ceremony was carried out on a much grander scale than that of Anuradha's (68).

The novel moves on highlighting many other gendered issues such as the masculinity which suggests the dominance of the patriarchal mind-set of men folk. To Hemant his business is above all while Astha's teaching job is nothing. He said blatantly, "Oh—ho, what is there in teaching? Hardly a serious job, you just go, talk to some children about poems and stories, organize a few clubs, and come back" (68). Moreover, once an all-American father who didn't care about the sex of his first born child now changed to an all-Indian one who considered rearing of children a woman's job. Astha, thus, a single mother strived at domestic and professional levels as well. Kapur peers into the soul of her protagonist and finds in her the seeds of a 'new woman' who has strong urge for financial independence which may culminate in her freedom from social conventions which in Indian societies have become the behavioural norms. The novelist reports, "...between her marriage and the birth of her children, she too had changed from being a woman who only wanted love, to a woman who valued independence. Besides, there was the pleasure of interacting with minds instead of needs" (72). The economic independence won Astha self-confidence because now she need not ask Hemant for every little rupee she spent. She could spend money on herself—her jewellery, her clothes, etc. Nevertheless, loneliness in Astha's life escalates day by day. She says complainingly, "when I come home I want the children. I hardly have you, I should have them" (78). In her fits of depression, she begins to suffer from severe headaches. Eventually, the loveless marriage ends on estrangement between them where not only the wife feels lonely but the husband also complains of his loneliness: "I am the one who is lonely and without company", (79) says Hemant.

It's a global phenomenon that woman is supposed to be inferior to man and she has no say in important matters. Women, especially in India, are not considered as beings to be consulted. Astha's mother donated her husband's books without consulting her daughter. Astha got more hurt when her mother told her that it was Hemant's house and he said that there was no room for the books. Astha could not control her anger, "Then who am I? The tenant" (87). Women in traditional Indian milieu have been trained to create comfort for their children, husband and in-laws and if ever a woman transgresses these unwritten social code of conduct, she is rebuffed. Hemant teaches Astha the behavioural norms of a decent family woman, "You seem to forget that your place as a decent family woman is in the home, and not on the streets" (172).

Traditional thinking of males deprived womenfolk of their right and they are on and off marginalized. They cannot be free to complain as their husbands do rather they always try to be conciliatory. Astha's mother sold her plot and delivered money in the hands of Hemant as if it is the prerogative of men. Poor Astha had no say in what her husband did with that money. She didn't have any access to it.

Manju Kapur's novel *A Married Woman* abounds in various instances of the gendered roles which are prevalent in a conventions bound Indian society. Astha seemed to have a good life but it was good because she never questioned. Can such marriage be the source of bliss where the wife and husband are not equals but master and slave? Hemant, the husband of Astha, spent Astha's money on a plane ticket and that too without her consent. The upbringing of Hemant in a patriarchal set-up made him arrogant as he flatly refused Astha to buy an antique silver box, priced at five thousand rupees. Astha got hurt "The tone, the refusal both hurt her. She was an earning woman, why couldn't she have a say in how some of their money was spent?" (165). She said, "I also earn. Can't I buy a box if I want, even if it is a little overpriced?"(165) Hemant retorted angrily, "You earn! What you earn, now that is really something, yes, that will pay for this holiday" (165). Thus Astha and Hemant began to have emotional gaps and at last she could not get into his frustrations (caused due to problems in business) and he could not share her enthusiasm. Astha's mode oscillated between depression and elation.

Astha is in the state of flux. She, on the one hand, strives for her independence while, on the other, she tries to be conciliatory with her husband and her in-laws. Her husband objected to her going out of the house since it never brought her enough money. But Astha, on the other hand, was reluctant in leaving her job since it is a means to her to assert her identity. She wanted to earn money which would be her own though she knew it was contrary to the spirit of good marriages for a wife to hang on to things and say they were her own. Job to Astha represented security, not perhaps of money but of her own life, of a place where she could be herself. She wanted to emerge from the image of an ideal wife and ideal mother. She got sick of sacrifices (168). To her it was better to break a marriage where it turned to be terrible, where the wife and husband could not live on equal emotional and psychological plane.

Kapur minutely observes the mind-set of Indian men-folk to whom a woman is a slave, an unpaid servant. And in such societies often economic independence does not work. It cannot make women less trapped than those who are without job. It's a woman's lot to bear pain whether caused due to menstruation (as does Anuradha) or any social customs. A long speech delivered by Astha throws light on the lives of women in India. She started, "In essence women all over the world are the same, we belong to families, we are affected by what affects our husbands, fathers, brothers and children. In history many things are not clear, the same thing that is right for one person is wrong for another, and it is difficult to decide our path of action" (197). She adds, "We judge not by what people tell us, but by what we experience in our homes. And that experience tells us that where there is violence, there is suffering, unnecessary and continuous suffering" (197).

Astha's quest for identity led her to take part in politics, do painting and take interest in Aizaz. She refused to live the way people like her lived. She became assertive so much so that she didn't respond favourably to the sex routine. She said, "Then what? Do I have to give it just because you are my husband? Unless I feel close to you I can't—I'm not a sex object, you have others for that" (224). To her marriage is not simply sex but something which provides interest, togetherness and respect which she failed to enjoy in her marriage with Hemant. Sex without love is not acceptable to her. She wishes, "I have to feel it is me you want" (176). Eventually, Astha's search for love dragged her to lesbianism. She felt completeness with Pipee, "She thanked God again for this love in her life, when she had thought all chance of love was over" (235). And this love was a precious gift of God to her.

Like the heroines of Shashi Deshpande, the female protagonists of Manju Kapur also reach to self-realization at the end. Astha also realized how it was better not to advance into those murky waters. She went back to the image of a traditional and devoted wife and mother, she decided not to abandon her children and stay with her husband. She realized, "I live my life in fragments, she (Pip) is the one fragment that makes the rest bearable. But a fragment however potent, is still a fragment" (264). Her search of a safe place, a warm place, a loved place and a life of stability forced her to stay with her husband and children. Like Pipee she could be free, she knew if she wanted, she too had choices yet she stayed with Hemant with whom she always, "felt like a woman of straw, her inner life dead" (287).

A description of these novels of Manju Kapur shows that the novelist exhibits clearly how in Indian society marriage is not always a means of deliverance from social constraints nor it ensures a sense of security and certainty. The heroines—Virmati and Astha—struggle between head and heart and finally yearn for autonomy which takes them to be a part of the political and intellectual movements of the day, at times, they become aggressive but finally they turn to passive acquiescence since marriage in India means 'accommodation' and 'acceptance', as taught by Astha's mother in *A Married Woman*, "Accommodation and acceptance keep families together (83). She adds, "What you cannot change accept gradually, cheerfully as Prasad for the Lord. Create a home where you are. Such a person is free from sorrow. Every understanding requires composed mind. Worst thing in life is anger" (83-84). True only women in India are home makers. They are supposed to accommodate and accept even the worst thing in their lives they are not supposed to be sensitive towards the fraudulent and apathetic behaviour of their husbands. All such descriptions show the masculine superiority in India which no body can ever dare challenge and under whose burden women have been groaning for ages.

WORKS CITED

Kapur, Manju. *Difficult Daughters*. New Delhi: Penguin Books, 1998.

——. *A Married Woman*. New Delhi: India Ink, 2002.

Malik, Seema. 'Partition and Women writers: A Reading of Anita Kumar's *The Night of the Seven Dawns*, Mehr Nigar Masroor's *Shadows of Time* and Shauna Baldwin's *What the Body remembers?'*. *Discussing Indian Women Writers: Some Feminist Issues*. Ed. R.K. Dhawan and Mohini, New Delhi: Prestige Books.

Singh, Veena. 'How Difficult are Difficult Daughters? Sunlight on a Broken Column and Difficult Daughters as female Bildungsroman'. *Contemporary Indian Literature and Expositions*. Ed. Santosh Gupta. Jaipur: Rawat Publications, 2000.

Navigating Myth and Tradition in Feminist Emirati Poetics: An Intertextual Approach

15

Saddik M. Gohar

Introduction

Though she is not yet a popular poet in the sense that great numbers of people read her works, one could praise Saleha Obeid Ghabesh for the thematic diversity of her poetry, her brilliant use of language, her structural inventiveness and subtle depiction of Arab dreams and frustrations as well as her exploration of revolutionary feminist issues. In addition to its feminist perspective, the poetry of the female Emirati poet is imbued with lyricism and textual complexity that resist generic categorization. Besides an engagement with social and political issues, Ghabesh's poetry is characterized by its existential concerns and universal motifs which make it appealing to those interested in promulgating historical and universal pursuits. Since she is largely unknown in the Arabic literary canon, her poetry, particularly her anthology *Beman Ya Buthayn Taluthin* (2002) requires critical explication and analysis. Capturing the catastrophic history of the Arab world at present, the poet reconstructs episodes from the history of Islamic Andalusia engaging into intertextual dialogues with feminist Andalusian poetry in which narratives of exile, defeat and subordination occupy the foreground.

As a whole, Ghabesh's poetry examines reconsiderations of contemporary problems of domination and hegemony playing a conspicuously prominent role in the formation and dissemination of notions of reform on the political and feminist paradigms. Serving as a potential signpost in Emirati cultural criticism, her poetry attempts to abolish all distinctions between men and women in the Arab world as well as other binarisms that constitute a legacy of patriarchal ways of thinking. Incorporating feminist and social issues rooted in the collective consciousness of the Arab people, Ghabesh attempts to place contemporary Emirati poetry in the context of current transformations in global relationships linking local cultural discourses with the intellectual concerns and orientations originating at the central sites of western literary canons.

Therefore, one of the central features of Ghabesh's poetry is an extensive use of myth and legend adapted and recycled to incorporate themes of contemporary significance in modern Arab contexts. In her preface to *Ya Beman Buthayn Taluthin? / Who will Secure a Safe Haven for Buthayn?*, she establishes an analogy between herself and the Andalusian princess, Buthayna bint al-Mutamed, the central female voice in the anthology. The links between the Emirati poet and her Andalusian counterpart are subtle and intricate to the extent that "they become one personality, one woman" (Ghabesh 2002: 5). Apparently, the Emirati poet is interested in the eventful life of her predecessor, Buthayna, because "her biography includes myth and tradition" according to Ghabesh. The life story of Buthayna, the Andalusian princess and the daughter of al-Mutamed ben Abbad, the king of Seville, a city located in Southwestern Spain, is the central inspiration for the Emirati poet.

During the Muslim occupation of Southern Spain (Andalusia) which lasted more than seven hundred years (755-1492), Arabo-Muslim rulers established several kingdoms which were subsequently dismantled after the restoration of Spain. In the aftermath of the collapse of the Muslim empire and the loss of Andalusia, Buthayna's parents were exiled to Morocco, however, the princess and the harem in her father's palace were sold out in slavery. Unaware of Buthayna's royal origin, a slave merchant from Seville gave her as a present to his son but she rejects to surrender her body to him. After the revelation of her identity and noble descent, Buthayna gained the admiration of her captor who, due to her beauty and virtues, proposes to her. Falling in love with him because of his kindness and respect for her, Buthayna accepts the engagement but refuses to consummate their marriage until she gets the consent of her father, the exiled king. But since Buthayna's decision to marry the young Spaniard is considered as an enormous transgression which goes counter to the dictates of an Islamic patriarchal society, she decides to negotiate with her domineering father rather than to clash with him. Using her feminine powers of negotiation, she is able to gain the sympathy of her father who inevitably accepts her marriage from someone who belongs to the camp of the enemies.

Being aware of her father's fascination with eloquent poetry and being a poet herself, she sent him a captivating poem explaining her predicament and persuading him to bless her marriage:

> Do not deny my ordeal
> I was sold out into slavery
> it is God's will that the great
> king has lost his throne
> in the era of corruption
> we were separated to taste
> the flavor of distress
> when the forces of hypocrisy
> deprived my father of his kingdom
> we were forced to leave each other
> I attempted to escape
> but I fell into captivity. (cited in Ghabesh 2002: 8)[1]

The references to "the era of corruption" and "the forces of hypocrisy" allude not only to catastrophic events leading to the fall of the Arabo-Muslim dynasty in Andalusia but also to contemporary and similar circumstances threatening to disintegrate the Arab nation. After an exploration of her own ordeal, resulting from the collapse of her father's kingdom in Seville, Buthayna appeals to her parents to accept her marriage from the son of the Spanish slave merchant because she fell in love with him due to his sense of morality and good manners: "Dear father, I hope you bless our marriage / since he adores me / Dear royal mother, the descendant of kings / I hope you wish us happiness and good luck" (cited in Ghabesh 2002: 9).

According to the Emirati poet, Buthayna, who was sold out into slavery, "was able to win the battle for freedom and life" (Ghabesh 2002: 9). Moreover, Ghabesh reveals her personal admiration of Buthayna because she insisted on marrying the man she loved without violating the moral codes of her family and society.

The encounter with Buthayna's story, particularly her strength to convince her parents of her marriage from someone who belongs to the hostile tribe or the enemy state, makes a clear shift in Ghabesh's poetic orientation. In other words, the crux of *Beman Ya Bathayn Taluthin*? centers around a climatic incident—the Emirati poet's identification with Buthayna's narrative which had a profound impact upon her inner transformation. Functioning as a kind of metonymy for Ghabesh, Buthayna's story forced her to confront the repressive constructions of a contemporary male-oriented society with narcissus and hostile attitudes toward women. In her attempt to transcend the intersecting sites of oppression that Arab women experience, she challenges politics of sexual subjugation and discrimination based on race and class. Regardless of her condemnation of a patriarchal and phallocentric system, her attempt to change reality seems to be dedicated by an ever-respectful, non-violent feminine desire for a dialogue with the other which does not seek to appropriate or obliterate him. However, her preoccupation with the complexities of power relations in contemporary Arab contexts makes her poetry rich and challenging. Therefore, an appropriation of western feminist theories carried over into analysis of Arabic literature may lead to enormous evaluation of Ghabesh's poetics.

For example, the feminist critic, Debra Castillo, in her discussion of feminist literature, argues: "as far as I'm concerned, a work is feminist insofar as it attempts to explain the mechanics of cruelty, oppression and violence through a story that is developed in a world in which men and women exist" (Castillo 1992: 189). Obviously, the story of Buthayna with her parents and her experience of slavery constitutes a point of departure for the Emirati poet, preoccupied with a construction of feminist poetics able to confront current domestic challenges and international transformations sweeping the Arab world. In spite of belonging to different backgrounds and histories, Ghabesh and Buthayna share common experiences which undoubtedly yield a more grounded, more incisive feminine implications and signifiers. In other words, there are common ties which bind Buthayna and the Emirati poet together in relation to their feminine heritage but they also have in common the shared history of subordination. Exploring the power of Buthayna as a symbol of female rebellion against patriarchal authority, Ghabesh, in a parallel process, probes a culture that seeks to mute her banishing her outside human history.

Engaging into dialogues with Buthayna, the Emirati poet is able to hear her voice, speak to her and the voice answers in return. The moment of epiphany in *Beman Ya Buthayn Taluthin?* is Ghabesh's realization that Arab women will inevitably be able to gain their freedom if they follow the example of Buthayna refusing to become part of the historical ghetto—the harem mentality perpetuated by a patriarchal culture. In this context, Buthayna's voice becomes the voice of the oppressed women in the Arab world functioning as a trope, a refuge and creating a tone of familiarity and intimacy which gives Ghabesh the authority to link her own history with the ancient/feminist Andalusian tradition. Like Buthayna, Ghabesh's existential anguish is originated in the dialectics between her desire to be released from a patriarchal culture and her fear from the consequences of revolt against a tribal tradition which subjugates the female for a long time. Encouraged by Buthayna's treatment of her ordeal, Ghabesh questions the patriarchal/tribal assumptions which shaped her life penetrating into the core of a tradition that seeks to banish the female subaltern outside the realm of humanity.

Intertextuality, Tradition and Transcultural Literature

The use of the Andalusian heritage and mythology in Ghabesh's poetry brings to the forefront the issue of intertextuality as an aspect of a transcultural literature that transgresses linguistic and cultural boundaries and disciplinary barriers. Explicitly, the term intertextuality was introduced for the first time in 1929 by Mikhael Bakhtin, in his book *Problems of Dostoevsky's Poetics*, which contains a collection of essays. The concept was developed in 1981 in Bakhtin's study *The Dialogic Imagination* where he argues that the functional text is a hybrid entity, not a single whole, it is a composite amalgamation of a variety of formulae (Bakhtin 1981: 76). Bakhtin's argument in *The Dialogic Imagination* advances the theory of intertextuality underlying the existence of a dialogue between the writer and early writers not just between texts as subsequent theorists such as Roland Barthes seemed to think. At the core of Bakhtin's theory lies an equation between a writer and other writers, a text and other texts in addition to a kind of human participation integral to the dialogues taking place between writers.

Historically, it is relevant to argue that T.S. Eliot was a precursor of the theory of intertextuality. As an advocate of allusiveness and interextuality, Eliot, in "Tradition and Individual Talent", underlines the temporal relationship of one writer with other writers and of one text with others. Eliot argues that the literary heritage of nations forms an organic whole and no single poet is able to make a complete meaning alone because his/her genius is the result of other works: "the most individual parts of work may be those in which the dead poets, his [her] ancestors, assert their immortality most vigorously" (Eliot 1972: 71). Therefore, poets should work within tradition described by Eliot in "The Function of Criticism" as paradigms or "systems in relation to which, individual works of individual artists have their significance" (Eliot 1972: 77).

From a theoretical perspective, intertextuality designates vast and undefined discursive spaces and it is a way to "dissipate the many ambiguities and errors such as those brought alone in the wake of the notion of influence" (Guillen 1993: 244). In the same context, Jay Clayton and Eric Rothstein point out that in modern critical canons, the premise of influence contingent upon the author or authorial intentions and background is substituted by the concept of intertextuality (Clayton & Rothstein 1991: 3). In addition to the aforementioned argument, intertextuality is a two-sided issue and the intertextual explication of a contemporary text with references to an old one should illuminate both texts because the knowledge of the old text supplements the understanding of its contemporary counterpart. Thus, prior knowledge of both texts are central for the reader in order to create analogies and bring to focus parallel connections and common issues. Therefore, it is convenient to compare a text, for explicatory purposes, with other texts by the same author or other authors from the present or the past taking into consideration inherent affinities and intertextual comparabilities. On this basis, Jonathan Culler identifies intertextuality as a literary technique dealing with specific analogies and establishing linkages between texts:

> Intertextuality is less a name for a work's relation to particular prior texts than a designation of its participation in the discursive space of a culture. Study of intertextuality is not the investigation of sources and influences as traditionally conceived, it casts its net wider to include anonymous discursive practices, codes whose origins are lost, that make possible the signifying practice of later texts. (Culler 1981: 103)

In a related context, Roland Barthes identifies the literary text as network of "multiple writings" which come from a variety of sources and discourses already in circulation in some form or other. To him, the writer is a synthesizer who deliberately reworks and echoes other texts because "the text is a tissue of quotations drawn from the innumerable centers of culture" (Barthes 1977: 146). Moreover, an intertextual study of two texts or more in terms of their allusive connections may not always lead to a full understanding. Thus, the domain of intertextuality extends beyond the limits of time, place, acquaintance, allusions and influence. The intertextual closeness between a text and another may be determined by their exploration of similar issues, projection of identical motifs, portrayal of similar characters, depiction of parallel situations and treatment of common problems. As expression of resembling themes, the texts, approached from an intertextual perspective, may be close or remote in time and place and the authors may or may not have alluded to or influenced by or even heard about each other. According to Paul Ricour,

> each text is free to enter into relation with all the other texts which come to take the place of circumstantial reality referred to by living speech. This relation of text to text engenders the quasi-world of texts of literature. (Ricour 1981: 149)

The Use of Andalusian Narratives as Intertext in *Beman Ya Buthayn Taluthin*?

Since texts resist simple clear-cut interpretations, Ghabesh's poetic discourse in *Beman Ya Buthayn Taluthin*? is revelation of intersections of motifs, narratives and myths integral to the Islamic literary tradition in Andulasia (ancient Spain). In her anthology, Ghabesh aesthetically transforms Andalusian history into a contemporary poetic construct incorporating Andalusian literature as intertext to explore political and social issues of great significance. An intertextual reading of Ghabesh's poetry provides an entry into her appropriation of Andalusian cultural heritage as a vehicle to express the dilemma of contemporary Arab history. Reflecting a range of trans-textual relationships with Andulasian culture and highlighting significant thematic parallels which link the past with the present, Ghabesh creates a hybridized poetics deeply rooted in classical traditions. In her attempt to reshape Andalusian historical narratives into a revolutionary dynamics, the Emirati poet attempts to develop a counter feminized mechanism to subvert a decadent patriarchal culture which drags the Arab world backward toward the Stone Age. In her feminist poetry, Ghabesh attributes contemporary deterioration and recurrent defeats integral to modern Arab history to the same hegemonic system which gives birth to the Arab patriarchal tradition.

In Ghabesh's opening poem "Do not deny that I was sold out into slavery / La tunkiro anny sobeit", the poet evokes the themes of female subordination and sexual slavery linking the past with the present in a unique poetic structure. The title is explicitly quoted from Buthayna's poem to her father, the ex-king of Seville when she appeals to him to approve her marriage from a man who descends from European origin. The analogy between Buthayna's story and the argument of the female persona, in Ghabesh's aforementioned poem, reveals common concerns about women's freedom and human rights. The Emirati poet's incorporation of the Andalusian narrative functions as a cry of anger in the face of a repressive tradition and a submissive society which attempt to marginalize the female subaltern. In this context, the Andulasian legend is reshaped to serve as a call for reform and social change in the Arab world. Subsequently, Ghabesh's poem becomes a cry within a cry against a decadent culture which robs women of their innocence and little dreams. Using myths and symbols acquired from Andulasian history, the poet enhances the central features of the poem by incorporating imagery and metaphors of anxiety and sorrow:

Taken as a captive
as if I were part of a language[2]
inconceivable to the passersby
whose statutes are formed
by the flames of an arid fire
and a storm dying on our distress
taken as a captive
as if I were a fading night
approaching sunrise but
my appearance is denied
by the rising morning
forcing me to regress into my cloak
scolding me:
"this morning is not for you".
(Ghabesh 2002: 14)

Utilizing a complex pattern of legends and symbols borrowed from Andalusian history, Ghabesh expresses her vision of female enslavement and displacement through allusive references which enrich the thematic range of the poem. The recurring references to aridity, death, distress, captivity and enslavement motifs in addition to themes of denial and regression underline the extreme pain and suffering inflicted on women in repressive societies:

Here I buried the tears
of my patience dispersing
the leaves of promises
that scorn my fidelity
I was gradually turned into

an ice statute, colonized
by the frost of my naïve expectations (14)

The female persona in the above-cited lines describes an experience of great agony in which the female body is colonized by a masculine structure and her humanity is violated by a patriarchal tradition until she is transformed into a statute of ice. In a poem comprising allusions and references to Andalusian narratives of oppression and revolt and standing as a testimony of contemporary patriarchal hegemony, the poet transforms history into a feminist construct interrelated with other tales of female persecution:

The Andalusian nights are making a confession
but there is no one to hear
all the maids and servants are gone
departing the kingdom of al-Mutamed
accompanying him to his Moroccan exile
surrounding his defeated throne
setting it in order
and filling his Diaspora palace
with wounded songs which
turn into tears in Buthayna's eyes (15)

Engaging themes of defeat, exile and exodus, the poet apparently points out that the Arab rulers did not draw moral lessons from their ancient history in Spain or elsewhere: "the Andalusian nights are making a confession/but there is no one to hear". The fall of the Muslim dynasty in Andalusia, accelerated by Arab-Arab wars and conspiracies, is considered as a turning point in Arabo-Islamic history. Therefore, the explicit references to "the Andalusian nights", the "defeated throne", the "Diaspora palace" and "the wounded songs" not only recall the collapse of the Muslim empire in Andalusia but also hint at further losses at present: 'All hearts turn into wooden soldiers / safeguarding the palace of al-Mutamed / the Andalusian nights make a confession / in languages written with hybrid letters / and glorified by the advocates of treason' (15).

Evoking the loss of Andalusia and the exodus of the Arabs from Spain in the fifteenth century, the Emirati poet predicts the emergence of more catastrophes at present, as long as the Arab region is dominated by a repressive/patriarchal tradition which ignores the female subaltern traditionally considered as a second class citizen. Using images of humiliation and defeat as a metaphoric equivalence of contemporary Arab history, the poet links the tragic consequences of female oppression and subordination in the Arab world with other aspects of backwardness and defeat on the political paradigm. For example, the recurrent allusions to the political corruption associated with the Arab kingdoms in Andalusia bring to the forefront the dictatorial/oppressive policies advocated by contemporary Arab regimes. While the Arab-Arab conflicts in ancient Spain brought about the fall of the Arab dynasties in Andalusia, contemporary Arab policies of oppression and the rising dictatorial regimes, in the era of post-colonization, were responsible for Arab defeats and the loss of Palestinian territories. Apparently, Ghabesh incorporates Andalusian history to invoke new assumptions using a poetic language which cuts across myth and history.

Nevertheless, the strength of her poetry lies in the way in which she manages to push aside unnecessary details removing the arbitrary and the accidental. Confronted by a society battered by humiliation and defeats and a culture mutilated by patriarchal constructs, she attempts to restore a world out of ruins. Castigating a world at odds with the modern concepts of equality, freedom and democracy, the poet wants the current way of life radically charged, if not completely destroyed. This process of destruction of male-oriented traditions which marginalize the female subaltern involves the use of poetry as a weapon of resistance, a premise which dominates the poetic text of Ghabesh's anthology. In this context, the Emirati poet emerges as a politico-feminist poet whose textual polemic, outlined in the paper, is an analogy of her creative appropriation of Andalusian history. Unlike parasitic appropriations, performed by other poets, her literary project offers insights into the present and the future of a feminist poetics in UAE, the Gulf region and the Arab world.

Incorporating Andalusian heritage, Ghabesh takes the title of her poem "What you Might do my Father / Fa-asak ya Abati" from Buthayna's verses of appeal to her father in which she begs him to bless her marriage to the man she loves. In the poem, Ghabesh's female persona, twice marginalized on account of her sex and her social status, grapples with concepts and constructs implicated in the patriarchal and hegemonic power relations denouncing a tradition which seeks to mute her in the era of gender and race consciousness. Confronting hegemonic structures which attempt to isolate Arab women by assigning them conventional feminine traits such as silence and weakness, she purports to explore the limitations and dangers of a reactionary culture which aims to obliterate the female identity. Identifying herself with Buthayna, the Emirati poet (or her female persona) says:

The tears of Buthayna recognized me
when I entered the door
the tears reveal the secrets of my silence
like Buthayna I am scared
of the well-dressed people
who set the trap for me
I am scared of the necklace of illusion
you put around my neck
scared of the sudden interest in me
when you gave me as a gift
to a very old man
whose body is ploughed
by coldness and frost
Father, I thought you have known me! (17)

Obviously, 'the tears of Buthayna' and the persona in the poem become the tears of all oppressed women in societies which obliterate female identities. The references to the female persona's fear of 'the necklace of illusion' and the indications implied in 'the sudden interest in me' are testimonies of a marriage bargain in which the father accepts to give his young daughter 'as a gift/to a very old man/whose body is ploughed/by coldness and frost'. Lamenting the unjust treatment of girls in conservative Arab communities, the poet castigates conventional marriage traditions which totally ignore the female. Describing marriage as a kind of trap and denouncing a society which forces girls to marry against their will giving them as gifts to old men or sacrificing them as scapegoats on the altar of a decadent tradition, Ghabesh contrasts the tale of female oppression in the Arab world with the narrative of resistance and revolt embedded in Buthayna's story.

After her address to her father, in the aforementioned poem, Ghabesh "or her persona" engages herself into a one-sided dialogue with Buthayna: "I thought he knows me, Buthayna / like the birds which know you / when you walk on the Andalusian coast" (18). Apparently, a juxtaposition is established between the tolerant behavior of Buthayna's father,[3] in the Andalusian myth and the patriarchal/hegemonic attitude of contemporary Arab parents toward their daughters who are forced to marry against their will:

You lost your father, Buthayna
and he lost you, the notebook
which he reads to the city
you are the best word in his alphabet
until your features are lost in alien contexts
the pulpits of Seville are waiting anxiously
for the return of al-Mutamed
who may mention your name
in the coming sermon (19)

As a carrier of a repressive tradition and a symbol of rebellion against patriarchal hegemonic structures, Buthayna is resurrected from the past in order to enable the Emirati poet to probe contemporary female predicaments: "but he is unaware/that you were sold in auction/he does not know that you throw/your name inside the furnace of fear/He is still unaware that the girl has no genealogy (20).

In the preceding lines, the 'he' apparently refers to a contemporary father figure haunted by a patriarchal/tribal tradition that aims to crush the soul and the body of the female. Here, the voice of Buthayna and that of Ghabesh (or her persona) merge together constructing a cry of anger against the subordination of their biological and literary femininity by hegemonic cultures[4] Since Buthayna's story reproduces the same patriarchal hegemony that Ghabesh denounces in her poetry, the latter's narrative of victimization becomes an extension of the former's in a ritualistic manner reminiscent of Shehrazade's stories in *A Thousand Nights and One Night*. Therefore, the space created by the coordinates of the textual relationship between Buthayna and Ghabesh, identified and analyzed above, provides more insight into Ghabesh's exploration of the dynamic relation between self and other. This view is contingent upon the Emirati poet's entanglement with the Islamic history in Andalusia within the praxis of Buthayna's narrative.

Conclusion

The feminist French critic, Hélén Cixous[5] underlines the role of language and feminine writing as constructs for subverting patriarchal structures of domination in the areas of language, politics and society. In her feminist/critical studies, she attempts to introduce alternative discourses to patriarchal logo-centrism which reduces women to positions of subordination. Like Cixous, Ghabesh, through her poetry, attempts to dismantle an apparatus of suppression rooted in patriarchal ideologies which aim to mute the female subaltern assigning her a status of inferiority. In an attempt to undermine cultural and ideological hegemonies which seek to marginalize Arab women, the Emirati poet promulgates a feminine poetics perpetuating Andalusian heritage and subverting significant elements of local religious and cultural history.

In "Prior to the Final Fall / Qabl al-suqut al-Akhir", Ghabesh refers to her encounter with a male persona in the evening: "the evening will be under my disposal / and the meeting at the edge of fear is mine / I am another Buthayna / perfume springs from me / as well as love and Diaspra / at a time when the tribe gives up trembling / the river can never abandon a chaste body" (56). The references to anti-feminist tribal mentality, rooted in Arabic traditions, and the association of the poet with Buthayna underline a history of female oppression which extends from the Atlantic Ocean to the Persian Gulf. Like Buthayna, the Emirati poet, through her female persona, expresses agony and fear as a result of being involved in a new experience in a patriarchal society: "I am scared of the captivity of my soul / I took the initiative of coming to his prison / on the doorstep I left my crown / I entered his house as a servant / trembling out of coldness / after my confession he liberated me / then he orders me / to recite his song" (58). The fearful experience of the Emirati poet's persona and the allusions to prisons and captivity of the soul are indications of major social problems encountering women in the contemporary Arab society which forces them to surrender to an oppressive masculine tradition: 'he orders me/to recite his song'. Living in an internal Diaspora, the poet laments life in an alienated society where "stories are broken" and her hands are bleeding "in exile". Witnessing "the fading lights of the candles/ before the final fall" (67), the female subaltern has no option except to "set her tent in order/closing the door and remain there / waiting for the season of departure" (59).

In *A Map of Misreading*, Harold Bloom considers the attempt to evade earlier writing, produced by an author's predecessors, as a basic motivation in literary production. In this context, Bloom illustrates that in order "to live, the poet must misinterpret the father by the crucial act of misprision, which is the rewriting of the father" (Bloom 1975: 19). In *Beman Ya Buthayn Taluthin?* Ghabesh, unlike male poets who reconstruct the texts of their forebears in order to dismantle them, rewrites her female predecessor integrating her poetic narrative into the contemporary literary canon. Ignoring Bloom's call for contemporary poets to "differentiate themselves into strength by trooping or turning from the presence of other poets" (Bloom 1975: 80), Ghabesh reveals no sign of anxiety, toward her Andalusian forebear violating Bloom's paradigm of literary influence. In addition to her adaptation of the Andalusian narrative to explore contemporary socio-political issues, the Emirati poet does not perform a textual dismemberment of Buthayna, her female Andalusian predecessor, but she allows her to recur in the new contextual corpus.

In other words, Ghabesh, in *Beman Ya Buthayn Taluthin?* does not imply a privileged position for her own poetic discourse simply because Buthayna, the Andalusian princess or the dead narrator, reads Ghabesh as much as Ghabesh reads her. Apparently, the major inspiration and the guiding light which come to the Emirati poet from the history of Andalusia in general and from the story of Butayna in particular form an infra-poetic structure for her anthology, linking the fall of Seville and Grenada with contemporary collapses and catastrophes on different fronts in the Arab world. The Emirati poet, in her anthology, explicitly associates the loss of Arab glory in ancient Spain and in contemporary history to the domination of decadent patriarchal traditions which subjugate Arab women. Struggling to save an entire history from oblivion, Ghabesh resurrects Andalusian myth linking the miserable end of al-Mutamed, king of Seville, with the potential destiny of contemporary Arab rulers engaged in Arab-Arab conflicts and guided by a masculine mentality which breeds policies of oppression leading to recurrent defeats. In other words, the young Emirati poet courageously interrupts contemporary patriarchal practices which confiscate female freedom disseminating her attitudes toward current issues of great importance in the social and political arenas.

Due to her enthusiasm for Andalusian history, Ghabesh's poetry borders on exploiting or colonizing Buthayna's narrative to fulfill ideological purposes. In this sense, Ghabesh's modern alternative discourse becomes a story within a story and a new text is created and perpetuated as the Emirati poet deploys her feminist vision using another woman's narrative. Through her engagement with Buthayna's legend, a woman's voice come to the Emirati poet from remote destination giving her poetry renewed vigor and sparking in the readers an interest in Andalusian history. Entering the text of the Emirati poet in several guises, Buthayna and her story are transformed into significant indicators and signifiers at the disposal of Ghabesh's poetic neologism and creativity. Functioning ultimately as a guarantee of Ghabesh's own voice, the story of Buthayna is reproduced in intellectual and political terms to deal with local and contemporary matters. Thus, Ghabesh's experience of reading Andalusian literature becomes 'a catalyst', to use T.S. Eliot's term, prompting the Emirati poet to compose her own anthology in all its revolutionary and feminist implications and in its provocative and subversive treatment of a male-oriented tradition. In order to awaken the Arab people from "the long sleep of history", to use the words of Ali Ahmad Said (Adonis), she created an anguished portrayal of a nation on the verge of catastrophe. In this context, *Beman Ya Buthayn Taluthin?* becomes an appeal or a call for social and political reform in an era of desolation and collapse.

NOTES

1. All translations from Arabic sources including *Beman Ya Buthayn Taluthin?* is done by the author of the article.
2. Historically there are controversial arguments which consider the Arabic language as anti-feminist and masculine.
3. While the poet appreciates al-Mutamed's treatment of his daughter's marriage issue, she criticizes his policies which participate in the fall of his kingdom in Andalusia.
4. It is relevant to argue that the term "feminine" in Ghabesh's anthology does not always imply a biological determinism but it transcends it.
5. For further details see Helen Cixous. *Coming to Writing and Other Essays*, ed. Deborah Jenson, tr. Sarah Cornell, Debora Jenson, Anne Liddle, Susan Sellers. Cambridge: Harvard University Press, 1991.

WORKS CITED

Bakhtin, Mikhael. *The Dialogic Imagination: Four Essays*, ed. Michael Holquist, tr. Caryl Emerson and Michael Holquist. Austin, Texas: Texas University Press, 1981.

Barthes, Roland. *Image, Music, Text*, tr. Stephen Heath. London: Fontana, 1977.

Bloom, Harold. *A Map of Misreading*. Oxford: Oxford University Press, 1975.

Castillo, Debra A. *Talking Back: Toward a Latin American Feminist Literary Criticism*. Ithaca: Cornell University Press, 1992.

Clayton, Jay and Eric Rothstein, ed. *Influence and Intertextuality in Literary History*. Madison: The University of Wisconsin Press, 1991.

Culler, Jonathan. *The Pursuit of Signs: Semiotics, Literature, Deconstruction*. Ithaca: Cornell University Press, 1981.

Eliot, T.S. "The Function of Criticism", in *Twentieth Century Literary Criticism*, ed. David Lodge. London: Longman, 1972, pp. 77-84.

——. "Tradition and Individual Talent", in *Twentieth Century Literary Criticism*, ed. David Lodge. London: Longman, 1972, pp. 71-77.

Ghabesh, Saleha. *Beman Ya Buthayn Taluthin? / Who Will Secure a Safe Haven for Buthayn*? Sharijah, UAE: Culture and Media Department Press, 2002.

Guillen, Claudio. *The Challenge of Comparative Literature*, tr. Cola Franzen. Cambridge, Mass.: Harvard University Press, 1993.

Ricour, Paul. *Hermeneutics and the Human Sciences: Essays on Language, Action and Interpretation*, ed. J.B. Thomson. London: Cambridge University Press, 1981.

Re-Configuration of Colonialism or the Negation of the Self in Postcolonial Cameroon in Bole Butake's Plays

16

Emmanuel N. Ngwang

The legacy European colonialism left on African countries is not only incontestable but lasting. Such legacy is manifested in the so-called civilized ways of constructing European style of houses, formal educational systems, the imposition of foreign languages on the business and administrative spheres of life, and a lifestyle at variance with the indigenous African lifestyles. While some African scholars and philosophers have welcomed these elements as beneficial to Africans, others have eschewed them as destructive of the African way. There has, therefore, arisen a continuous tension between the two groups whereby those who favour the foreign ways point to the advantages that accrue from colonialism, and, on the other hand, those who despite this unfortunate historical era point to the exploitative nature of the new ways. The latter group tends to point at the true face of colonialism which had almost nothing positive to offer Africans. Khapoya points out that the main objective of colonialism was the destruction of the colonized: "Colonial administrators often pursued policies that totally disregarded African interests and opinions—policies that removed colonized Africans as active participants in shaping their own history" (110). Joseph Harris confirms Khapoya's theory by asserting that

> The establishment of European colonial rule in Africa placed ultimate power in the hands of aliens who came from a cultural background that traditionally had denigrated African people. Thus, the dominant long-range force became the

> colonial state that emphasized modern forms of... bureaucratic rule. Indigenous political and economic structures lost their legitimacy and authority. (206)

It is, therefore, obvious that colonialism was the imposition of the will of the colonizing Europeans on the formerly independent African people, based on the explicit or sometimes implicit intention of exploiting the Africans both economically, culturally, and politically. To succeed in doing so, the imperialists found it necessary to defend colonialism by promising the colonized "a higher order of existence" and by re-assuring the domestic critics that, on the balance, the gains of the colonized far outweighed their losses; and by contending that at any rate the colonized were being saved from the brutality of their old life and that they were being offered the blessings of a morally and technologically superior civilization. This concept was a very potent psychological propaganda which had a way of working on the minds of the colonized, destroying the confidence the colonized had in their way of life, institutions, and their creative abilities within their own cultures. The educated or rather literate elite, therefore, saw colonialism as conferring on them a higher social order, a higher and more advanced civilization, and a means of upgrading and maintaining their newly acquired status at the expense of their indigenous cultural values. The colonized started off by acquiescing to the new dispensation through servitude with the aim of eventually inheriting the ways of the masters. Hence, the struggle for independence in the 1960s seemed to have been carried out with two objectives: on the one hand there were those who sacrificed their lives to acquire genuine freedom from the colonial masters to truly liberate their lands from the domination of these foreigners, and on the other hand, there were those opportunists who saw in this struggle an attempt simply to supplant the colonial masters in order to attain to the status of their former masters with all the collateral benefits that accrue from such positions. This contradiction shocked Ernest A. Champion who had thought that "colonialism ...was never meant to be a perpetual institution; it was not a timeless adventure" (77). Unfortunately, he continues, "colonialism not only appropriated land from other nations, but there was also an attendant colonization of the mind, so much so that even after the demise of colonialism, the colonization of the mind continues" (73). It is indeed this "colonization of the mind" that negated and undercut the original concept of the fight for freedom, a fight which was meant to free the Africans of colonial rule and colonial mentality.

At independence, the hope of many African nation states was that they would extricate themselves from the inferiority mentality by replacing the colonial masters with their own educated sons and daughters, many of whom had been educated and trained in Europe and the Americas. So independence was to spell the total death of colonialism and the colonial mentality. Unfortunately, this was not to be the case in most nation states. This situation was particularly pervasive in Francophone Africa where the French colonial policy of assimilation attempted to create French people out of Africans. As President Paul Biya of Cameroon was to assert some years ago after having a working session with the former French President Mitterrand, the so-called independent leaders of French Africa remained students and stewards of their colonial masters. Paul Biya said over Cameroon radio television transmitted from Paris, after meeting with Mitterrand after the La Baule meeting convened by Mitterrand for francophone African leaders to implement and pursue democracy in their countries (1991), that "Je suis un bon étudiant" (I am a good student) (Takougang and Krieger 109). Though, he might not have meant it in a literal sense, such a statement validates the colonial masters' stereotypical approach to Africa as a lost continent, where the natives are incapable of ruling themselves or understanding the concept of democracy. It is this same mentality that the prolific essayist and critic philosopher Frantz Fanon observed in Algeria in 1962 in the unfortunate turn of events following Algerian independence:

> [After the French were forced to leave], the elite layer of Europeans in Algeria was promptly supplanted by an elite layer of bourgeois Algerians who sought little more than to snatch appropriated privileges into their own hands. In this sense, colonialism went undefeated. Widespread poverty and social inequity persisted, and the manipulation of power

> ensured that the FLN remained an unchallenged political party in democratic Algeria in the following decades. Throughout the rest of Africa, similar tales played out: internal conflicts arose, mostly from economic and political strangleholds exacted upon these small nations by their former or continuing colonizers. (Ehlen 167)

Fanon's experience was equally shared by the African American dramatist LeRoi Jones whose inspiration for and "commitments to cultural nationalism" based on Africa's "successful rebellions against colonial rule" was frustrated when he visited Africa in October 1974. He abandoned his stance when he saw that "a simple change in the complexion of power would not bring about the transformation for which he looked" (Bigsby 285). Furthermore Khapoya, in his analysis of political instability in Africa concluded that "the transfer of power by European colonialists did not lead to changes in the political institutions that the Africans inherited or in the basic orientation of ordinary people toward their new leaders wielding authority and power over them, whose primary objective was to serve vested interest rather than the country as a whole" (190-91). We now have a breed of African leaders who are corrupted by power and fueled by greed. It is, therefore, Frantz Fanon's reference to the new class of Algerians as "continuing colonizers" and LeRoi Jones' disappointment with postcolonial political configuration that has given rise to this research project entitled "Re-Figuration of Colonialism or the Negation of the Self after they had left".

As Fanon eloquently alluded to in the passage above, the African nations were now to confront another colonial monster, the able students of the Masters who had so learned the tricks of the masters and combined with the native knowledge of their people that they set up themselves against their own people, exploiting and enslaving the people for their own personal gains, thereby undercutting the whole concept of political and economic freedom and independence. In the end, they find themselves isolated by the local citizens but surrounded by their political stooges who clamor for the proverbial crumbs that fall from the masters' tables. This, in a way, was not only a re-figuration of colonialism or what has become known as neo-colonialism, but equally a negation of the self, a self denial of sorts. In other words, the new leaders betrayed the political, economic, and cultural platforms on which they had campaigned against the colonial masters. They now become the Black (as opposed to the white) masters, and experts in the game of colonialism. This situation is vividly captured by Shey Ngong in Bole Butake's *And Palm Wine Will Flow* as he bewails the state to which the village has degenerated under their ruler:

> What a land! What a people! To think that people in other lands...
> Oh! Nyombom!
> Creator and guardian of the land,
> Grant me strength and wisdom
> To weather the surging storm.
> The Fon has lost vision.
> The noble men and elders of this land
> Now listen only to the inner voice
> Of greed, and fear of a man who has
> Surrounded himself with listeners
> And watchdogs to do his bidding. (89)

Later, Shey Ngong characterizes the land where the transvaluation of values has become the norm: "Today, nobles have become slaves and slaves nobles" (92), and the land has become one of "drinking and feasting where there is too much in the belly...[and the] head becomes an empty shell". Shey Ngong's use of the imagery of drinking and eating here, is indeed a metaphor for the exploitation of the people by their own leaders which is given prominence in Armah's *The Beautyful Ones Are Not Yet Born* (1968).

The protest literature of post colonial Africa, and by extension, Cameroon is replete with attempts of writers to re-evaluate the fallouts of independence and to identify and apportion blame for the failure of dreams of freedom, liberty, equality, and the pursuit of happiness for all and sundry that had been promised at independence. The political leaders have become so comfortable with their positions that they have resorted to exploiting the local people through fear, intimidation, coercion, bribery and corruption and the outright rigging of national elections to ensure their continuity in power. This has sometimes taken the form of regional, class, ethnic, socio-economic status, language, and sometimes religious marginalization, from one country to another. These colonial tendencies sometimes take the form of one group (region, ethnicity, class) imposing its will on the rest and thereby betraying the fundamental trust and confidence that had constituted the foundation on which the national unity was built. The other citizens who do not share the same ideology with the ruling class are automatically referred to as foreigners or strangers as was the case between the ruling Beti ethnic group, on the one hand, and the Anglophone and Bamilike groups on the other (Tarkougang and Krieger 95-97). I clearly remember when the late Mayor of Yaounde Emah Basile, who in reaction to launching of the Social Democratic Front in Bamenda and the attendant uprisings, referred to the politically astute Anglophones as "les énemies dans la maîson" "les étrangers, les Nigériens" (translated as "the enemies in the house", "the strangers, the Nigerians", 94-96). The English speaking Cameroonians, now the British Southern Cameroonians, could no longer accept the second class status that was assigned to them and the resultant marginalization they suffered. In such cases, and when the people are political sensitive (like in the Southern Cameroonian situation against La République du Cameroun), this has given rise to secessionist tendencies manifested in public demonstrations and culminated in the All Anglophone Conference I and II which took place in Buea and Bamenda in 1993 and 1994 respectively (Aka 291, Tarkougang and Krieger 168-69). In Bole Butake's play "Shoes and Four Men in Arms" (a play set in a military dictatorship where the soldiers are sent to quell a popular uprising with unprecedented brutality), the people come out shouting: "We want freedom! We want jobs! We want our salaries! Give us freedom! Liberty now! Freedom! Liberty! Freedom!" (141). In the late 1950's and early 1960's, one would have conceived this attitude in the context of the colonist rising against their foreign imperial overlords, but it is ironic that in this play, the natives are rising against their own national leaders; in fact, they are clamoring for freedom and liberty from their own leaders who have literally reduced them to second class citizens, slaves, and colonists. This political strife and unrest are the citizens' reactions to the exploitation they now suffer in the hands of their new "colonial" masters, their supposed leaders whom Butake now refers to, in Dance of the Vampires, as the vampires. In a conversation between Nformi and Albinia (a nickname for Caucasians), Nformi uses this vampire imagery to draw an analogy between the exploitation of the natives both by the colonial masters and their protégé who have now constituted the ruling junta: "Albinia and their emissary, Albino, are only interested in sucking the wealth of our land. While Psaul Roi and Song are sucking the blood of the people" (172).

This "sucking" imagery is symbolic of the relationship that existed between the colonized and the colonizers wherein the colony existed to serve the material well-being of the colonizer. However, a much more devastating relationship now exists between the ruling elite and the natives where in the absence of "the wealth of the land" (which has already been sucked by the Albinia, the white colonizers), Psaul Roi, the ruler, now sucks the blood of the people. Instead of giving life to the people, as has been the traditional role of the king, the king sucks life out of the people. This, in effect, is the negation of the self, as this action is tantamount to self-destruction. In the African cultures, the king usually stands for the people, and that is why he is usually addressed and referred to in the collective third person plural pronoun "they" or first person pronoun plural "we" or "us" even when he is alone. In fact, Albino refers to this self-destructive tendency of the king when he compares his foreign home palace (or seat of government) with that of Psaul Roi's:

> My assignment as an emissary to your kingdom was to explore the possibility of doing business with your people. After my brief stay here, there is no doubt that business opportunities abound. Even the insignificant but humanitarian affair of the incinerators has yielded and is still yielding a lot of dividends. Just as a ruler without the ruled is no ruler, so is the land without people, no matter how rich it may be. Your Most Royal Majesty, you turned

> against your people and now they won't come back in spite of your instruments and proclamations urging them to do so. Where I come from the palace is a market place where people converge to dialogue with their king. But here, the palace, like the land, has become the evil forest where people fear to tread. (171)

Albino's observation is an accurate depiction of the presidential palace in Yaoundé which is protected by mounted armed presidential guards, whose fearful presence has turned the palace into a proverbial "evil forest". It also adumbrates the theme of alienation which eventually resulted in separatist movements like the Southern Cameroons National Congress (the SCNC), now known as the British Southern Cameroons Nation (BSCNATION), clamoring for independence from La République du Cameroon on the bases of regional and linguistic marginalization.

It is the same image and impression we have of the palace in Bole Butake's *And Palm Wine Will Flow* where people go to, not for advice and wisdom, but one where, according to Shey Ngong, people "come to [the Fon] with gifts in return for the red feather" (91). The Fon is equally referred to as "Holy one, the lion of Ewawa" who has pronounced that "the farmlands of [Shey Ngong's] revered wives now belong to Kibanya's wives" (93). There is also the prevalence of what the soldiers in Shoes and Four Men in Arms refer to as "Social malaise, agitations, and demonstrations" (140) resulting from the failure of the government to pay salaries, the rising unemployment, poverty, and military brutality on the unarmed civilians. University female students are mercilessly raped by the half educated soldiers who force the students and university graduates to denigrate university education and literacy. They tell the unemployed graduates:

> Where are you, vandals? Subversive over-sabi bookshops! Come out and I will show you something. Standard Seven is better than big, big certificate. Big certificate, no work to do. So you become subversives and vandals and terrorists. (119)

The above situation, which incidentally happened at the University of Yaounde in 1991-92 when I was teaching there and witnessed it, approximates, though on a minor scale, the complaint raised by the American colonies against the British colonizers in 1776: "the turning of the local soldiers against their people making the soldiers to become the executioners of their friends and Brethren, to fall themselves" (22). Butake may not have had this analogy in mind by the time of writing, but one will be remise not to see this parallel. The gravity of the whole situation in the play does not only lie in the barbaric treatment the natives are subjected to, but in the fact that, unlike in the American colonies where the ruler was foreign, in this play, the King here is one of them. The King has turned against his own people. The number of shoes gathered by the soldiers signifies the number of students who have been savagely disposed of as revealed in this gory conversation between the merciless soldiers:

> First: How many did we capture during the operation?
>
> Third: Who cares to count? Four or five truck loads. Something like that.
>
> First: Any girls?
>
> Second: Plenty. You know they are more easily affected by tear gas. And since we surrounded them completely it was by far better to catch a girl. (118)

The soldiers then proceed to loot the shoes, appliances, and extort money from the helpless civilians under the guise of quelling an uprising. It is indeed a misreading of the play to conclude that "these soldiers serve their country by standing guard over a pile of shoes, the only visible trace of the demonstration" (Breitinger 14). This myopic approach begs the question, whose interest are the soldiers serving and what do the shoes represent? The soldiers serve a double interest here. In the first place, the soldiers are there, as Albino says, to execute the orders of the General (President) whose survival is threatened:

> [The Chief Commander] means privileges and honours which regular soldiers like you don't have and will never dream of having. Yet, he and the monarch are completely dependent on the army, on you, to do their dirty job of keeping the people under an iron heel. We are talking about the plight of your people. The manipulation of you soldiers by one man,

> an alcoholic who happens also to be drunk with power even if he doesn't know what to do with it. (167)

Secondly, the soldiers want to use this opportunity to rape the girls, loot property from houses they have broken into for their insatiable sexual and material greed. These soldiers are indeed a refined rendition of the Police Officer in "The Survival" who uses his position of power to rape and extort sexual favors from Mboysi. Mboysi's reaction to and description of the situation parallels the despicable and nauseating language Armah uses in "The Beautyful Ones Are Not Yet Born" to describe the corrupt belly-pot politicians. After having outwitted the Police Officer, Mboysi addresses him:

> You would kill me, would you? You crawling, thieving maggot. Growing rich on the misfortunes of others. Stuffing your decaying stomach and your bulging pockets on the calamity of my people. Never again shall you live to perpetuate our misery. It was better for all of us to have been killed than to be treated like caged animals. (83)

And where the officers cannot rape or extract sexual favors from the poor women, they openly ask for bribes to perform the duties for which they are paid; sometimes, they flagrantly break or operate above the law. This is the case with the "practical philosopher" in Butake's "The Rape of Michelle" where, without any moral compunctions, the police officer asks for a bribe from Akwen who wants to visit her incarcerated husband:

> **Policeman**: Madam, I will not do you a favour for nothing. You think I am alone on duty? There are three others out there. What you are giving me cannot buy a bottle of red wine.
>
> **Akwen**: Alright, here is something for all of you. And, please, treat my husband well.
>
> **Policeman:** It all depends on you, Madam. Our treatment of your husband depends on you.... Don't stay too long. Or you will put me into trouble. The law says that criminals must never be left alone with visitors. (180)

Later, Policeman reports to Mikingdong (Akwen's husband) that he had told the latter's wife that everything depended on her, "And she did her duty. And now you are happy. That is how life should be. You make me happy. I make you happy. One hand washes the other. And that is how things should be" (183). This is a case of extreme perversion of justice. In fact, Policeman schools Mikingndong on the practical philosophy:

> Teacher, let me tell you something. Whether you did it or not does not really matter. If you do not make contacts, you are going to stay in prison for a good part of your only life.... But with money...you can move mountains.... Contacts. That is the right word.... A telephone call from above to the magistrate! An envelope from below to the magistrate! And the deed is done. The case is closed or simply thrown out of court. Contacts.... Oh yes! We must be practical and realistic. You think the magistrate eats truth? You think the prosecutor eats truth? You think the commissioner eats truth. But people need a drink now and again. They need money to do things. That is what I call practical philosophy. (182, 186)

The soldiers, the police officers, and the court system who constitute part of the legacy bequeathed by the white colonial masters are used here not to preserve order or guarantee and uphold justice like the colonial masters had conceived (Sandbrook 147) but rather to intimidate and punish the political agitators and supposed criminals who are fighting for their legitimate rights and to enrich themselves. They are a reflection of a system of governance that is self-destructive, one that negates the very concept of a government of the people, for the people, by the people. Again in Dance of the Vampires, Albino reiterates the King's responsibility: "Your Excellency the Most Royal, there is no business without trust, without goals. Your goal is your throne, power. Mine is gain. Shall we seal with a handshake?" (166). Albino understands the desire of Psaul Roi's mind, which is to attain absolute power over his impoverished subjects, rather than to protect them. Later, Albino underscores the nonchalant attitude of the King and his supporters in these words:

> What wonderful predators you are! Preying on your own kind. Don't you see the consequences of your own folly? I have had to bring in specialists from Albinia to build the

> incinerator and to fell the trees for wood and transport it to the various locations. And here you are asking me for more compensations. You ask your Chief Commander here, or your Commander-in-Chief who has barricaded himself in his palace and is drinking himself to certain death, what the real situation of your beloved country is. (166)

We are confronted here again with the image of eating, if not cannibalism: "predators", "preying on your own kind" and "drinking"—a callous disregard of the well-being of the citizens, a scene of plenty in the midst of poverty. The answer to Albino's worry about the true state of the beloved country is obvious: abject poverty, social unrest, and rebellion. This is a country ruled and where the soldiers are manipulated by "one man, an alcoholic who happens to be drunk with power even if he doesn't know what to do with it..." and "many intelligence sources report the refugees [say] that until the monarch leaves they will remain refugees. They have never been ruled by a vampire king" (167). This, indeed, is the land of the big dogs where the concepts of freedom, equality, and the pursuit of happiness have been negated, a self-negation of sorts.

WORKS CITED

Banham, Martin, James Gibbs, and Femi Osofsan, eds. *The African Theatre: Playwrights and Politics*. Oxford: James Currey Ltd., 2001.

Bigsby, Christopher W.E. *Modern American Drama: 1945-2000*. Cambridge: Cambridge University Press, 2000.

Butake, Bole. *Lake God and Other Plays*. Yaounde, Cameroon: Editions CLE, 1999.

Breitinger, Eckhard. "Bole Butake's Strategies as a Political Playwright." *The African Theatre: Playwrights and Politics*. Eds. Martin Banham, James Gibbs, and Femi Osofsan. Oxford: James Currey Ltd., 2001, 7-17.

Champion, Ernest A. *Mr. Baldwin, I Presume: James Baldwin–Chinua Achebe: A Meeting of the Minds*. New York: University Press of America, Inc., 1995.

Ehlen, Patrick. *Frantz Fanon: A Spiritual Biography*. New York: The Crossroad Publishing Company, 2000.

Fanon, Frantz. *The Wretched of the Earth*. New York: Grove Press, Inc., 1968.

Khapoya, Vincent B. *The African Experience: An Introduction*. Second Edition. Upper Saddle River, NJ: Prentice Hall, 1998.

Lazarus, Neil. "(Re)turn to the People: Ngugi wa Thiong'o and the Crisis of Postcolonial African Intellectualism." *The World of Ngugi wa Thiong'o*. Ed. Charles Cantalupo. Trenton, NJ: African World Press, 1995.

Martin, Phyllis M. and Patrick O'Meara, eds. *Africa*. Third Edition. Bloomington, IN: Indiana University Press, 1995.

Sandbrook, Richard. *The Politics of Africa's Economic Stagnation*. New York: Cambridge University Press, 1985.

Nature and Man in Seamus Heaney

17

Anju Bala Agrawal

Heaney's poetry is quite near to Romanticism. He may appear as hero in Byron and in Goethe, but his retreat is most evident in Wordsworth. Heaney writes most intimately of poets whose imagination accord with his own imagination. He withdraws from the world into a sacred area of personal sensitivity and in Nature, a subjective, irrational self. Wordsworth's more particular 'self' found in childhood and nature a solace for frustrated revolutionary idealism. "As Nature was for Wordsworth, the Bog People were for Heaney."[1] Heaney chose bogs as a landscape icon for Ireland. Like Wordsworth, Heaney retreats into an area of personal sensitivity.

Heaney's description of nature started with its physicality. In *Death of a Naturalist*, we see a large amount of imagery of touch, taste, smell and synesthesia (the buzz of bluebottles visualized as gauze) as the flax is with sods. Heaney is on firmer ground when he describes the processes of earth and how man interacts with nature through ritual, custom and work. His poems are not only about manual work on farm like ploughing, planting, harvesting horse-shoeing but they are themselves manuals also on how the work is done. Heaney is one with his rural origin, so his rehearsal of the customs he witnessed or participated as a child assumes the quality of incantation and commemoration. His subject matter is often loud with the slap of the spade and sour with the stink of the turned earth. In *Door into the Dark*, he moved beyond himself and looked at the mysterious life-cycle of the eel and the compulsive work-cycles in the eel-fishermen's life as in the poem "Lough Neagh Sequence".

Heaney returns for peace to Northern Ireland people to reestablish the rhythm of the natural world. The strongest figures in *Death of a Naturalist* and *Door into the Dark* are those, like Heaney's father, who were devoted to land and whose lives were ritualized in harmony with their environment. Seamus Heaney does not have the naïve romantic notion that nature never betrays the heart that loves her. His poems present nature as a random power that sometimes rewards but more often frustrates human efforts. The poet in these two books is walking the land, training his eyes, getting the measure of things right. Landscapes are tactfully moralized, pressed to disclose values and meanings so gracefully reasonable that they hardly need pressure at all, only a few of Heaney's "time-turned words".

Heaney chose bogs as a landscape icon for Ireland. He calls the bogs a sort of Jungian as well as geological memory bank as it is like a dark casket where we can find many of the clues to our cultural identity. Certainly bogs, like Wordsworth's Lake District, do not conjure up the romanticized tourist version of an Ireland with rolling green hills, rippling brooks and lush vegetation. At other places Heaney has described the romantic beauty of this region like Wordsworth. The second book ends with the poem "Bogland". This poem also presents an Irish folk lore:

Butter sunk under
More than a hundred years
Was recovered salty and white.
The ground itself is kind, black butter.

(*DD*, 41)

Bog hoards the treasures of the past. It has several mysteries and miracles like the elk and the butter. Heaney "delighted in the 'visual surprise' of the bogland, like Hardy's Egdon Heath, with its changing patterns of purple, yellow and ochre in different seasons. His awe at the bogland did not spring so much from its size and colour, but from his 'sense of its ancient life'."[2] In fact "Bogland", the last poem in *Door into the Dark* made a new promise that Heaney would go further and dig more deeply into

Ireland's past. Heaney writes in *Preoccupations*, that the bog serves as "the memory bank of the landscape, or as a landscape that remember(s) everything that happened in and to it" (54).

Bogland is presented as an insatiable and consuming ground. It indiscriminately swallows all that comes to it and preserves it intact as a kind of treasure that can be yielded up in time. Heaney's first attempt to present bog is the poem "Bogland" which closes *Door into the Dark*. The preservative power of the bog is graphically indicated in the third stanza:

> They've taken the skeleton
> Of the Great Irish elk
> Out of the peat, set it up
> An Astonishing crate full of air.
>
> (*DD*, 41)

Here the massive frame of an Irish deer rises out of the land. In contrast to the grandeur of this image, the next object to emerge from the bog in the poem is butter, 'recovered salty and white'. Taken together, the elk and the butter signify the heterogeneity of the bog, its tendency to preserve everything without selecting out a particular set of objects. Heaney continues with the bog theme in *Wintering Out*. In *Wintering Out*, Heaney reached down into the bog and magma of the Ulster region. He first takes up the issue in "Bog Oak". Bog oak is a piece of seasoned wood retrieved from the bog and used as a building material. The poem "Bog Oak" describes the folk practice of the considerable use of buried timber dug from the bogs for roofing beams and of pine for kindling:

> A Carter's trophy
> split for rafters
> A cobwebbed, black,
> Long-seasoned rib.
>
> (*Wintering Out*, 4)

The memory of this rafter calls up images of an entire native community, not just the speaker's own immediate family but it stretches back into a communal past, a gathering of his ancestors. In the final two stanzas, Heaney presents an image of the sixteenth century English poet, Edmund Spenser, who wrote a political treatise entitled, A View of the Present State of Ireland, in which he advocated the deployment of extremely harsh measures against the native Irish. In the beginning of the poem, the poet calls the bog oak as 'A carter's trophy' to be 'split for rafters'. The poem indicates that we can read the colonial history of the country within the grains of the retrieved timber.

In Heaney's third volume *Wintering Out*, a revaluation of the powerful picture of rural Northern Irish life has been presented. A group of poems is concerned not only with deep reading of the earth but also with topography. Heaney has great fascination with the earth. He uses various metaphors for the earth and gives a vivid description of activities involving the earth. Heaney has rich vocabulary for earth terms such as mud, mould, silt, slime, slicks, etc. These terms are used for different kinds of landscapes such as fens and bogs as well as for singular weather events and how they transform the earth's surface. Heaney has described earth in mythological way. He has written a short but significant poem describing Nerthus—Mother Earth:

For beauty, say an ash-fork staked in peat,
Its long grains gathering to the gouged split;

A seasoned, unsleeved taker of the weather,
Where kesh and loaning finger out to heather.

(*WO*, 38)

In the form of 'Bog', he describes earth as 'quagmire, swampland, morass', all three traceable to Germanic roots. Though, he does not settle on any of these, he likes more neutral, less exotic bog. The bog is 'ruminant ground', a marvelous double entendre, a place that swallows its cud ('mollusc/and seed pod') only to yield it up again. This part of earth is reflective, thoughtful and a storehouse of memory.

Earth-pantry, bone vault,
Sun-bank, embalmer
Of votive goods
And sabred fugitives.

(*North*, 34)

The poet also describes that the vowel of earth is the root of flowers, snow, weather, seasons, etc. In the end of the poem, he is sorry to think:

Our mother ground
is sour with the blood

(*North*, 38)

"Heaney's gaze as a poet is characteristically focused, not on the skies, on the stars or clouds, but downwards, earthwards, on the bog, the ditch, the dark well, the river, on graves and tombs."[3] Heaney describes this sequencing of bog landscape formation fairly accurately in this excerpt from his poem, "Kinship":

This centre holds
and spreads
sumpand seedbed
a bag of waters

and a melting grave.
The mothers of autumn
Sour and sink,
Ferments of husk and leaf

Deepened their ochres
Mosses come to a head
Heather unseeds
Brackens deposit

Their bronze
This is the vowel of earth
Dreaming its root
In flowers and snow.

(*North*, 36)

He continues to trust in his homeland. His poetry is grounded in actual, local detail, often in memories of Derry or observation of his adopted home in the Republic of Ireland. In later volumes, he wants to learn more about himself and his society in relation to the archaeology of that land. "Kinship" again celebrates intimacy with land, language and family. In the narrowed world of family and self, life-enhancing relations are still possible.

Kinship begins characteristically with Heaney walking in the bog searching for "antediluvian lore".

Heaney has great fascination with the earth. He uses various metaphors for the earth and gives a vivid description of activities involving the earth. Heaney has rich vocabulary for earth terms such as mud, mould, silt, slime, slicks, etc. These terms are used for different kinds of landscapes such as fens and bogs as well as for singular weather events and how they transform the earth's surface.

In *North*, Heaney's poetry gradually moves away from the direct sensuous encounters with Nature of the earlier work, towards a natural world, which while still insistently and materially present, is increasingly medicated by verbal categories. In *Field Work*, Heaney uses the natural world and his relationship with it in order to express how as a result of age his views on the natural world changed. In the beautiful "Glanmore Sonnets" he stays alert, watches the way steam raises from the plow, crouches "where small buds shoot and flourish in the hush", outstares a black rat swaying on the briar "like infected fruit". He is not a man to worry about the precise relation between nature and culture; it is enough for him if they seem continuous, so that the analogies can go both ways. He takes pleasure, as in "The Guttural Muse", in showing how both worlds meet. The poem refers to the noise of young people leaving a discotheque:

> Their voices rose up thick and comforting
> As oily bubbles the feeding tench sent up
> That evening at dusk-the slimy tench
> Once called the 'doctor fish' because his slime
> Was said to heal the wounds of fish that touched it.
>
> (*Field Work*, 28)

Heaney addresses many aspects of nature in his writing. In his poems, he encounters such things as man's relationship with nature, what he believes nature may be, and where in nature he thinks man belongs. Elmer Andrews comments:

> Dominated by a sense of nature's powers, he sees history, language and myth as bound up with nature, with territory and landscape. The landscape is sacramental. He is peculiarly

> responsive to the emblematic character of natural objects and processes. They evoke in him a deep sense of the numinous.[4]

Heaney's love of nature is not limited to earth only. He is equally in love with the sea also, but he uses the sea to depict his personal life. In "Lovers on Aran", Heaney presents the eternal embrace of land and sea gradually. It seems a personal symbol. The sea, the rocks and landscape are a symbol of love. The concluding lines of the poem show the completeness in his relation with Marie Heaney.

> Did sea define the land or land the sea.
> Each drew new meaning from the waves' conclusion.
> Sea broke on land to full identity.
>
> (*Death of a Naturalist*, 34)

After reading poems by Heaney, I feel that they try to convey the idea of nature being beautiful to the reader, something that in its untouched wildness can still look astounding and marvellous, without being altered or changed in any way. It is this beauty found in nature's wildness that causes the writers to also relay the idea that nature can sometimes be threatening.

We don't find any violent aspect of nature as we find in Shelley and Byron. But the political situation, violence, massacre, etc. depict a kind of storm in poet's life. Heaney has written several elegies mourning at the death of his friends and relatives in this political storm. We also get a description of pathetic condition of potato gatherers in the poem "At a Potato Digging". From September 1945 to February 1946 three quarters of the crop were destroyed in 323 counties in Ireland. This famine shattered the mind and soul of Ireland. It is said that one million died due to hunger and a half a million left their homes and went to other places in search of some job, bread and butter. During these years of famine and in later years Gaelic language, Gaelic culture and folk tradition lost their very existence. Estyn Evans in his book Irish Folk Ways has described that each member of Irish family ate eight ponds of potatoes every day out of despair. In his poem, Heaney has described the poor plight of agriculture.

He says that poor potato gatherers first appear like insects and then as crows attacking crow-black fields:

Labourers swarm in behind, stoop to fill
Wicker creels. Fingers go dead in the cold.
Like crows attacking crow-black fields,

(*DN*, 18)

In *The Haw Lantern*, we have a glimpse of storm in the "Hailstones", where he describes the memory of a sudden storm of childhood:

Nipple and hive, bite-lumps,
Small acorns of the almost pleasurable
Intimidated and disallowed

When the shower ended
And everything said wait.
For what? For forty years.

to say there, there you had
the truest foretaste of your aftermath—
in that dilation

when the light opened in silence
and a car with wipers going still
laid perfect tracks in the slush.

(Selected Poems, 221)

Heaney is widely read and respected due to his detailed and sensuously vivid evocation of rural Ireland and childhood. In early poems while describing his father as Daedalus of the fields, he introduces himself as a boy, a clumsy disciple, 'stumbling', 'yapping', 'tripping' like a puppy. As a child, he aspires to grow up and plough. Soon he realizes the superiority of his father and lives in a state of eclipse.

All I ever did was follow
In his broad shadow round the farm.

(*DN*, 12)

In his early volumes, his poems commemorated activities and trades of common persons like thatchers, blacksmiths, water-diviners, threshers, turf-cutters, ploughmen with horses, churners, hewers of wood and drawers of water. He also describes the victims of historical disasters, the croppies of 1798, the famine victims of 1845-47. They are ancestral presences and kin to parents and grandparents, part of the deep hunter land out of which modern Ireland emerged. In commemorating them, Heaney forms an alliance between his own poetry and the experience of the oppressed culture they represent. The thatcher leaves people 'gaping at his Midas touch'; the blacksmith goes in from the sight of motorized traffic 'To beat real iron out'; the diviner 'gripped expectants wrists. The hazel stirred.' These figures have skills which are mysterious, even occult. Heaney had a reputation for digging:

> By God, the old man could handle a spade.
> Just like his old man.

Heaney is not uncritical of rural life. In 'Follower' and in 'Thatcher', each vignette of anonymous labour has its distancing moment: 'I wanted to grow up and plough', says the adult poet remembering his child-self. He is a little critique of potato diggers when he says: 'Processional stooping through the turf / Recurs mindlessly as autumn'. He does not want to follow this life but labourer with a spade remains forever a part of his inner landscape. Heaney compares his pen with spade. He provides too much importance to spade. He is surprised at the use of spade by his father. "By God, the old man could handle a spade / Just like his old man". Heaney's father uses spade to dig a long trench to plant potato seeds in while Heaney is also digging but for words to plant into his poem instead of literally digging into the ground. Heaney's father is trying to dig deeper and deeper into the earth to try and obtain the best possible soil in which to plant the potato seeds.

Heaney delineates with child psychology in his poetry again and again. Piety to the terrain of childhood and terrified helplessness both have been expressed by him. In the poem "Death of a Naturalist", references to Miss Walls, to the 'daddy frog', and 'the mammy frog' and the information that 'that you could tell the weather by frogs', Heaney cleverly conveys a child's psyche and the pleasures of his initiation into the mysteries of nature.

In the poem "Punishment", Heaney's description of the woman victim retrieved from the bog provides an image for those young catholic women in Heaney's own Northern Ireland subjected to 'tarring and feathering' by members of their own community. Heaney's intense emotional touch with history, myth and symbols is presented in the poem "The Tollund Man". A man was deposited in the bog as sacrifice to the fertility goddess 'Nerthus'. The poet has described this man in the poem "The Tollund Man" who is a symbol of Irish people. He comes before us a modest saint symbolizing the triumph of nature over art. Heaney appeals to this man having spiritual existence to plead for Ireland. In the last stanza of the poem, Heaney has expressed his powerful thoughts through "The Tollund Man".

Out these in Juteland
In the old man-killing parishes
I will feel lost
Unhappy and at home.

(*WO*, 37)

"The Tollund Man" is also a powerful symbol of men sacrificed to inscrutable forces and to the community's needs. This poem twinned by "The Grauballe Man" and other two poems are of female bodies "Bog Queen" and "Punishment". These bog bodies are the symbols of cultural predicament.

The poem "Wolfe Tone" reaches back to a historical personage and to the complex historical events of the Irish 1790s. Tone attempted a union of Catholics and Protestants against England and was captured in 1798 after his invading fleet was defeated. He committed suicide in prison. He symbolizes the reformer estranged by his gift, his style and his daring from the very people he attempts to serve.

Light as a skiff, manoeuvrable
yet out manoeuvred
I affected epaulettes and a cockade
wrote a style well-bred and impervious
To the solidarity I angled for,
and played the ancient Roman with a razor.
I was the shouldered oar that ended up

far from the brine and whiff of venture,
like a scratching—post or a crossroads flagpole,
out of my element among small farmers—
(Selected Poems, 235)

Here the 'cockade' and 'razor' are like saint attributes and oar is also a symbol. Tone invents a metaphor for himself—that of a 'shouldered oar'. At this parabolic moment, the persona of Wolfe Tone and the person of Seamus Heaney converge.

Heaney is so much attached to his native Ulster that in order to examine his vocation as a poet, Heaney employs a persona from folk tradition. In "The Last Mummer", a companion piece to "The Servant Boy", we find the mummer 'shrouded' 'in mist and mystery. The mummer is bearing an ash plant as a stick; a cattle dealer would carry a stone, a contemporary native weapon. He arrives at a modem equivalent of the Big House. Unable to lure the occupants, he beats against their iron gates and hurls the stone onto their stone roofs in a gesture of frustration. Parker, in this respect comments, "like Heaney, he is 'trammelled / in the taboos of the community he serves, and he too is forced to pick a nice way', through the ritual dramas of 'blood / and feuding' which make up the national repertoire."[5]

Heaney's love of man reaches new heights when he commemorates the memories of the dead. He has written several elegies in memory of his friends and relatives. In Haw Lantern, he has presented several elegies which combine the density of living with the bleakness of loss. "The Stone Verdict", an anticipatory elegy for Heaney's father and other elegies commemorating the death of his young niece, 'Rachel', his wife's mother, his colleagues at Harvard, Robert Fitzgerald, affirm that the absence of the dead leaves a space in life but it takes a shape so powerful that it becomes a presence in itself. People of any culture share standards and beliefs. The artist's inner drama goes beyond the personal to become sympathetic and therefore political. If we ascribe immense and unforgettable value to the missing human piece, we ascribe value squarely in the human sphere.

Thus, Heaney has given a description of various aspects of nature, but the background is mostly ulster. In his later volumes also, Heaney returns again and again to the familiar landscape and human beings. He gets an effective metaphor to communicate the sense of a living landscape, continually in process, responding to topography, changing climate and human influence.

NOTES

1. Tony Curtis (ed.) *The Art of Seamus Heaney*, Ireland, Wolfhound Press, 1982, p. 49.
2. T.P. Flanagan, in an interview with Michael Parker, 27 November, 1985, quoted in Michael Parker, *Seamus Heaney: The Making of the Poet*, Dublin: Gill an Macmillan, 1993, p. 87.
3. Alan Warner, *A Guide to Anglo Irish Literature*, New York, Gill and Macmillan, St. Martin Press, 1981, p. 263.
4. Elmer Andrews, *The Poetry of Seamus Heaney*: *All the Realm of Whisper*, quoted in Contemporary Literary Criticism, Vol. 74, p. 178.
5. Michael Parker, *Seamus Heaney: The Making of the Poet*, p. 97.

WORKS CITED

Works by Seamus Heaney:

Death of a Naturalist, London: Faber and Faber, 1966.

Door into the Dark, London: Faber and Faber, 1969.

Wintering Out, London: Faber and Faber, 1972.

Stations, Belfast: Ulsterman Publications, 1975.

North, London: Faber and Faber, 1975.

Field Work, London: Faber and Faber, 1979.

Selected Poems 1965-1975. London: Faber and Faber, 1980.

Preoccupations: Selected Prose 1968-78. London: Faber and Faber, 1980.

Among school children, AQ John Malone Memorial Lecture, Belfast, 1983.

Station Island, London: Faber and Faber, 1984.

Sweeney Astray, London: Faber and Faber, 1984.

The Haw Lantern. London: Faber and Faber, 1987.

The Government of the Tongue, The 1986 T.S. Eliot Memorial Lectures and Other Critical Writings. London: Faber and Faber, 1988.

New Selected Poems 1966-1987. London: Faber and Faber, 1990.

Seeing Things, London: Faber and Faber, 1991.

The Spirit Level, London: Faber and Faber, 1996.

Beowulf (1999).

Electric Light (2001).

ABBREVIATION OF SEAMUS HEANEY'S BOOKS

DN = Death of a Naturalist
DD = Door into the Dark
WO = Wintering Out
N = North
S = Stations
FW = Field Work
SI = Station Island
SA = Sweeney Astray
HL = The Haw Lantern
P = Preoccupations
GT = Government of the Tongue
ST = Seeing Things
SL = The Spirit Level
EL = Electric Light

Need for Racial Harmony and Universal Brotherhood: A Critical Response to *The Nowhere Man*

18

S. John Peter Joseph

> Novels are the mirror of the age, but a very special kind of mirror, a mirror that reflects not merely the external features of the age but also its innerface, its nervous system, coursing of its blood and the unconscious promptings and conflicts which sway it. (Walter Allen 18-19)

Literature is a manifestation of the cultural, social, political and spiritual growth of a nation. It embodies not only the long-cherished and the deep-rooted traditions but also a comprehensive perception of the changing aspects of life and true reality of a nation. To understand the customs and cultural modes of a nation, one should study its literature. In the words of Paul Verghese, "there is no better yardstick to measure the culture of a nation than her literature which is an expression of society" (110). Literature, therefore, is the most specific and precise record of the history of a nation and the essential characteristics and spirit of its people. Undeniably good literature is always concerned with significant socio-economic and political problems and it acquires its essential unity when a genuine writer gains an insight into the basic social and historical trends of his times. While highlighting the true and serious purpose of a work of art, Anita Desai remarks: "Literature should deal with more enduring matters, less temporary and less temporal than politics. It should deal with life and death. It should be too ironical and also too mystical to accept the world at face value and regard it as the whole or the only truth" (1).

India which is known for its vast treasure of spiritual wisdom and cultural heritage has significantly contributed to the growth and development of world literature. Indian Literature in English occupies a renowned place among English and other literatures of the world. Fiction, being the most effective and impressive form of literary expression today, undoubtedly occupies a significant position in Indian Literature in English. As a unique and remarkable literary form, it has gained maturity and inimitable identity. The real maturity and success of fiction in Indian Literature in English can be gauged both in quality and quantity.

As the Indian English Novel has made a rapid and phenomenal progress and achieved excellence in the present literary scenario, the Indian English novelists have perceived in fiction a true and authentic vehicle for the representation of their literary genius and for revealing their sensibilities. The novelists, who belong to the pluralistic and multilingual Indian society, represent the ethos, image, traditions, conventions and glorious heritage of India in their novels. The fiction writers of recent times have been tirelessly experimenting with new thematic concerns and innovative writing techniques. Themes concerned with social evils, historical romance, social realism, hunger, poverty, tradition versus modernity found in the novels of earlier periods are being replaced by themes related to psychological issues like isolation, alienation, frustration, rootlessness and search for identity. With new trends in themes and stylistic techniques the corpus of Indian English fiction has been steadily and rapidly expanding. Remarkable novels have been written by illustrious novelists like Vikram Seth, Salman Rushdie, Arundhati Roy, Amitav Ghosh, Shashi Deshpande, Bharati Mukherjee, Shobha De, Nayantra Sahgal, Kamala Das, Khushwant Singh, Manju Kapoor and Mahesweta Devi. These writers along with the well-established novelists of earlier decades have not only succeeded in translating their vision of life into works of art but also in taking fiction to new vistas of thought and idea.

The depiction of the two opposite culture and value systems of India and Britain happens to be one of the most prominent thematic concerns of Indian English novelists. The confrontation between the East and the West at social, cultural and political levels has been viewed from different perspectives. Several novelists have even attempted to portray artistically the possibilities of mutual understanding between the East and the West. Commenting on the treatment of the East-West theme by Indian English novelists, Meenakshi Mukherjee observes:

> The definition of 'East' as well as of 'West' varies from novel to novel, but each tries in its own way to grapple with the problem that has continued to concern the Indo-Anglian novelists for more than fifty years. One is struck by the unabating interest shown by these novelists in the interaction of the two sets of values that exist side by side, and often coalesce, in the twentieth century. (65)

Some of the best novels which deal with the theme of confrontation between the East and the West are Santha Rama Rau's *Remember the House*, G.V. Desani's *All About H. Hatterr*, Raja Rao's *The Serpent and the Rope*, Monohar Malgonkar's *Combat of Shadows*, Ruth Prawer Jhabvala's *Esmond in India* and *Heat and Dust* and Bharati Mukherjee's *The Tiger's Daughter*. B. Rajan's *The Dark Dancer* and *Too Long in the West* depict the cultural and the social conflict between the East and West and the reaction of an Indian on coming back home after a brief stay in England. Novels such as Timeri Murari's *The Marriage*, Reginald and Jamila Massey's *The Immigrants*, Sasthi Pratha's *She and He*, M.V. Rama Sarma's *The Stream and Look Homeward*, Romen Basu's *A Gift of Love*, Anita Desai's *Bye-Bye Blackbird*, Dilip Hiro's *A Triangular View*, Chaman Nahal's *Into Another Dawn* and Kamala Markandaya's *The Nowhere Man* focus on different aspects of the East-West encounter by analysing the problems arising out of Indians' inadequacy to adjust themselves to the alien culture while they are in England.

The East-West dichotomy, as illustrated by the Indian's acquaintance with England constitutes a significant area of concern in the fictional works of Kamala Markandaya. She reveals her serious and vital artistic preoccupation by examining various factors that hinder cordial relations between the two different races and cultures. With great historical consciousness, she delineates graphically the tensions and conflicts between people of two diverse races and two entirely different attitudes of life from various perspectives by bringing them together in different relationships and situations.

Eastern in cultural and religious heritage and Western by inhabitation, Kamala Markandaya possesses a sort of "mixed sensibility" (Harish Raizada 37) with which she depicts judiciously the confrontation of the two modes of living. Her thorough knowledge and perception of both Eastern and Western values of life enables her to portray the personal, political and cultural interactions between the two. Undeniably, she is a sensitive writer and her accurate depiction of the juxtaposition of two diverse civilizations is a true accomplishment because her own creative and aesthetic personality is a unique combination of opposite qualities and values of two cultures. Harish Raizada rightly points out:

> Like a double—faced Janus, she can look at both ways of life with keen discernment and dispassionate objectivity. Her treatment of racial relationships is therefore realistic and unbiased. Englishmen and women portrayed by her are also not mere types but individuals infused with vitality of their own. (37-35)

In *The Nowhere Man* (1972), Kamala Markandaya deals with the theme of East-West encounter from a new perspective by portraying the miserable plight of the Indian immigrants in England from pre to post-Independence. In the words of B. Krupakar: "Kamala Markandaya's novel *The Nowhere Man*... is a compassionate and distressing tale of an aged Indian immigrant who becomes a martyr to racial hatred" (24). The novel illustrates the author's "continued concern with cultural values in the context of racist attitudes in England following the decline and defeat of British imperialism" (A.V. Krishna Rao and Madhavi Menon 105). Markandaya artistically presents the dichotomy of the East-West confrontation "which is shown through the undeserved plight of an old and friendly Indian immigrant in England; the portrait of his misery is probably the result of a deep study of the helplessness of Indian expatriates in Britain" (105). The Indo-British interaction is depicted mainly through the experiences of Srinivas, an Indian immigrant in Britain. Srinivas becomes a 'disoriented' person and is considered to be a trespasser. He, even after living for half a century in England, tends to feel like a "nowhere man, looking for a nowhere city" (*The Nowhere Man* 166). Being cut off from his well-founded traditional and cultural roots, he tries to get sustenance from his adopted country.

After his emigration from India in his youth, Srinivas lives in England for half a century and almost becomes a "naturalized Briton" (*The Nowhere Man* 93). Unlike Dev and Adit in Anita Desai's *Bye-Bye Blackbird* and Val in *Possession* who are young and have two options before them: whether to go to India or to remain in England itself, Srinivas, being an old man, has no such choice except to stay in England. He has spent several years of his life there and has started looking upon it as his own country. Considering England as his own country, he is very careful not to hurt or offend his hosts in any way. He tells Mrs. Pickering with pleasure. "This is my country now...my country! I feel at home in it, more so that I would in my own" (*The Nowhere Man* 58). He shows similar feelings to his friend, Abdul Bin Ahmed telling him that England is his country, "This is where I live, in England" (75). He does not agree with him that Britain would one day like to turn him out at any time.

The East-West confrontation as treated in this novel arises mainly from the economic pressure faced by Britain in the wake of the disintegration of the British empire. The post-War England with all its immigration problems is not safe for people like Srinivas. With the Depression, the two World Wars and the loss of companies, the British have started treating the immigrants in London as mere trespassers. Unemployment and housing have become the most acute problems. The British tend to view the outsiders with great suspicion and are very much afraid of the prevalent economic competition as they fear that sooner or later they will transgress their rights. According to them, the immigrants without money are animals and at no level is it possible to treat them as human beings. Very often the interests of the British and those of the immigrants clash with regard to job or housing or cultural activities.

The young men of England like Fred Fletcher, Mike, Joe and Bill who undergo the tremendous strain of being unemployed look upon the immigrants as the cause of their miserable plight and turn hostile towards them. They hold them responsible for "they came in hordes, occupied all the houses, filled up the hospital beds and their offspring took all the places in schools" (163). Fred finds that a large number of African and Asian immigrants are blocking the way of the English youth to economic security. He blames people like Srinivas for the miserable plight of the wandering and unemployed English youth "and becomes a self-styled champion of the cause of the English youth, campaigning systematically against the foreigners whom he wants to go back to their own countries" (Rangan 190). Fred, behaving like a racist demon, challenges a coal-black man who is sweeping the street: "Here you. You got no right to be in this country. You bugger off, see" (*The Nowhere Man* 164). Similarly, when he meets Srinivas, he tells him without any reservation, "You got no right to be living in this country" (164). When Srinivas tells him that he is British "by adoption" (165), Fred tries to assault him. Fred begins to feel that "he hated that colour and the man, and the untold evil he and his kind were letting loose in his country, his beloved England which he felt he had never loved so much before, not even where he left its shores for Australia" (165).

Ascribing the miseries and the predicament of the unemployed English youth to people like Srinivas, Fred becomes a professed defender of the cause of the British youth crusading systematically against the foreigners. "He shone, Fred felt: was born to lead, he knew with utter conviction. So he would. He would lead his countrymen in the fight to overthrow the evil, hidden forces that were threating them in their homeland (279). As the intensive agitation against the black mounts, posters begin to appear in different parts of London carrying "man-sized messages of hate, BLACKS GO HOME" and opening new hells of "fear and desolation in those at whom they were aimed" (168). Srinivas is able to understand the veracity of Abdul's words when he is tormented by Fred and his friends. He, no doubt, looks upon himself as an unwanted man and pathetically tells Mrs. Pickering

"It is time...when one is made to feel unwanted, and liable, as a leper, to be ostracized further, perhaps beyond the limit one can reasonably expect of oneself" (193). The West, in fact, has made him a nowhere man. He sadly realizes that he has nowhere to go to if at all he leaves England.

> Nowhere, he said to himself, and he scanned the pale anxious eyes which were regarding him for reasons that might drive him out, a nowhere man looking for a nowhere city. (166)

Srinivas thinks over his situation as "an alien, whose manners, accents, voice, syntax, bones, build, way of life—all of him—shrieked alien!" (230). Brooding over the uncongenial climate prevailing in England, he voices his miserable condition to Mrs. Pickering: "The people will not allow it. It was my mistake to imagine...I am to be driven outside, which is the way they want it. An outsider in England. In actual fact I am, of course, and Indian (231-32).

It is quite evident that Srinivas and Vasantha have different attitudes towards England. While the former entertains a kind of cosmopolitan outlook in life, the latter remains wholly an Indian till her death. Even after settling down in London she never compromises her orthodox Indian ways. Though living on the British soil, she adheres to her Indian ways of living, dressing, eating and even dying. As a typical Indian woman, she never compromises with her rich religious tradition. Despite acquiring property and financial status Srinivas and Vasantha cannot fully identify themselves with the alien culture. Wholesome integration with a foreign environment and its socio-cultural atmosphere is not possible for them because they cannot give up their deep-rooted native traditions and religio-cultural systems. Srinivas tells Mrs. Pickering: "One does not realize when one leaves one's country, how much is chopped off and left behind too" (67). When Mrs. Pickering tells him with a note of consolation, "There can be compensations. If one is cut off from one's culture there is always the adopted one to draw upon", he replies. "But you see, we—that is to say, my wife and I—I do not think we did" (68). Srinivas, in the midst of agitations arising from racial prejudice and discrimination, tries to accept his position as an outsider in Britain.

The reaction of Srinivas's son, Laxman, to the problem of racialism is quite different from that of his father. He, who has never known India, has his education in the Christian schools. His participation in the War and marriage with an English woman makes it clear that he has totally identified himself with the English society. And that is why the racial discrimination against the blacks shocks him profoundly. When an English woman tells him in a spirit of racial antagonism, "Go back where you belong" (261), the enraged Laxman retaliates, "I belong right here" (262). When accused by her husband of total ungratefulness of England for its aid to India, he retorts "Loans totalling one quarter of one per cent of the gross national product lent at rates of which a back-street money-lender would be ashamed. It is, in any case,...less than a hundredth of what has been lifted or looted" (262). As a reply to the rude remark of his adversary, "You're going to cause an explosion, you and your sort" (262), he says with contemptuous spirit, "You mean you are. You'll be blown up with it, what's more, you and your sort" (262).

The sudden and unexpected demise of Seshu and the death of Vasantha prove a great blow to Srinivas. Vasantha has been a source of great strength to him. With the death of his wife, Srinivas finds life quite empty and barren. His business starts failing and the house becomes what his elder son, Laxman, contemptuously calls a 'pigsty'. Srinivas's loneliness is very much caused by his severance from his kith and kin who leave one by one from his life forcing him into a predicament against an alien and hostile environment. He feels terribly lonely and rootless and often resorts to the memories of the past. He feels frustrated and even thinks of returning home. He wishes to return to India but he cannot do so. He can only make an expedition to the land of his birth only in imagination. In the words of Rangan, Srinivas is "a rootless restless individual, dispossessed of India and disowned by England" (186). To R.S. Singh, Srinivas is "a rootless creature, a product of the meeting of the East and the West" (147).

The delineation of the relationship between Srinivas and Mrs. Pickering after the death of Srinivas's wife, Vasnatha, transforms the entire novel into "a perceptive work of art" (K. Madhavi Menon "The Vision in Kamala Markandaya's *The Nowhere Man*" 29). Their relationship is undoubtedly built on an unswerving commitment to human values based on true freedom. True freedom is essentially commitment without either force or compulsion. The novel holds out the possibility of intercultural meeting through this relationship founded on profound human sympathy, care and compassion to the exclusion of racial and cultural barriers. Mrs. Pickering tries to alleviate Srinivas's sufferings. She is extremely kind, understanding and helpful. A divorce of middle age, not physically attractive, enters his house and gradually influences him. Though Srinivas meets her by chance, the meeting develops into a warm relationship. She cooks, cleans, mends his clothes, sometimes even spends her own money and helps him with good counsel. Srinivas admires her and later she becomes a sort of common-law wife to him.

Through the cordial relationship between them Srinivas realizes his responsibilities to Mrs. Pickering and also to the country he has adopted as his own. He begins to feel that he has a duty and an obligation to the society which has given him refuge. Therefore, he has to remain passive and calm though he suffers a lot in the hands of fanatics like Fred and his people. His spirit does not give up its strength completely even though he seems to be undergoing a lot of racial conflict. Fred's diabolic nature seems to be quite boundless. He finds pleasure in tormenting Srinivas in several ways. He puts faeces, dead mice, etc., at his door step. Srinivas is abused and scandalised and eventually Fred sets fire to his house to burn him alive. While trying to set fire to the house of Srinivas, he himself gets caught in the flames and is charred to death. Srinivas is finally saved from the burning house, but soon dies of shock.

Despite his sincere efforts to integrate into the alien culture and the life of the country of his adoption, Srinivas is not allowed to do so. Ever since he reached England, he has tried his best to feel one with the people of the country of adoption. But unfortunately, the English community had failed to absorb him into its mainstream. The pertinent comment of Rangan deserves to be mentioned here:

> Srinivas represents millions of men who for some reason or other leave their own roots and fail to strike roots in the alien soil, and die as rootless and restless individuals. Srinivas lives in England for one full generation of thirty years only to be a nowhere man. (192)

A.V. Krishna Rao finds certain similarities between *The Nowhere Man* and *The Plague* (1948) of Albert Camus. Rambert, the principal character, feels terribly miserable and totally isolated in the oppressive situation which arises out of the plague. The faltering emotions and the harrowing experiences of Rambert in exile can be easily compared with those of Srinivas, who is also undergoing tremendous ordeal due to racial hatred and animosity. Though he feels homeless and uprooted by being cut off from his native traditions and ancient heritage he, unlike Cross Damon, the outsider in Richard Wright's novel, *The Outsider* who advocates violence against the racial aggression of the Whites, follows the principles of tolerance and non-violence. Firmly believing in the concept of love and ahimsa, Srinivas seems to agree with Rambert when the latter says: "And that's my point, we—mankind have lost that capacity for love... Let's wait to acquire that capacity..." (*The Plague* 65).

The Nowhere Man shows that in spite of the presence of fanatical racialists and their sympathizers England does not certainly lack men of good sense. On the one side, there are self-appointed hard-core racial champions like Fred who, while referring to immigrants, bursts out, "He is a devil. They're all devils", or like Mike who bellows, "Bloody Swine. Deport the whole bloody lot" (*The Nowhere Man* 205), or like Mrs. Glass who comments, "It's these people, these immigrants. They keep coming here, who asked them? One day they're poor, living off the rates, the next day they could buy us all up" (197). On the other side, there are people who are able to understand the process of history and the genuine spirit of the times. They are Dr. Radcliffe, Mrs. Pickering, Mr. Glass, Mrs. Fletcher and the constable Kent. Mrs. Fletcher feels extremely sorry for the misconduct of her son and even apologizes to Srinivas on behalf of her son. These people, no doubt, stand for the highest British traditions.

Kamala Markandaya's frequent return to the theme of the East-West encounter and especially of the Indo-British meeting and her masterly treatment of it in great depth and seriousness shows his genuine and resolute concern for the global and contemporary situation. As a sincere student of history, she is quite aware that the contact with the West is really conducive to the growth and development of a new angle of vision in the life of the East. But she knows that cultural pride, sharp political disagreement, colonial domination, racial consciousness and the subsequent tension kept the twain apart. Unlike other writers, who are of the opinion that the gap between the East and the West can never be properly bridged, Kamala Markandaya seems to suggest in her novels that cultural and political synthesis and a compromise between the two modes of living are always possible. She endeavours to establish the point that a harmonious union and lasting relationship between the East and the West can be established only through mutual respect, appreciation and understanding and not through domination.

The Nowhere Man undoubtedly proves to be a testimony of the novelist's widening awareness of contemporary developments in race relations at the international level. Thakur Guruprasad observes that the novel "is a very objective, balanced and truthful account of Indo-British relations...filtered through the genuine artist's imagination..." (200). Markandaya in the novel attempts to convey the idea that senseless racial animosity and global violence will be fatal to the entire mankind. She decries racial violence and aggression and convincingly emphasizes the need for racial harmony, tolerance and universal brotherhood. She firmly believes that racial bigotry is a serious menace to human existence.

WORKS CITED

Allen, Walter. *Reading a Novel*. London: Phoenix House, 1940.

Camus, Albert. *The Plague*. Trans. Stuart Gilbert. New York: Random House, 1948.

Desai, Anita. "Replies to the Questionnaire", *Kakatiya Journal of English*, Vol. 3, No. 1, 1978.

Guruprasad, Thakur. "And Never the Twain Shall Meet: Kamala Markandaya's *The Nowhere Man*". *Language Forum*, Special Issue on Modern Indo-English Fiction, 7, 1-4 (April 1981-March 1982).

Krupakar, B. "Race Relations and *The Nowhere Man*". *The Literary Endeavour*, 2.283, n.d.

Markandaya, Kamala. *The Nowhere Man*. Bombay: Orient Longman Ltd., 1972.

Menon, Madhavi K. "The Vision in Kamala Markandaya's *The Nowhere Man*". *Commonwealth Quarterly*, 13.34 (December 1986-March 1987).

Mukherjee, Meenakshi. *The Twice Born Fiction,* New Delhi: Arnold-Heinemann Publishers (India) Ltd., 1974.

Raizada, Harish. "East West Confrontations in the Novels of Kamala Markandaya". *Perspectives on Kamala Markandaya*. Ed. Madhusudan Prasad. Ghaziabad: Vimal Prakashan, 1984.

Rangan, V. "*The Nowhere Man*: A Critical Analysis". *Perspectives on Kamala Markandaya*. Ed. Madhusudan Prasad. Ghaziabad: Vimal Prakashan, 1984.

Rao, A.V. Krishna and Madhavi K. Menon. *Kamala Markandaya: A Critical Study of Her Novels, 1954-1982*. New Delhi: B.R. Publishing Corporation, 1997.

Singh, R.S. *Indian Novel in English*. New Delhi: Arnold-Heinemann, 1977.

Verghese, Paul. *Problems of the Indian Creative Writer in English*. Bombay: Somaiya, 1971.

The Diasporic Poetry of G.S. Sharat Chandra

19

Basavaraj Naikar

G.S. Sharat Chandra (1945-2000) was a poet of Indian Diaspora living in America. He has published five collections of poetry namely, *April in Nanjangud* (1971), *Once or Twice* (1974), *Heirloom* (1978), *Immigrants of Loss* (1993) and *Family of Mirrors* (1993). Recently, he has also published a short story collection entitled *Sari of the Gods* (1998). He hails from Nanjangud in Mysore district of Karnataka State, India. After his education in Law at Pune (India) he went to Canada and received another law degree from Osgoode Law School in Toronto. There he felt that "lawyers were pompous asses... There was racism in Canada then and no one would hire me. I left Canada and went to Iowa City."[1] It was there that Chandra began to realize an ambition cherished since his days as a teenager—to become a poet. This was his greatest achievement. Later, he became a Professor of Creative Writing in the University of Missouri, Kansas State, USA and practised the genre of poetry, fiction, and short fiction. In the early seventies, he published interesting translations of a few vacanas of Sarvajna in London Magazine. A brief look at his career is enough to show how he was compelled by the contingencies of his life and quirks of fate to leave his motherland and settle in America in search of better material comforts and recognition. Obviously, he was destined to be an expatriate poet who was to oscillate between two cultures, i.e. native Hindu culture and American culture at least in the initial stage of his migration. In the later stage, he was slowly absorbed by the American culture, which diminished his attraction for the native culture and nostalgic attachment. As the poet's vista of experience grew wider, his perceptions of life grew sharper and his dilemmas also might have multiplied. A migratory bird has to keep on adjusting itself to ever-new atmosphere without losing its basic identity. "We are all, he seems to say, immigrants in the land of imagination."[2] He believes that "It is human to miss something that was there before—country, town, place, street, wives, husbands."[3] Thus, we may trace an evolution in Sharat Chandra's poetic career, which begins with native experience, passes through immigrant experience and ends up with American experience.

Sharat Chandra's early experience in his native land may be seen in his early collections of poetry. In his interview with Mary Vasudeva and Deepika Bahri, Sharat Chandra clarifies his views about his native place and childhood experience as follows: "No neglect or abandonment by family, as Bruce King erroneously speculates in his book *Modern Indian Poets in English*. I had a wonderful childhood in a large family. But the sense of being lost is a quest for answers not simply for myself, but for understanding the conflicting psychological selves we possess."[4]

In the present article, an effort has been made to understand the major themes articulated in *Heirloom* and *Once or Twice*. The poems in this collection show not only his native and homely experience in India especially in Karnataka, but also his separation from his motherland and the consequent nostalgia. Like many globetrotting poets, Sharat Chandra also has the advantage of adopting a contrastive mode of perception, i.e. east- west encounter. Familial relations happen to be the dominant themes in the poems in *Heirloom*. Family, therefore, becomes a dominant metaphor controlling the poetic perception of Sharat Chandra. While in India, he prepares himself to go to America and while in America, he nostalgically remembers India and corresponds with his father and other relatives. "I feel terribly nostalgic and miss everything that was part of my life. But it is important that this sort of nostalgia shouldn't overwhelm the sense of universal aesthetics. Poetry is art and art doesn't accommodate sentimentality."[5] Chandra's particular hell, like Dante's, is centred in his sense of displacement...Dante himself, banished from his beloved city of Florence, demonstrated that one of the essential qualities of all damnation is homesickness. Chandra, in his updated way, knows exactly what he means."[6]

Most of the poems in *Heirloom*[7] and *Once or Twice*[8] deal with Indian, especially South Indian, more especially South Karnatakian life—like painting, sculpture, beggary, bureaucracy, funerals, holy shrines, fishermen, farmers and other details of cultural environment. Family or familial relationships happen to be the dominant metaphors in his Indian poems. The relationship between father and son in its various manifestations is an important motif in some of his poems.

In "Poems for My Father", the poet recounts the last moments of his father and his attachment with the latter and the former's expectations about the latter. The first stanza describes the illness of his father and how the entire family is silently worried about it:

> In the kitchen my father
> squats as usual,
> the family gathers around
> to discuss his last illness,
> my father looks well,
> he scoops up the rice and curry
> eats it calmly,
> he too is talking of his illness.

Then he describes how his father's disease was not diagnosed properly, how it was malaria and not cancer, which enervated him and how he appeared to be recovering. The poems, obviously, articulate the poet's nostalgic memory about his father, the concern of the members of his family for the father's health and their anxiety about his imminent death. The poet, who has been living in America thousands of miles away from his motherland, feels a special bondage to his family and the head of the family, i.e. father. What is admirable in the poet is that in spite of being in America and enjoying a very comfortable life there, he cannot afford to forget his father as the Indians, especially Hindus attach a great deal of importance to the father because father and mother happen to be gods for the children.

But when the poet goes away from India to America, he receives a letter from his mother that the father has started bleeding. The poet is unable to reconcile himself to the harsh reality and has a wishful dream. He suffers from deep anxiety about his father.

Again the father appears to be temporarily better and wants to wait for the poet's publication of his book of poems named after his native place, i.e. Nanjangud, for a hearing aid and a little port wine. But before the father's expectations are fulfilled, he is overtaken by death. After his death in Mysore, he appears to the poet in America (i.e. Mount Pleasant) and seems to talk with him telepathically.

The expatriate or diasporic experience consists in one's going away from one's country and coming back to it nostalgically and to notice the change that has been brought about in the native country by Time. It is this experience, which has been recounted in the "Return" section of the poem. When the poet lands in India, perhaps at Bangalore or Bombay, he feels the torrid heat of the tropical country, which provides a sharp contrast to the cool climate of America:

At the airport
The family Fiat
crackles in the heat,
the doors are hot
as the underside
of an electric iron.

The backwardness of the village, hence of the country stares hard in the poet's face:

The roads to home
are scant bound as ever
coolies move along the potholes
with gravel pans on their head
bullock carts trundle
in and out the car's wheel-span.

The effect of Time on life may be felt conspicuously. His mother has become old and looks as frail as a sparrow. His father is dead and cremated according to the customs of his caste:

My father
cremated by the river's bend
then transferred in a basket
skull pelvis femur
lies under the mango tree
free of caste and skin.

Life continues and modernity has crept into the town. The rich have bought air-conditioners and the poor are reconciled to their lot. The poet plans to go for a pilgrimage. The mother is reconciled to her widowhood and loneliness. The idea of the father's death makes the poet aware of the possibility of reincarnation, which is part of Hindu faith.

In the poem entitled "Consistently Ignored", the poet shows the boy's curiosity, seriousness and the maternal humour and myth-making capacity. In the villages of Karnataka and also perhaps in India, the mothers tease their children by saying that they bought them from some beggar or caught them from the sky. It is this collective myth that the poet tries to deconstruct in the present poem:

Consistently ignored in a family of ten
I asked mother, 'Am I your real son?'
She paused from grinding spice,
'No, I bought you from a beggar
For a bushel of rice'
From behind sisters giggled.

The boy (i.e. the poet) unable to distinguish between humorous myth and reality takes it very seriously and begins to search for the beggars from whom he might have been bought:

I matched features, spied on beggars
Roamed the backyard thinking
Of distant huts, certain
My mother sat busy in one
Scheming to trade another son
For fish to add to that bushel.

The boy's inability to understand the parental humour is itself quite humorous and throws light upon the working of a boy's psyche.

The metaphor of the family is conspicuous in "Brothers". The brothers, who are brought up together and grow together, are separated by the contingencies of life like marriage and jobs at different places. Perhaps, the separation is part of one's growth in life. The poet deplores that:

My brothers come visiting less and less
they come
leaving their wives and children
in sleep.

The poet wants to be close with them once again and longs for the bliss of childhood marked by fraternal affinity and cordiality:

I hold their hands
we are children once again
this is the dream I understand
which takes me
to places where I would stay
places
I would not want to leave.

The poet longs to recover the lost affinity and cordiality:

We should go on this way
forever
I tell them they listen they listen
they promise to be closer.

In this poem, Sharat Chandra obviously shows the universal experience of man in very simple terms. He has shown how the process of growth in life involves the loss of childhood paradise and the distancing from the close relatives and how a sensitive soul longs for the recovery of that paradise. The poem remotely brings to our mind the poems of similar themes by Wordsworth.

In *Heirloom*, there are a few poems, which are autobiographical in nature and give expression to his thoughts about his personal predicament and dilemmas. In "My Thirty

Third Morning" Sharat Chandra offers an autobiographical picture about himself. He turns thirty-three on a grey morning and dreams of a song, of a crow, of ducks with silent squawks and thrushes with suspended whistles and imagines himself to be a crow being scared of squawking ducks. His thirty-third birthday is marked by a sort of fear and mechanical living without any grand or colourful dimension to it:

> The crow crows at the break of light
> Who would say it has inclinations
> Scares easily of squawking ducks
> Head-on thrush collisions,
> It's none of these but myself
> Turning thirty-three on a grey morning.

"My Thirty-Fifth Birthday" is a nostalgic evocation of the poet's childhood in Karnataka, India and also shows a contrast between the Indian past and the American present. He, for example, remembers his vernacular medium of instruction and his slips in the recitation of Sanskrit hymns from the Veda for which he is disliked by his High School teacher. Likewise, he remembers his chaste aunt, who used to sniff a brand of snuff named after a goddess. Similarly, he remembers the old gramophone records of military hotels blaring their sound and chasing his car. He also remembers Mahatma Gandhi, who taught him the lesson of native life:

> Inside a touring talkies
> Gandhi himself pointed
> his fingers at me from a slide
> which read
> 'Be worthy of your mother country.'

The irony may be in the contrast between the past days spent in India and the present stay of the poet in America:

> All this
> just because
> until late in the night
> in this American town
> I drank scotch
> and cursed in English.

In "Buckled to My Waist", Sharat Chandra recounts his close relationship with his father and the importance of paternal advice. He seems to request his seven-year dead father to forgive his mistakes as well as his longing for perfection. He confesses that it took him fifteen years to realize the truth of his father's advice:

It has taken me fifteen years to learn
the wisdom of your last whisper,
fifteen years of dragging a makeshift
bridge of words buckled to my waist.

The poet seems to be disillusioned with poetry, which has become a commercial affair, 'a chase of ordeals without hoof'. Although the eyes travel freely, the mind cannot do so as it is anchored to its bone. Similarly, the poet may be engaged in the free exercise of his imagination, but he cannot soar in the sky, as he is earth-bound. The over-all vision of the poems seems to be the striking contrast between the harsh reality and the unshackled play of imagination.

In the epistolary series of poems entitled "Letters from My Father" Sharat Chandra offers details of his family background in Nanjangud, the Government of Karnataka, their problems and concerns and socio-religious problems, etc. In the first letter, the father writes about the three ministers or politicians, who wear the Gandhi-cap and control the government and debate over the use of English language. Then, he writes about his poverty:

Today we had no rice
so we ate green beans and curd
the milkman is out looking for a patch of grass,
it has not rained since 1973.

Then, the father writes to the son about the failure of rains in Karnataka and the effort of the government to get some artificial rains with the American help:

our government has proclaimed
they'll make rain
the eldest son of our chief
is already in America
to ask the President for some clouds.

The ironical contrast between the scientific method of attracting the clouds and the religious especially superstitious method of conducting some ritual to attract the rains is suggested in a very subtle fashion by the poet. The hunger of the people is described in a very ironical tone by the nephew of the poet:

Your nephew says
if the government cordoned off
the hungry millions together
over a parched field of wheat
they'd cry enough to make bread.

In the second letter, the father informs the son about the effect of political life upon the civilian life. The poet's doctor-sister is transferred to some other place simply because she made the Deputy Minister's wife wait for some time.

In the third letter, the father informs the son about the geographical and social changes, which have affected them adversely. The heat is terrible hence 'sacrificial'. The effect of Time on human age is described by the father:

This afternoon my skin hangs heavy on my back.

The economic poverty has brought about a lot of change, almost degeneration in the society of Karnataka. It is indirectly described by the poet:

The washerman's donkey hops
round and round in the alley
it isn't convinced
the garbage pail is empty of dinner leaves.

This description is followed by an ironical one:

No one eats with leaves any more
it's faster from hand to mouth
if there's enough to hand
to mouth...

The fourth letter recounts the father's mystic experience so common in old age among the Hindus:

I have a strange feeling
someone sits in the front-room
fanning the heat from his face:

do you think it is Him?
Perhaps he took a shortcut by draught...

The mystic experience is accompanied by a philosophical reflection in a Hindu's life. The father asks such a philosophical question:

Isn't the body a wrap within a wrap
folds of goatskin
hiding the dark it hides from
the dark it'll accompany?

In the fifth and last letter, the father writes about the poet's mother. It easily shows the mother's religiosity, concern and affection for the son:

Your mother sends dried camphor
from the feet of the Lord:
her eyes still light up at your letters
though she fails on her feet.

The father further advises him to go to the third country for better prospects and nobler ways of living. The last section looks like an anti-climax on account of its note of practical suggestion:

If you don't hear from me
do not be pensive
it only means
I've run out of ink...

The lengthy epistolary poem, thus, offers a varied picture of the Hindu family, socio-political, financial and mystical aspects of life. All these details are part of the poet's diasporic nostalgia for his motherland and his desire to keep in touch with his roots lest he should forget or lose them as he is overwhelmed by the American culture.

"The Black Deity" depicts the superstitions of the Hindus in an objective fashion. When the poet watches the black idol of a goddess on the Mylapur hill of Madras, he notices the hot afternoon and the drying trees. The horrid summer of India creates the problem of water and food for the natives. The villagers, who cannot understand the irregularities of Nature, blindly attribute them to the wrath of a goddess in accordance with their anthropomorphic religious belief:

At the village men whispered
Of the black deity's wrath -
Pestilences or death in the family.
The priest counselling sacrifice
Kept glancing at the tree
Where the batu-birds stilt-walked.

The poet, who understands the superstitious belief of the Indians, tries to visualize the scene of people getting ready to offer the sacrifice:

Now, miles away from the tree,
I have a vision of a posse
With lanterns and axes
Creeping up the hill.

"Vendor of Fish" offers a beautiful picture of the life of a fisherman marked by hard labour and hope of security and comfort so essential for human happiness. The poet describes his diary of hard work in the first stanza:

All night he waits at the harbour
his eyes the colour of sea
the sea the colour of trawlers
he grabs the finest wipes them
on his shawl his shawl
the colour of blood.

One may easily see the unifying bond between the fisherman, the boat, the sea and the fish in the stanza. There is almost a religious devotion in the fisherman for the whole phenomenon of his profession.

The fish that the fisherman catches has a practical, especially a commercial value for him. It is inevitable for his survival, i.e. for his food:

Fish the colour of rupees
he thinks of the meal he'll buy
the meal of chapatis and kurma
the fish in the smell of kurma

he packs them in the basket with ice
his hands the colour of fire.

It is the dream of a better life that galvanizes him and quickens his movements. The dream also enhances his aesthetic sensibility thereby enabling him to appreciate the beauty of the fish. His joy of life expresses itself in the form of a song:

He leaps on the tar road faster
than sweat can print his feet
the distance is the colour of dreams
the fish in the basket shine
sawdust daubs their fins
he sings in praise of their colour.

In "Self-Portrait" Sharat Chandra offers an autobiographical picture. He claims that he has no belief in astrology and does not have a clear picture of his future life:

There are scars instead
of lines on my palm
I've no biography
only remembrance.

He is aware that he life is marked by a sense of emptiness:

I say
leaves have a habit
of giving in to emptiness
like oysters with pearls
missing...

When he encounters an astrologer in a nameless street, who holds a horoscope to his face, he bares his shirt and shows them his bony body and walks away from them.

"Relatives" (*Once or Twice*, 11) happens to be an imaginary picture about the poet's own future life. When he writes his last poem, his relatives come to him and ransack his body for the last poem and try to arbitrate over his art. The poet seems to be satirizing the possessiveness and the greed of the relatives, who want to derive some profit or even reputation from the poet, but alas, without trying to understand his heart:

His manuscripts fly around

like feathers of a shot bird
his love spreading
her long dress her hair.

They try to understand some hidden message in his tears and examine his cheeks. They seem to be in a hurry to understand him:

he examines the cheeks as he wipes them
he stomps his boot with urgency

When they cannot understand the meaning of the live poems, they believe in the afterlife of the same and therefore, seal them in transparent wrappers and send them to lawyers:

He believes in the afterlife of the poem
as silverfish eggs of moth
he seals them in cellophone
he sends them to his lawyers.

Finally, when they cannot understand the meaning of the poem in their lifetime, they leave it to their children to pursue it:

We'll bequeath our search
to our children they say
owning the last poem
will be its own reward they say.

But they feel proud of the physical possession of the poem, though they can never enter its semantic heart.

In "Tirumalai" (*Once or Twice*, 18), the poet highlights the contrast between religious faith and the harsh and ugly reality in the Hindu context. Venkateswara happens to be the Lord of Seven Hills and attracts thousands of devotees every day. The poet also being a Hindu is naturally inspired to visit the deity:

Lord Vishnu's place
Also known as Lord Venkateswara
He turned stone on the seventh hill
While visiting earth on a curse
He ran into woman trouble.

After explaining the mythical background of Lord Venkateswara's descent to the earth, the poet describes various aspects of the deity's role. He is known as a rich-god in South India:

Since then he's grown famous
As arbiter of disputes
Bribed with rubies and emeralds
By those who can afford such bribes.
Politicians speak well of him too
So do government servants
Wanting promotion or increment
Women wanting child or husband.
Some visit incognito
Others with bare hands
Or faceful of tears.

Thus, people have pitched their faith in the Lord of Seven Hills for various reasons. The poet also is made by the circumstances to believe in it:

I, when I was four,
Gave the Lord my head of hair
I was told that would make me rich
My hair prosperous.

But the irony is that the poet's faith is totally nullified by the harsh reality of his experience:

The father who said that is dead.
My mother who held me to the barber
Ails with age and despair
The hills have changed hands
I have grown bald
And owe two payments
On the alimony.

The brief examination of the Indian themes in Sharat Chandra's poems shows how the opposite pulls of longing (for India) and belonging (to America) control his emotions and perception and how he has to strike a balance between physically going away from the native country and emotionally coming home repeatedly. This paradoxical experience of going and coming happens to be an important aspect of diasporic experience.

NOTES

1. Mackle, Lynn. "Features", University News, October 7-13, 1996.
2. Russ, Biff. "The Kansas City Star", Sunday, October 24, 1993.
3. Mackle, Lynn. "Features", University News, October 7-13, 1996
4. "Swallowing for Twenty Years/the American Mind and Body: An Interview with G.S. Sharat Chandra" by Mary Vasudeva & Deepika Bahri, *Journal of Commonwealth and Postcolonial Studies*, Vol. 5, No. 1. Fall 1997, published, April 1998, Georgia Southern University, Statesboro, USA, p. 13.
5. "An Interview with G.S. Sharat Chandra: A Poet of Indian Diaspora," Basavaraj Naikar. *Literary Vision* (New Delhi: Sarup & Sons, 2005), p. 116.
6. Russ, Biff. "The Kansas City Star", Sunday, January 15, 1995.
7. Sharat Chandra, G.S. *Heirloom*, Hippopotamus Press, Surrey, 1978.
8. Sharat Chandra, G.S. *Once or Twice*, Hippopotamus Press, Surrey, 1974.

Equating 'the other half of her equation': An Appraisal of Androgynous Subsistence in *Wuthering Heights, Debi Chaudhurani* and *Sula*

20

Koyel Chakrabarty

The expression 'other half' always seems to bring to our minds a very clichéd expression that is used for introducing one's spouse as the 'better half'. Interestingly enough, the expression which actually talks of fulfilling a whole, unbalances itself with an element which is 'better' and not present in the first half. Ironical nevertheless, like the Victorian 'angel of the house', the expression 'better half' loaned from a gender oriented relationship like marriage, misbalances the attempt to balance the equation, between a husband and his wife, that it at all tries to establish. And here lies the ogre of social hegemony and change that tries its best to mis-equate an equation leading to the development of phenomena like feminism.

Feminism is no more in its first or second wave of its evolution where girls would undress like boys and fight for equal political and economic rights but rather has turned into a proposition deep rooted with logical stances and a blend in relative persistence in humanity. On this, Anna Quindlen, famous twentieth century bestseller author and journalist, in one of her interviews rightly comments "It's important to remember that feminism is no longer a group of organizations or leaders. It's the expectations that parents have for their daughters, and their sons, too. It's the way we talk about and treat one another. It's who makes the money and who makes the compromises and who makes the dinner. It's a state of mind. It's the way we live now." Being born in a semi-equal boy-girl world today, our duty lies in accelerating this semi-equal state to a balanced whole where every human being will not be endangered by the past concepts of gender differentiation but an equation within themselves that proclaims in it two halves one man and one woman. This concept of 'androgyny', as popularized by Simone de Beauvoir as 'brotherhood' or masculinity in woman, have urged critics, like Carolyn Helibrun in her *Toward a Recognition of Androgyny,* to examine concepts of androgyny to subvert existing representations of masculine feminine traditional literary criticism. She claims referring Woolf that 'androgyny' is useful to feminism because it moves away from Freud's notion of bisexuality, which reinforces gender difference as binominal. She further asserts, androgyny circumvents literary patterns of dominance and submission associated with rigid gender paradigms.[1] However, the representations and interpretations in feminism has not restricted itself to 'androgyny' or 'brotherhood', since then, rather it has taken greater shapes in the nineteenth and the twentieth century in the works of Ursula LeGuin and others who carry the concept of androgyny further from Helibrun to its hope for a Utopian future.

The concept of androgyny as established by the first wave feminists can be associated, with the Hindu mythology, through the icon of Ardhanarishvara, also known as Parashiva. It is a general signification of Lord Shiva and his wife Parvati, also taken as Shakti, as a whole. The idol of Ardhanarishvara, with a definite equity of Shiva and Shakti, Shiva in the right half and Parvati being the other half, represents power and energies to destruction and creation, rage and calmness all in one. It represents the harmony of the opposites into a single whole. Shiva and Shakti is one and the same Supreme. On Its own free-will for the benefit of *pashus* (souls), which are drowned in *pasha* (bondage), It believes to create the living and non-living world. Its dynamism of creation thus springs out of It, which is called *shakti.* Shiva and Its power, Shakti create everything. This is the form of their togetherness that springs out of Lord Shiva. Shiva and Shakti are one and different in a single entity. They are ratiocinated equally as the person and his action. They are one and the same like the ice and the water—one becomes the other. The Ardhanari form thus, illustrates how the female principle of God, Shakti is inseparable from the male principle of God, Shiva.

Ellen Goldberg in her book, *The Lord who is half woman Ardhanarisvara in Indian and Feminist Perspective* makes an extensive study of Ardhanarishvara: the Lord Who is Half Woman. She examines the influence of Ardhanarishvara through iconography, mythology, devotional poetry and the role of Ardhanarishvara in Hatha Yoga practice. She provides a critical analysis of the image in terms of the gender construction of 'male' and 'female' and androgyny across cultures. For Goldberg, Ardhanarishvara represents "a paradigm of sacred human knowledge—a symbolic cultural landscape, formulating, regulating and legitimising religious and ideological presuppositions including gender, on the one hand, while also providing a diagnostic paradigm for mapping the transformations of human consciousness through the subtle conjunction of the male and female form."[2]

The concept of androgyny, as represented by the literary writers, face variations worldwide as writers with different visions and missions sketch out their female-heroes in such a manner that they represent her masculine-matriarchy over her tender and traditional woman-ness, thereby asserting her uniqueness and identity in a society which is unravished and unblemished by social constructs of feminine subjugation. But it is not surprising that most of such literary instances bear a definite pattern among them ascertaining the feminist proposition world wide. This paper will hope to establish the androgynous pattern and existence of Prafulla in Bankim Chandra Chattopadhay's Bengali novel, *Debi Chaudhurani*, Catherine-Heathcliff two-in-one existence in Emily Bronte's *Wuthering Heights* and Sula-Nel androgyny in Toni Morrison's novel *Sula,* irrespective of their cultural, socio-economic structure and background.

The three novels taken as cases for study, though literary products of entirely different races, decades and nature, have in them, the theme of androgyny lurking in respective individual patterns. Emily Bronte's *Wuthering Heights*, published in the Victorian limelight, portrays the story of an inseparable pair-Heathcliff and Catherine who perish, unable to fight separation of their selves, not only in love but also psychological and existential, thereby representing the harmony of opposites in one spiritual existence irrespective of the gender constructs of society. *Debi Chaudhurani*, by Bankim Chandra Chattopadhay, the first novelist in proper in Bengali and Indian English Literature, on the other hand, portrays the struggle of a simple rustic girl, Prafulla to establish her identity by adopting a life of a dacoit when deprived by her in-laws. The novel is important in the sense of its chronological placement as the feminist assertion of Prafulla seemed unthinkable in the then socio-economic scenario in India. Published in 1884, just two years later to his magnum opus *Anandamath*, which set in the anti-colonial protest and its hue in entire country with the cry of expression "Vande Mataram", *Debi Chaudhurani* had clearly an undercurrent of anti-colonial assertion beneath its domestic set up and representation of Dionysus energies in women. *Sula*, a novel of entirely different kind, represents and deconstructs the mammy existence in Afro-American society, portraying the unconventional carefree male-like existence of Sula who finds her counterpart in Nel; another could be unconventional character, who in the end of the novel understands the equation of the other half prowling within two soul mates. It is interesting that all three novels represent women existence as somewhat androgynous, either representing it as a blend of male-female entities as divided into two bodies or both in female fortitude or in a singular androgynous existence within oneself, despite their racial and cultural differences.

Wuthering Heights represents a synonymous entity within a male-female existence between Catherine and Heathcliff, the inseparable personalities who are spiritually bound despite their opposite natures. In deciphering the texture of relationship between Catherine and Heathcliff, critics have been hovering all over centuries to produce different interpretations pertaining to their queer bonding. Terry Eagleton in analyzing this relationship comments that, "the curious impersonality of the relation between Catherine and Heathcliff" has a famously "ontological or metaphysical quality".[3] Their relationship as Catherine tells Nelly, "I cannot express it" (102), very closely corresponds to the readers' conclusion to the birth and continuance of the nature of relationship, that they cannot too express it. Catherine, as the novel progresses, narrated by Nelly, is passionate, happy natured, sensitive petulant, diabolical and a careless pretty young girl. Heathcliff, on the other hand, is a cold-blooded, ill-natured uncouth boy who never shows his warmth, but only his hatred and anger. When angered, Catherine, on the other hand, becomes defiant, headstrong, and cruel. Heathcliff is sullen, and is capable of vindictiveness but when exposed to empathy and love becomes docile and innocent like a child.

Catherine, though psychologically and spiritually bound to Heathcliff, marries Edgar because of her class consciousness. Unable to realize the patent and portent bond between her and Heathcliff, she considers her marriage from the materialistic and socio-conventional point of view and marries Edgar who lives in the drastically opposite precinct, in the Thrush cross Grange which is elegant, lighted, set in a lush green environment and stands as a veritable contrast to Wuthering Heights which is characterized by darkness, clumsy atmosphere and a sinister feeling. Catherine, who used to live in the Heights accustomed to its evil grandeur, was akin to Heathcliff's positive attachment to the sinister self in the house itself. Despite the contrast, Catherine, soul-bound to Heathcliff and therefore Heights, retains the same notorious and chaotic sensibility in her which she had cherished long and simultaneous with Heathcliff from her childhood. Heathcliff on the other hand, lacks in him the softness and delicacies of nature and for that he clings to Catherine for its extract. They realize that they are one and unassunder and same to each other's soul. After her marriage with Edgar, Catherine is disillusioned by her thoughts of her sunny life in Grange as she realizes too late that it is the dark primitive consciousness that exists in her and forms a cumulative whole only together with Heathcliff. All her thoughts and tasks remain incomplete, vacant and void to a certain extent only because the other half is detached from her. It is after three years when Heathcliff suddenly returns back rich and gentlemanlike and upturns the existing roles by becoming the master of Heights and beservanting all members of Heights. He now goes to meet Catherine to prove his capability and right over her. Catherine eager and exited to see Heathcliff wants to simplify relationships with her husband

and past lover, but fails in vain because the conflict of super-ego over id, as represented by the two characters respectively, is unsolvable. Linda Gold in her renowned essay, "Catherine Earnshaw: Mother and Daughter", sees in the symbiosis of Catherine, Heathcliff, and Edgar the relationship of Freud's id, ego, and superego.[4] At a psychological level, they merge into one Personality with Heathcliff's image. Heathcliff, the id, expresses his most primitive drives like sex, seeks pleasure, and avoids pain; the id is not affected by time and remains in the unconscious appropriately. Heathcliff's origins are unknown, he is dark, he runs wild and is primitive as a child, and his three-year absence remains a mystery. Catherine, the ego, relates to other people and society, tests the impulses of the id against reality, and controls the energetic id until there is a reasonable chance of its urges being fulfilled. Edgar, the superego, represents the rules of proper behavior and morality inculcated by teachers, family, and society; he is civilized and cultured. According to Freudian analyses, the ego must be male to deal successfully with the world and a female ego would have to live through males to survive. This Catherine does, as Linda Gold puts it, by identifying egotistically with Heathcliff and Edgar. After her marriage, she expects Edgar to accept Heathcliff in their household and to raise him from his degraded state; this would result in the integration of the disparate parts of her personality—id, ego, and superego—into one unified personality. She realizes the loss of her self after being away from him and in a fit of profound pain and physical closeness, tells that she cannot survive without him and it is he who is her soul mate. She refuses to elude with Heathcliff thinking of her present bonding with Edgar and her raised social status. Catherine dies unable to bear on the agony of confrontation within her in the hope of a sum total psychological integration between the id and the super ego.

Shocked by Catherine's death, Heathcliff implores her to haunt him: "I *cannot* live without my life! I *cannot* live without my soul!" He feels devastated by the death of his one true love whom he could neither imbibe nor nurture. Heathcliff remains a barren heath at the end of his pleas and forsakes Catherine for Isabella though he really could never remove his self from

Catherine. After Catherine's death, Heathcliff is haunted by Catherine's ghost and he becomes mad and animal-like as because he has lost the other tender half of his self and sorrow stuck spend his last days on Catherine's burial until he becomes one with the sod that covers Catherine.

The relationship between Catherine and Heathcliff, in Jungian readings, as aspects of one person; which may be the archetype of the shadow and the individual or the archetypes of the animus/anima and the persona, take the form of a "soul-image" in the personal unconscious. When a man projects his anima onto a real women or a woman projects her animus onto a man, a triad arises, which includes a transcendent part. In *Wuthering Heights*, Catherine for whom Heathcliff is the animus, and to Heathcliff, for whom Catherine is the anima, the latter expresses anger and hostility, freedom, command, irresponsibility, rebellion, and spontaneity. For Heathcliff, Catherine is beauty, love, status, and co-ordinate, all that he lacks in him. Catherine's love for Edgar "is like the foliage of trees in the woods", subject to change of time but her love for Heathcliff "resembles the eternal rocks beneath-a source of little visible delight, but necessary". He is her "own being" (100). The projection of their soul-images explains their profound sense of connection or identity with each other. Catherine's words, "I am Heathcliff", "Whatever our souls are made up of [Heathcliff's] and mine are same and Linton's as is different as a moonlight from lightning" (100) or "I think therefore I am Heathcliff", and Heathcliff's comment to Nelly later on, "Catherine has a heart as deep as I have, the sea could be readily contained in that horse trough, as her whole affection be monopolized in him [Edgar]...It is not in him to be loved like me, how can she love in him what she has not?" (182) and Heathcliff's references to Catherine as his 'soul' and his 'life', all signify to the fact that there is a undivided two-in-one existence in them, which is equally ratiocinated by the qualities of hardness and softness, brute and kind, love and hate, God and Debil, Heaven and Hell. The power of the two comes from one will, one soul—the soul which has one existence and that finds fulfillment in the culmination in the energies produced from a neuter suit, androgynous in nature, unhampered by gender discrimination and society. One is complementary and purposively supplementary to the other in life and death and so Heathcliff and Catherine's love only finds fulfillment in the dark unconscious self, either in dreams or in death.

The most interesting part that *Wuthering Heights* as a Gothic novel explores is the ambience of thrill and intense passion among the characters that let critics brainstorm issues of androgyny in it. Catherine and Heathcliff, the two equal consciously unconscious halves of a definite circle, later distorted into a disproportionate triangle, with the presence of Edgar and class relations, misequates the geometry among them that lead to their extinction and unfulfillment in love and relationships. Here the change of role or situations could easily turn Catherine into Heathcliff and Heathcliff into Catherine as there lay between them the same fundamentals of existence, the power to adopt something and nullify it all at the same time. The concept of Ardhvanari or androgyny as represented in the two characters, Heathcliff and Catherine, works in that subtle alchemy in their relationship that lets one attract and repel each other at the same time. The presence of particular opposites, of black and white, poise and wrath, good and evil in both characters bring in a disposition of harmony without loosing hold on each other thereby demonstrating a whole like existence in the two, characterized by same yet different rudiments of human physical and psychological existence.

In decoding *Debi Chaudhurani* as a novel encompassing the theme of androgyny, one must deeply scrutinize the protagonist's actions that are essentially fatalistic. Prafulla becomes *Debi Chaudhurani* when she poses herself as masculine, taking up an outrageous step from a housewife; of becoming a dacoit, a leader not only because it was the only left over alternative to survive, and retain her self but also for the country. As noted earlier, *Debi Chaudhurani* is set in the paraphernalia of colonial domination where women are called for participation in the anti-colonial movement against British. Prafulla, an ordinary illiterate village girl, incidentally married to Brajeswar, gets rejected by her in-laws because of a sudden spread rumour, at the occasion of her marriage, that she is a low caste and a liar.

When she arrives at her in-laws, she is rejected outright by her father-in-law. She also finds during her one night's stay, that her husband has also two more wives, one of who is jealous and a bit eccentric and another very friendly and kind but deprived of the sexual happiness from her husband. Even though she confesses the truth that she belongs to a Brahmin family and pleads shelter as a servant in the house, Haraballav Roy, her father-in-law, a capitalist *zamindar* orders her out of the house the next morning. Prafulla, hopeless and hapless, for the last time questions how should she feed herself when exiled from home, the hard hearted man only replies that she could do any thing to feed herself—be it theft or dacoity. The words of her father-in-law proves proleptic to her coming fate as Prafulla meets Bhabani Pathak, the leader of the gang of infamous dacoits soon after.

Bhabani Pathak, who is well-known as the most powerful dacoit in Bengal, notices the poor destinationless girl's potential to social good and masters her to rise up to her personal situation. Bhabani Pathak grooms her to marshal training, teaches her to read and write, and counsels her to shooting, fighting and horse riding. After a vigorous training of five months, Prafulla becomes ready to face the masculine world masculine-like. Pathak renames her as Debi Chaudhurani and sets her free to act for social good of all thereby destroying the social evils, run free by the rich landlords and the British officers.

'Debi Chaudhurani' the name despite its female sagacity does not feature any feminine or masculine trait but carries in it a sense of upgraded status and social consciousness. 'Debi' in Bengali language is added before the name of a woman to show respect and her social position. Here the concept of 'Debi' is someone like Queen Elizabeth who has a royal existence defying any gender roles. Debi does not cross dress but she proves herself as a magnificent manager of the dacoit fellows who loot the rich and distribute the riches among the poor. Instances of social service and economic assistance become common to Debi and she emerges as a mother of all rustic poor, crossing all boundaries of past, present and future, her personal and domestic existence, gender construction, class and society. She is someone who is strong and protective as a father but soft and empathetic like a mother.

The theme of androgyny in *Debi Chaudhurani* can be discerned most prominently in the protagonist in a form of binary existence, as because she exhibits tender grace, vulnerability and qualities of humanity as Prafulla on one hand, and intelligent, militant and managerial like a queen, on the other, voicing herself and asserting her position in society and before her in-laws. She befools her in-laws by raiding Haraballav's cargo ship and looting him to poverty. This she does purposely to trap them into her notions and bring her in-laws under her control. Her actions here remind us of Prospero, in Shakespeare's *The Tempest,* who too had created a magical tempest through a well-planned a stratagem to capture his kinsmen to regain his position as a king and teach them a moral lesson. Debi by her intelligence spins tales and events in such tactful manners so that she is able to gain back her position and dignity in her in-laws. Looted and debt stricken Haraballav fails in paying the taxes to the Company. Debi rises up to the situation, hijacks Brajeshwar to her *bajra* (boat) and economically helps her husband with gold coins as loan. But Brajeshwar is too callous to recognize her behind the curtains.

Debi has more reasons to appraisal from a feminist point of view because she not only exults her own position and steals respect and dignity from others, but also helps others retain the same. Debi assists Sagar, the third wife of Brajeshwar, in getting back her love from her husband and also in getting back her lost self-esteem. In this, she is selfless, wise and exhibits her intellectual skills. She incurs a voice over game to answer back her husband through her rival, Sagar. After Brajeshwar fails to pay the Company taxes, he goes to his rich father-in-law, as a last refuge. As the Marriage between Sagar and Brajeshwar was economically arranged for business motives between the fathers, Sagar was deprived from the love of her husband. Now that Brajeshwar was a pitiable fellow who never took care of his daughter, his father-in-law refused any favour. Furious over his father-in-laws refusal, Brajeshwar literally kicks Sagar aside and promises her never to come back. Instantaneously, an unrecognized woman voice from outside asserts that one day she will take over the revenge on her husband's act of kicking by beservanting him and making him massage her feet. This is Debi voicing over for Sagar who discloses her identity and takes her to her boat and harasses their pauper husband to fall to Sagar's feet as a servant so that he recognizes his fault and succumbs to her love and dignity. Here Sagar can be called as an alter-ego of Debi who participate with Debi to run over the show as a perfect partner in cowing the male ego and atrocity. Her interactions with her rival, both as Prafulla and Debi, have provided her with new experiences which will now help her in establishing a better future.

The plot of *Debi Chaudhurani* revolves on its central protagonist Debi and it is Debi who leads the plot after Pathak handovers the rung of plot. To wind up, she calls Brajeshwar at Sandhanpur Kalsajir Ghat (a local Indian jetty) to return his debt on their first marriage anniversary. Debi plays over her masterstroke now. Haraballav calls the British for assistance, with a hope to gain British favour, as Debi had been trotting over the territory without any proof and is one of the most wanted contemporary criminals. Debi befools the British officer in charge in disguise by presenting three Debi Chaudhuranis at a time. Tactfully she manages a way out of her whole unit of the British enclosure capturing the officer instead, in her boat, thereby proving herself politically sound over the male 'Others'.

The boat comes to Bhutnathpur, the village where her in-laws live and Debi surrenders herself to Brajeshwar, who is also very much ready to accept her with unaccountable apologies for the past. She while leaving her troop greets her master Bhabani Pathak and tells that she has decided to return to her husband. The theme of Debi Chaudhurani finds a summation in Pathak's speech. He blesses her and says as war is needed, peace is also crucial.

Prafulla finds her deserved place back in her in-laws, in the end, with a ceremonious reception, one like a queen. Her position now in the in-laws becomes no more like a stereotyped wife in the household but she transmutes her Debi Chaudhurani self into mind and action thereby creating a conscious figure of her new self, in others minds. She now will receive a position far more crucial and increased status as a decision-maker and can voice out her needs and feelings. What Prafulla could not, Debi Chaudhurani could. The note of androgyny becomes all the clear in the voice of her mother-in law who jeers at her husband and points out his misconception and unjustness. She asserts that a woman can win over many things if she feels, she can captivate men, liberate and be his master all at a time. She can be man and woman at the same time. Prafulla as Debi Chaudhurani finally transmutes the Hindu social standards of being accepted as a helpless wife in laws and conforms to the Para Shiva myth proving her creator a progressive mind.

The context of *Sula*, when compared to the early two novels is very different. Sula is a modern novel, set in a black Afro-American, describing the upcoming changes in the black community and the need of an unconventional 'New Woman' to pinpoint the deprogrammed traditional existence. Sula though a novel of high feminist assertion and ironic representation of Afro-American existence of the blacks, as racially and socio-politically distressed beings, *Sula* deconstructs the role of a woman as a mother, mammy, sister, daughter, friend, and lover giving her a chance to express her soul's choice to find her real soul mate the 'other half' of her equation. *Sula,* in an open text, represents the story of a black girl, Sula, who born in a small town Ohio, at Medallion, proves her unconventional self through her queer ways of life, love and marriage. Sula, who is born of a sturdy mother and inherits the hard, cruel yet an over sensitive grandmother, can go beyond boundaries set for women and society and can disappear suddenly one day only to come back as ill omen and destroy the subtle relationships cherished by long deliberations of friendship. Sula represents that deprogrammed self in a mammy-society where now not only men but also women have the rights to change one's sexual mates more than once and go off for a while to some other land to upgrade oneself and be unaware of the social restrictions imposed by the prehistoric past and can take up modern ways of life and living according to one's convenience. "She is new world black and new world extracting choice from choicelessness responding inventively to found things. Improvisational, daring, disruptive, imaginative, modern, out-of-the-house...outlawed, unpolicing, uncontained, and uncontainable. And dangerously female."[5]

Sula, the daughter of Hannah and grand daughter of Eva Peace, inherits in extremes all hard and subtle tricks to existence in an Afro-American society at Bottom, a place which is again an outcome of a colonial hoax. From her very childhood, Sula is unconventional for her absurd ways and behaviour. Inheriting the abnormal strength to suffer and persistence from Eva, Sula lacks that gentleness that Eva at least seemed to have. Morrison incurs an open text method, full of holes and gaps, in narrating *Sula* but adopts a mini Chinese Box technique in delivering the story of five women, Helene, Nel, Eva, Hannah, Sula, one by one steadily and in a interesting manner so as to bring a distinct ironic contrast in representing the Afro-American society and the lives of the girls. After her husband leaves the house with four children, at Eva's custody to feed, Eva suddenly vanishes one day and returns after eighteen months later with one leg and crutches, with the insurance money to feed her family. Later when her loving son, Plum comes back mentally crippled unable to lead a normal life, from the First World War front, Eva sets her dear son to fire so as to relieve him off the pain of survival and her pain to witness. Even later, when Hannah, her daughter, catches fire, Eva jumps out in rescue but fails. It is so assumed that Eva had mercy-killed her daughter in the ambulance itself unable to see Hannah wriggle in pain and lost physic. But Sula is unreadable. Everybody seems to hate Sula except Nel. Nel, another young girl same in age as Sula, who decides in her childhood not to lose her 'me-ness', befriends Sula for the likeliness in them. She and Sula from their childhood stayed and played together discovering themselves as two individuals with one soul thereby forming in them inseparable bondings. Sula represents that masculine energy and courage that can slash off the tip of her finger before the white boys who have come to eve-tease them. Nel becomes the other half of her equational existence as she imbibes in her the tendencies of her mother to be good. The good-woman convention in the society for a girl to adhere to the existing norms of the society, playing the stereotyped roles of a daughter-wife-mother was forcefully imposed on Nel by her mother's influence, with her marriage with Jude and because of this self-resignation to the social laws, Nel fails to become Sula, negating the girl-girl bonding that was easily possible. Lesbian interpretation of Nel-Sula relationship, though not uncommon and unnatural in Morisson's critics, fail to attain its totality as Nel negates Sula from believing and seeing her 'self' from within as she tries to submit to the conventions of her mother. The novel explores in it the umbilical theme of mother extraction or a non-verbal inborn link derived from the mother in daughter, thereby constructing a mother-daughter inseparable bonding consciously or unconsciously. Nel's inheritance of her mother's goodness and her utmost struggle to submit into the moral conventions make Nel become more isolated from her self and thus Sula, who constituted of her other half. It is in every aspect that Sula is Nel's other half and consciously opposite. Sula's accidental overhearing of her mother confessing a neighbour that she loves Sula but dislikes her, consciously cuts of the mother-daughter bond between them. On the other hand, Nel's too much of mother closeness kills her 'me' unconsciously and she consciously seems to conform to the norms of a good woman. But ironically the scenario of both the girls changes in the end of the novel. When Sula dies on her death bed, she crumbles into a fetal position, tired and disillusioned by her love and life, unconsciously connects back to her mother. Nel, on the other hand, who had always been a darling for her mother, unconsciously hates her mother in the end. With Sula's death, she understands that it was Sula that formed her other half and fulfilled her 'me'-ness and not her mother whom she tried to imbibe in so much so as to exterminate Sula from her. She now unconsciously starts releasing herself from her mother's existence.

Both Nel and Sula successfully balance the equation in them into a total circle only before their maturity. Sula's accidental killing of Chicken Little makes her cry and afraid but she manages in concealing the truth. Sula's unrestricted cruel and absurd means of life fascinates Nel so much so that when Chicken Little, slips off from Sula's hand and falls into the pool and gets drowned, Nel enjoys the scene of Chicken's death as 'thrilling'. This corresponds to the thrill that Sula feels when she watches her mother burn accidentally by fire. Nel realizes this only in the end when after Sula's death she goes to meet Eva and discovers her real self torn apart with Sula's demise. She now, on the burial of Sula gives a final cry of realization that it was not Jude that she had missed for so long but Sula whom she could neither receive nor reciprocate but only tended to. "We was girls together,"... "O Lord, Sula", she cried, "girl, girl, girl girl girl" (174). The poignancy of her cry is of the loss of her soul, her misunderstanding, her sacrifice of that me-ness that she cherished in her and had given up for false conventional roles which got her nothing but pain and exile.

The theme of good and bad in *Sula* is ironically treated as it raises question towards the existing norms of the society that brings to our mind the famous Shakespearean quote, "fair is foul and foul is fair". Nel on Sula's deathbed finally asks the question, why she had slept with her husband; the question that had been tearing her ever since Jude left. Neither repentant nor apologetic, Sula tells her that Jude simply "filled up the space". The feminist interpretations for a perfect androgyny is complete here between both girls which Nel fails to understand; her mind is veiled with the misconceptions of social constructs and concepts like goodness and badness. Sula whispers a final haunting and ambiguous question to Nel, asking her to consider which of them is the good and which one is the bad. Sula suggests "I mean maybe it wasn't you. Maybe it was me." Rebuffed and shaken, Nel leaves. Since Jude's abandonment of her three years earlier, Nel has lived a hard life, working to support her children and maintain her home. She has done what was expected of her as a deserted wife and mother, and has taken her place with the rest of the women in the community. Likewise that she has been a "good woman", never betraying her husband; she is, again, a good friend to Sula, whom she never betrayed; Sula betrayed her by sleeping with Jude.

They are at odds, still opposites who, together, form a whole. Nel extols the virtue of hard work; Sula rejects it. Nel blusters about Sula's man-like independence; Sula acknowledges it with pride. In contrast, Morrison suggests that the distinction between good and evil is rarely so clear-cut as Sula and Nel suppose; consequently, there is some good and some evil in both Sula and in Nel. "The most significant difference between the women might be that Sula accepts the fuzziness of moral categories with her usual good humor, whereas Nel refuses to look at the unacceptable aspects of herself, aspects which confound her cliched thinking. In fact, Sula's ability to laugh at herself may be her most redeeming quality."[6]

The androgynous subsistence in both girls existentially continues even after the expiry of one half of the equation. Nel after Sula's death understands Sula in a new dimension, in a new way and discovers herself as the perfect balance in framing their whole equation. She now is more close to Sula, the entity, the soul rather to the body which is no more, paradoxically now completing the whole, the unbalanced equation of an existence, which is properly ratiocinated with male-female qualities, and unconventional conventionalities. Sula after her death in a way does not leave Nel as "You [Nel] and Sula what's the difference?" as Eva puts; they consist of a same soul. Sula just after death sees her body lying on the bed and her free soul now writhes in excitement to tell Nel that death does not hurt. Morisson is ironic as Sula reveals this philosophic truth that living hurts but death does not. Indirectly this is a call for Nel, a distant possibility for them to meet in a painless world. Even in death and after life Sula dwells in Nel. The unification of entities cannot be any stronger.

To sum up, all the three writers in the above discussed novels have portrayed their characters with distinctive androgynous qualities that produce the image of Ardhanarishvara as a blend of power and sensitivity. All the female characters imbibe in them something of the maleness either by being a part of another's soul and equation or by culminating in her male the like virtues proving their selves above the mundane gender constructs and assumptions of the society. No man is without a woman self and no woman is bereft with a man's. The interesting precision to optimism, despite the upcoming new feminist forces in the contemporary era, the writers have strikingly realized and explored the opposite selves in a woman and their power to ratiocinate. By this, they have not only set for them new patterns and paradigms that can raise them above the commonplace gender constructs but also voice her unconventional deprogrammed self globally.

NOTES

1. Humm, Maggie. *A reader's Guide to Contemporary Feminist Literary Criticism.* UK: Harvester Wheatsheaf, 1994, pp. 126-27.
2. Goldberg, Ellen. *The Lord Who is Half Woman Ardhanarishvara in Indian and Feminist Perspective.* New York: Sunny Press, 2002, p. 94.
3. Eagleton, Terry. *Myths of Power: A Marxist Study of the Brontes,* London: Macmillan Press, 1975, pp. 107-08.
4. Linda, Gold. "Catherine Earnshaw: Mother and Daughter", *Thematic Issue: Women's Studies and English Teachers English Journal,* 74.3. USA, March 1985, pp. 68-73.
5. Morrisson, Toni. "Unspeakable Things Unspoken: The Afro American Presence in American Literature 1989", *Within the Circle: An Anthology of African American Literary Criticism.* (Ed.) Mitchell, Angelyn. USA: Duke University Press, 1994, p. 390.
6. Bergenholtz, Rita A. "Toni Morisson's Sula: A satire on binary thinking." *African American Review,* 30.1. Spring, USA. 1996. See. http://findarticles.com/p/articles/mi_m2838/is_n1_v30/ai_18372105>http://www.bnet.com/

REFERENCES

Bronte, Emily. *Wuthering Heights.* (Ed.) Marsden, Hilda and Jack, Ian, UK: Oxford Clarendon Press, 1976.

Chattopaddhay, Bankim Chandra. *Debi Chaudhurani.* Calcutta: Sahitya Samsad Prakashani, 1884.

Gupta, Dinen. (Prod.) *Debi Chaudhurani. Bankim Rachanabal.* 15 reels. Calcutta: Indrapuri Studio, 1872.

Leselie, Julia. *Myth and Mythmaking.* India: Routledge, 1996.

Meese, Elizabeth and Parker Alice. *The Difference Within: Feminism and Critical Theory.* USA: John Benjamins Publishing Company, 1989.

Morisson, Toni. *Sula.* USA: Penguin Books, 1973.

List of Contributors

Neeru Tandon, Reader, Department of English, VSSD College Kanpur, Uttar Pradesh.

Tripti Karekatti, Department of English, Shivaji University, Kolhapur, Maharashtra.

Rani Nalawade, Department of English, Shivaji University, Kolhapur, Maharashtra.

Hariclea Zengos, PhD, The American College of Greece.

Sarbojit Biswas, Lecturer and Head, Department of English, Hiralal Bhakat College, Kolkata.

Garima Gupta, Lecturer, School of Languages, SMVDU, Katra, Jammu & Kashmir.

Esterino Adami, University of Turin, Italy.

Subir Dhar, Professor and Head, the Department of English, Director, the School of Languages and Culture, Rabindra Bharati University, Kolkata, West Bengal.

Gauri Shankar Jha, Head, Department of English, R.F. Govt. College, Changlang, Arunachal Pradesh.

K. Mishra, Reader in English, Sonarpur Mahavidyalaya, University of Calcutta.

Geetha B. Assistant Professor, Languages Group, BITS-Pilani, Rajasthan.

Mbuh Mbuh Tennu, Lecturer, Department of English, University of Yaounde I, Cameroon.

Vandana Datta, Department of English, College of Commerce, Patna.

John Nkemngong Nkengasong, University of Yaounde I, Cameroon.

Malti Agarwal, Reader & Head, Department of English, N.A.S. College, Meerut, U.P.

Saddik M. Gohar, United Arab Emirates University, UAE.

Emmanuel N. Ngwang, Associate Professor, Mississippi Valley State University, Itta Bena, Mississippi.

Anju Bala Agrawal, Reader, Department of English, R.C.A.Girls' P.G. College Mathura, U.P.

S. John Peter Joseph, Reader in English, St. Xavier's College, Palayamkottai.

Basavaraj Naikar, Professor & Chairman, Department of English, Karnataka University Dharwad.

Koyel Chakrabarty, Lecturer in English, BRCM College of Engineering and Technology, Haryana.